THE LINES WE DRAW

THE LINES WE DRAW

The Journalist, the Jew and an Argument About Identity

TIM FRANKS

BLOOMSBURY CONTINUUM
LONDON · OXFORD · NEW YORK · NEW DELHI · SYDNEY

BLOOMSBURY CONTINUUM
Bloomsbury Publishing Plc
50 Bedford Square, London, WC1B 3DP, UK
Bloomsbury Publishing Ireland Limited,
29 Earlsfort Terrace, Dublin 2, D02 AY28, Ireland

BLOOMSBURY, BLOOMSBURY CONTINUUM and the Diana logo are trademarks of
Bloomsbury Publishing Plc

First published in Great Britain 2025

Copyright © Tim Franks, 2025

Tim Franks has asserted his right under the Copyright, Designs and Patents Act, 1988, to be
identified as Author of this work

For legal purposes the Acknowledgements on pp. 259–89 constitute an extension of this
copyright page

All rights reserved. No part of this publication may be: i) reproduced or transmitted in any form, electronic or mechanical, including photocopying, recording or by means of any information storage or retrieval system without prior permission in writing from the publishers; or ii) used or reproduced in any way for the training, development or operation of artificial intelligence (AI) technologies, including generative AI technologies. The rights holders expressly reserve this publication from the text and data mining exception as per Article 4(3) of the Digital Single Market Directive (EU) 2019/790

Bloomsbury Publishing Plc does not have any control over, or responsibility for, any third-party websites referred to or in this book. All internet addresses given in this book were correct at the time of going to press. The author and publisher regret any inconvenience caused if addresses have changed or sites have ceased to exist, but can accept no responsibility for any such changes

A catalogue record for this book is available from the British Library

Library of Congress Cataloguing-in-Publication data has been applied for

ISBN: HB: 978-1-3994-2308-3; eBook: 978-1-3994-2304-5; ePDF: 978-1-3994-2305-2

2 4 6 8 10 9 7 5 3 1

Typeset by Deanta Global Publishing Services, Chennai, India
Printed and bound in Great Britain by CPI Group (UK) Ltd, Croydon CR0 4YY

To find out more about our authors and books visit www.bloomsbury.com and sign up for
our newsletters

For product safety related questions contact productsafety@bloomsbury.com

for Sarah
and for Leo, Harry & Aaron

Contents

Family Tree	viii
Introduction	1
Prologue: Birmingham	5
1 On Stories; The Refugee	9
2 On Prejudice; The Student	16
3 On Risk; The Risk-takers	32
4 On Facts; The Victorians	80
5 On War; The Soldier	117
6 On Precision and Concision; The Lost (Part 1)	142
7 On Justice; The Lost (Part 2)	180
Pause	194
8 On Trust; The Immigrant	197
9 On Joy; The Artists	213
Epilogue: Birmingham & London	247
Acknowledgments	259
Glossary	261
Endnotes	264

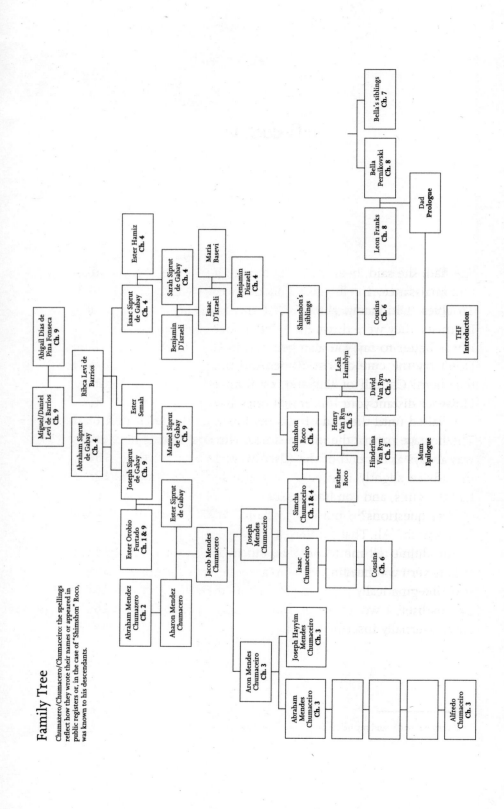

Introduction

She had, she said, been in 14 Company. It was the Special Forces' reconnaissance, intelligence and deep cover unit set up in the Troubles. Ultimately, she said, if the kidnappers were militant Islamists, they were threatening lethal force, and if they asked you, it was better to say you also believed in God. Don't be an atheist. Don't try the cute agnostic line. And then, if they ask you how, tell them: Church of England, or Roman Catholic, or whatever. However distant your link might once have been.

I waited until the end of this session with the High Risk team. The hostage part of the BBC hostile environment refresher course was always at the end of the day. Always a bit of a downer. Always the advice slightly imprecise. Because invariably the kidnappers had the guns, and you had value.

'Any questions?' I put up my hand. 'What should I say?' I said. 'I'm Jewish.' 'Ah. That's different.'

She didn't tell me to do this, but it became my private ritual. Whenever I was heading into a place where, as the High Risk advisors phlegmatically put it, there was an 'increased threat of kidnap by jihadists', I would grunt and tug and worry off my wedding ring, internally inscribed with

*אני לדודי ודודי לי

---

*'I am my beloved's, and my beloved is mine' (Song of Songs, 6:3)

As if my potential captors were unlikely to Google me. Or when a senior member of a very well-armed Islamist paramilitary group, on his turf, asked me where I was from, *really* from, and when that didn't produce much of any interest – 'Birmingham' – he asked where my family was *really* from. I knew what he was getting at, and he probably guessed that I knew, and I nodded and smiled and told him I was British. Which I am.

That was at the sharper end of my deployment in the Middle East. It was a different sort of risk mitigation to others that were more religiously indiscriminate: driving in 95 mph zig-zags down a deserted highway in Iraq while coming under small arms fire; taking cover in a ditch or under a table when you heard the scream and whistle of mortars incoming. No – this was the attempt to control the odds for Jewishness.

Far more frequent were the occasions when those factors were calculated by others, on my behalf. As I conceded in my valedictory *From Our Own Correspondent* from Jerusalem, from the moment that I was appointed the BBC's Middle East Correspondent it was clear – people stated as much – that the corporation had been strong-armed by the Israeli Prime Minister into taking the decision, or it was clear that I *would* indeed be tilting the balance of coverage (viewed variously as a good thing and a bad thing), or it was clear that I deserved sympathy for the impossibility of trying to occupy, in this region in particular, simultaneous states of Jewishness and journalism. *That* was just schoolboy physics.

And there were those who didn't know I was a Jew. At least, I can only assume they didn't. The top-ranking French official from a UN agency who, at a diplomats' dinner party in Jerusalem, told me 'everyone knows Jews run the BBC'. I pointed out to him that the Director-General of the time was Roman Catholic. That proves nothing, he informed me; we moved into the dining room, and I moved the conversation on, because the hosts were friends. Or the British bloke who was at the centre of a piece I had been commissioned to do for the *Today* programme – it was supposed to be about music and exile for pity's sake – telling me, as we wound through Damascus, wedged sweatily and interminably in the back of a packed public minibus, that 'everyone knows' the Rothschilds plotted and funded the Holocaust. I disagreed: no effect. I shut up: no effect. On and on, he waxed. Should I have got off the bus, walked off the job? Maybe. I didn't. I still don't know what the right answer was.

It wasn't all about being a Jew. There was also the original sin of working for the BBC. Often, so obvious, so quintessential was the bias, that it was a badge of honour not to have watched, heard or read output for years. To suggest that that might undercut the validity of the observation was, I would be told, missing the point.

Sometimes, I didn't even get that far. A friend from Brussels was visiting Jerusalem. He had invited me to his hotel, close to the Old City, for lunch. It was a Shabbat, the day of rest. I was not particularly rested. My wife Sarah had, several days before, nipped back to the UK to sit some professional exams. At which point an Icelandic volcano called Eyjafjallajökull started fuming, and the cloud of ash grounded aircraft across Europe. That Saturday came at the end of the normal, unpredictable, busy work week and an abnormal week of single-parenting three young boys. I was queueing for the hotel buffet balancing two plates for the older two boys on one arm, and holding perpendicularly under the other, à la ironing board, my youngest son, rigid with fury and hunger. I was tired, and deeply aware of my limitations. The queue was moving at geological pace, but I noticed out of my peripheral vision that a fast-moving object was approaching. 'Are you Tim Franks?' 'Yes.' 'I'm here from London. My husband knows your parents.' 'Hello.' 'You know that most Jews think the BBC is doing a terrible job?'

For most of the time, I tried to remain as inert, as non-reactive as possible. I was human landfill. This was not martyrdom. There was a certain pragmatism. It could also – whisper it quietly – have a satisfyingly maddening effect with the livid and the self-righteous: the equivalent of meeting bull-necked road rage with a benign grin.

Don't imagine I assumed that they were always wrong, and that – heaven forbid – I was always right. I questioned and I questioned what I was doing, how I was doing it. And – yes – why I was doing it: what might have been drawing me one way or the other, even subconsciously. Often the complaints might contain a kernel of truth, or at least a reasonable objection. But that might well involve finding that kernel buried in a slurry of causation: it was clear that I was a self-hating Jew, an Islamophobe, part of the BBC conspiracy, and an unthinking adherent to one of several mutually exclusive world-views.

It still happens. Less often, perhaps. But I also have less patience. At the end of pre-recorded interviews, now, however tough they've been, I generally try to ease the tension. The mics are off, there is nothing much to be gained. And, after all, asking – on occasion – disobliging questions, persistently: that is what I am paid to do. But when, recently, a senior minister from a polarising foreign government told me as we were saying goodbye to each other 'your views are extreme and radical', I was, to use the parlance, triggered. My smile disappeared and my handshake turned into something a little grippier, as I told him, quietly: 'You have absolutely no idea what my views are.' I fantasised about saying other things. I don't think I did. At least not out loud.

What happens, though, if I ask that question of myself: what exactly my views *are*? Hypocritical, you might think; or ill-advised; or unhinged, in the manner of someone talking to themselves in public. Certainly risky. Especially when it comes to that unwieldy idea of 'Jewishness', of what it means to be Jewish. Of how, even more fundamentally, even more contentiously, we construct identity.

And that is to suggest that I have an answer – or at least that I did before I started scraping the mud from the scattered, buried tiles of this family mosaic. These far-flung characters – many distant in time and place and relation – they are an accidental assembly, speaking languages I imperfectly understand. As I began to stumble across them, I never thought that they could coalesce to define not just my sense of identity, but an idea of identity. Even less, one that I might want to share.

It may have been professionally adroit, up to this point, to steer clear. But the disadvantage is that others then occupy the entire bandwidth. It is a little grandiose to compare myself to Eyjafjallajökull. But after being quiescent for decades, I am ready to start venting.

Prologue

Birmingham (1970s & 80s)

The first surprise is that there is a story, at all, to tell.

Because growing up, we didn't really do family. Close relatives, like Christmas, was what other people had. There were no grandparents around. Earlier ancestors were a mystery: lost, foreign, unknown. Ours was a pollarded family tree. There was, for a time, one eccentric aunt, but she disappeared when I was ten. No first cousins, other than those several time zones away. My parents, my sister and I were like a paramilitary cell. Maybe not in the sense of being Kalashnikov-toting outlaws sworn to ideological purity. But otherwise the analogy works: we were small, sealed, self-contained. Connections to others reportedly in the same group were vague or non-existent.

We did not even have that great, sustaining Jewish diet of words. There were few family stories, beyond occasional, vague hints. Sometimes a trace would surface, but only to show how deep the rest of the plot was buried: best to leave it that way. At least until a postcard arrived in 2017, I met an uncle I never knew I had, and a chapter of our history re-wrote itself.

What we had instead was routine. Friday evening: candles, *kiddush*, breaded plaice – one week hot, one week cold. Alternate Saturday mornings: swimming lessons (back of the class, and couldn't see anything without my glasses) or synagogue (adrift in boredom). Sunday morning: *cheder* – Sunday school. There, I gleaned early hints as to the history and duty of the diaspora Jew. At the age of eight, our class was given a morning of respite from learning liturgy. The respite was the Holocaust. I knew about it. But I hadn't — at that point — seen the black-and-white pictures of the mounds of naked corpses, which were wordlessly passed around. There was no introduction, no discussion. But, in its own way, it meshed with the more perennial message ingrained within us, from *cheder* onwards, that to marry out, to marry a non-Jew, was to give Hitler his posthumous victory.

Israel existed, but for our family it was distant. We had no immediate connection. We never visited: the furthest we ever holidayed was Suffolk. Belatedly, I started attending one of the two Jewish youth groups. There was *Bnei Akiva* for the more strictly orthodox. I was sent to *Habonim Dror* ('The Builders of Peace'), which met in a small hut in the back of an Edgbaston garden, and proudly proclaimed itself Socialist, Jewish, Zionist. I had some wispy ideas about Jewish statehood. What I did not have was a reflexive veneration of The Jewish State. In saying that, I am making no ideological declaration. It was just assumed that I would, and while I rather balked at the expectation, I had neither the wit nor the will to ask the questions which might have helped. All of which meant that when I attended what should have been the climactic summer camp — the four-week Israel tour at the age of 16 — the only time I went weak-kneed was getting dehydrated walking up Masada.

Outside our low-ceilinged, modern-build family home, it was Birmingham in the 1970s and 1980s. Jews were a minute minority in the second city. Anti-Semitism, like racism, ran bone-deep. I'm not sure whether it was thinking or unthinking. I would say that maybe it doesn't matter, but later chapters might suggest otherwise. Perhaps the clearest indication was the age of those willing to flaunt their feelings. Primary school offered a parade of teachers who struggled — actually, I'm not certain they did struggle much — to contain their contempt. Kids, meanwhile, were kids. 'Jew' was a flexible syllable of abuse: adjective, verb, noun. I wasn't unpopular. Socially, I was in the undistinguished middle. But for those few — especially at secondary school — who were more overtly bigoted, it would have been remiss to forego the opportunities. I was spared, by and large, the more physical abuse: one of my classmates of South Asian descent had a pipette of sodium hydroxide squirted in his eyes. But the same drag-knuckled klutz who went unpunished for that, would, along with his cackling helper, regularly draw 'DIY' in large letters on the blackboard before the start of a lesson. The teachers would mutely wipe it off, and then fail to crack the mirror-writing code which would connect the graffiti to the shouts of 'D-I-Y' each time the Yid put his hand up to ask or answer a question.

Beyond school, certain things were not so much accepted, as just understood to be so. The local golf club kept on turning down applications from Jews until the Jews stopped applying and set up their own club miles away. My father, who wrote the first textbook of geriatric dentistry, who pioneered clinical and inter-disciplinary care for marginalised groups when such things were not just unfashionable, they were pretty much unthinkable, who founded and edited a ground-breaking and long-running scientific journal, who was invited to lecture around the world at the most prestigious institutions – he was never offered a professorship at Birmingham University. Coincidentally, the powers-that-be there occasionally let slip within earshot what they thought of The Jews.

Despite the hum and sometime gust of anti-Semitism, we never denied our Jewishness. It would have been fruitless. We were, in our own way, proud, a little defiant. We also could wallow: my father and I loved our annual pilgrimage to London and to Bloom's Kosher Restaurant for tongue, chips (chips!), ketchup, gherkin and Coke (Coke!), hurled on to the table by the immaculately rude and ancient waiters. But that was a private ritual. The lesson learned from inside our house, and across our home city, was that you do not foist or intrude. Celebrate what is out there: the glittering achievements of artists, scientists, intellectuals, non-Jewish and Jewish. Join the academies of music and sport and learning, if you can. But be super-sensitive to the sensitivities of others. That way they may not poke at yours.

I remain, I think, quite shy. I do not have that easy swagger. I won't dominate the dinner table, the party venue, with anecdotes of dash and danger. (I have them, believe me, I have them. I just can't be doing with the 'I'll see your RPG and raise you a sucking chest-wound'.)

But that very reserve may explain the great appeal of journalism. The excuse I have to knock on doors and enquire within. It did not always come easily to me; sometimes it still doesn't. On one of my first visits to Northern Ireland during the Troubles, a colleague and I headed south to Crossmaglen, a crucible of Irish Republicanism. My youthful attempts to draw people out were painfully contorted and cack-handed. The producer – who happened to be Irish – turned to me later, in the car and said, very gently: 'Tim, stop fucking apologising every time you ask a question.' He has my thanks to this day.

Yet there is also a bloody-minded side to me, often roused by roadblocks or rudeness or dissembling – or just by those loud, braying voices of certainty. Some things *are* clear and obvious. But it is also a truism of reporting that the best stories often turn out very differently to how you first approached them. Which means that while risk should always be calculated, it should also be accepted. Curiosity is fundamental. That sounds trite. But some of the best journalism involves asking guileless questions and kicking against the rules. It is child-like. And by the end of this book, I suspect I will come to realise it is more than a method, a reporter's reflex. It can underpin the very construction of identity. Indeed, it becomes impossible to ignore the strong links between my Jewishness and my journalism – a symbiosis even. Each informs the other. Prepare, if that is your wont, to be infuriated.

ONE

On Stories; The Refugee

There is a fiction about the BBC. Well, there are plenty. Here are two.

One hardy perennial is that we all agree what the story is and what our line must be before we dare pick up a phone, a pen, a mic. We can't help ourselves. We can do nothing but sniff and scuff and paw and whine, before the email arrives from the News Lords' 09:00 meeting. Then we're off.

So, no: before I started my five-year tour of duty as Europe Correspondent, I didn't ask the high-up in Foreign News (back when we called it 'Foreign') what the line was. I did, though, ask him how he thought we were navigating the competing narratives. He brushed off the question. 'The only thing I care about,' he said, neither insightfully nor particularly originally, 'is why is this lying bastard lying to me?' This same manager – this was decades ago, before internet news websites had really got going, and he is long retired – later told me that he rarely read the newspapers ('Why would I? Yesterday's news.') and *never* read op-eds ('Why would I? Just opinions.')

It was, in truth, a decent impulse: to be devoted to the idea of fact, and willing to decry its absence. But there's an even more fundamental task in journalism. It is spotting that there is even a story to tell. And here, now, I so nearly didn't.

A second fiction, sedulously cultivated in my on-air persona, is that I'm a cool, stolid sort. Shrillness shall not move me. I have no idea if anyone is convinced by that, but the truth is I am a fan-boy given to adolescent passions. My latest infatuation – which may well have passed by the time this book is published – is for Hannah Arendt. Not only is it unseemly in a man of my age and my stature to write comments like 'oh heavens yes' in the margins of books by her and about her, but I am insulting schoolboys everywhere. It is just in my eternal adolescence that Arendt, despite some painful, even appalling mis-steps, seems to have something to say about so much today, and that – like the teenaged existentialist I once thought I was – I have the most superficial understanding of what that might be.

One thing she did say (I think) is that the way we insert ourselves into the world, that we are properly born into it, and that we have a lasting, maybe chaotic effect, on it – is through the stories we tell. 'Action and speech…contain the answer to the question asked of every newcomer: "Who are you?"'[1]

Traditionally, at this point, I should begin to answer that question by introducing a postcard, a photograph, a manuscript, or even just a relative's recollection. But this happenstance story turns on a void.

~~~~

THE REFUGEE (BORN C.1708)

> 'Inevitably, dreamy constructions of a possible ancestry for himself would weave themselves with historic memories which had begun to have a new interest for him.'
>
> GEORGE ELIOT[2]

It began with two hours of nothing. 'We think there was.' 'Beneath here.' 'No trace remains.' The path was well-trodden: settlement, development, exile. It was a tribute to the historian who took us on our oxymoronic tour around 'Jewish Lisbon' that she held our attention with words alone, and that at the end, I thought to ask myself the question that, until then, I had failed to.

Chumaceiro?

It could sound Portuguese. That 'ei', slung halfway between the 'ay' of 'day' and the 'igh' of 'night'. The 'o' that is 'oo'. I only knew it as the name of a wife, because that is how family trees and histories — perhaps most of History — have been constructed: stories written by men, about men. So Simcha Chumaceiro was not so much a woman in her own right, but the second wife of my great-great-grandfather Reverend Shimshon Roco, long-serving cantor at Bevis Marks Synagogue in London.

Great-great-grandmother Simcha had lived in Amsterdam, before she moved to London. Her Portuguese-sounding name was no coincidence. I was to discover that her great-great-grandmother, Ester Orobio Furtado, had lived in Lisbon, before she had moved to Amsterdam.

Those lines we describe, the schemata we draw — trunk-branch-trunk-branch — they are so useful and so misleading. They give us the clarity we need. I can count the stages: yes, that makes Ester my great-great-great-great-great-great-grandmother. But they don't tell the story of how tenuous, or in this case how flammable, the limbs of the trees were.

Ester was born in Portugal more than two centuries into the Inquisition. You will meet, later, a great-grandson of hers — also a Chumaceiro — who could claim a role in encouraging the end of Portuguese anti-Jewish statutes deep into the nineteenth century. By the start of the previous century — Ester's century — many Jews had already fled. Others had long been cowed into conversion. Some embraced their new faith; some repressed their identities to the point where no vestige was left; and some, somehow, not only concealed their Jewishness but sunlessly managed to nurture and propagate it.

These were the families that were *marrano* — the term of abuse which became a token of honour for these hidden Jews. Ester had to be from one of these families. There is no way in which she could otherwise have married her husband, a Jewish artist and calligrapher whom she and we have yet to meet. In any case, the Orobio Furtados were 'one of the most illustrious of the Marrano families', according to the historian Albert Hyamson.[3]

Ester's full surname is recondite enough to suggest she was part of this clan.

Ester must have grown up surrounded by prickling fear. Perhaps not always. Perhaps there were periods where you could ignore the wash of acid in your stomach, when there was no surge of terror orchestrated from above, no self-fulfilling denunciation from the street. But when Ester was born, the fires in Lisbon were still being lit.

They were called *autos-da-fé* – 'acts of faith'. Did God appreciate the irony? Ester herself had been 18 at the time of the 1726 *auto*. Among those in the dragnet, another Orobio Furtado, almost certainly a relation. Matheos was a merchant, inscribed into the ledger as a 'New Christian' (in other words, a Jew who had ostensibly converted). Still, he was now to be cleansed, koshered, reconverted. This was – stunning to relate – the fifth time he had been done for recanting his professed belief, and sliding back into Judaism. His sentence was listed as 'prison, wearing penitential garments in perpetuity, branding, and five years in the galleys'. There is a footnote in the inquisitorial records. Matheos should consider himself lucky. This was *'abjuraçam de leve'* – 'light punishment'.[4]

Apostasy could, indeed, provoke much worse. Matheos was one of dozens to be tried; three were sentenced to die by fire.[5] One was pardoned on recantation. A woman of 65, convicted a second time of 'Judaical practices' was strangled, then burned. A 44-year-old 'priest', 'Manoel Lopes da Carvalho', shipped over from Bahia in Brazil to the Lisbon inquisitors, 'obstinately persisted in his opinion, which was, *that Christ came to Perfect, not Abolish the Law of Moses.*' And also, for good measure, that '*the Inquisitors were not Christians, but Idolators*'.

Lopes da Carvalho's unflinching stance would be put to the most abominable test, as relayed in an accompanying letter, attributed to a Samuel Oppenheim, and dated four days after the *auto-da-fé*. 'They first put a slow fire, to see if he would Recant, and then they would have strangled him at once, and put him out of pain.' Lopes da Carvalho demurred, as he did later when the fire was fiercer and he was offered another chance. The only moment he cried out – but without vehemence – was to say '"*Accept this Humble Sacrifice thou God of Israel...*" During the twenty Minutes that he was alive at the Stake, He did not once Change his Countenance, nor give the least loud Cry. He only some times shrank up his Leggs, and put his Handkerchief to his Scull and Chin, till it was burn't away; He looked to the Kings Window, and round about upon the Mob...I never saw a Creature in their Bed dye so calm resign'd and intrepid a Manner.'

It was around this time – the first half of the eighteenth century – that Montesquieu, in *The Spirit of the Laws*,[6] summoned the character of a fictional Jew to relay 'a most humble remonstrance to the inquisitors of Spain and Portugal'. The philosopher explained that the argument had been prompted by 'a Jewess of 18 years of age (Ester's age at the 1726 *auto*), who was burnt at Lisbon at the last *auto-da-fé*'.

The protest is patient, mostly polite, but in the end rather pointed. It is also, in Montesquieu's acute view, 'the most idle, I believe, that was ever wrote. When we attempt to prove things so evident, we are sure never to convince.' One of the champions of the Age of Reason acknowledges there's no arguing with some.

The final 'act of faith' in Lisbon would be held in 1739, after Ester had sailed for Amsterdam. (The butchery would end; the institutionalised repression – the prohibition on the open practice of Judaism and permission even to re-settle in-country – would be what would last almost until 1870.)

When precisely Ester did leave, there is no record. But we can though guess that it would have been a journey saturated in fear. Michael Geddes, a contemporary English Protestant cleric seconded to Lisbon, wrote that the refugees could not risk going through Spain, and so had somehow to secure passage on an English or Dutch man-of-war. Even though once aboard they should have known they were safe, 'yet these poor Wretches...if they happen to hear Portuguese spoken upon the Deck, or in any of the Cabins, they tremble Hand and Foot, as if the Familiars of the Inquisition were come to carry them away.'[7]

Ester Orobio Furtado evaded the reach of the Inquisitors. On 21st August 1736, in Amsterdam, she married 41-year-old Joseph

Siprut de Gabay, nine months to the day after his first wife[8] had been buried. Before the witnesses, Ester scratches an X, and it is barely even that: trailing a tail, her sign is a knackered starfish below the handsome swirls of her husband.

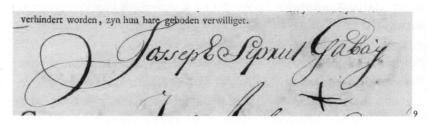

[9]

Ester bookends this story. That signature of her husband Joseph stands out not just against her 'X', but against all the other entries in Amsterdam's wedding register of that year. Joseph, after all, is a calligrapher. He is also a poet, an illustrator, a carver of tombstones, a kabbalist and a man who delights in the company of friends. His is a resolutely upbeat, sweet-tuned answer to the question of what Jewish identity – perhaps just identity – might comprise. With him, we will play out.

And from Ester and Joseph's branch, high up in the canopy of this family tree, will hang many of the stories, and some of the responses to the questions Jews ask themselves, and have asked of them by others. Who are we? Where do we fit? Do we fit? Some of it may seem familiar, as we tread the evergreen hunting ground of the anti-Semite: Jews are best when they're left out of power, out of literature, out of our country, dead. But let's not give the Jew-fearers, the Jew-haters all the tunes. What expectations do Jews have? What counts as a 'Jewish' story? What rules count in the construction and definition of identity? How do we shape our lives, and the life around us?

Lots of questions. You'll have noticed that. That's where I'm comfortable. I am a journalist, after all. I much prefer to interrogate the answers of others, than proffer my own. It's part habit, part cowardice, and – large part, I hope – my humourless and utter devotion to the idea that the BBC is better off when its staff don't mouth off.

Here, though, I'm planning to career right into religion, peoplehood and identity politics. And more: use thoughts on journalism as the starting points for how we can approach the stories of these variegated Jews, all relatives of mine.

Let's begin, then, with another question so often lobbed at us before we even open our mouths. Before you turn your gaze upon the world, have you looked in the mirror?

TWO

On Prejudice; The Student

'In case I have not said this somewhere earlier in the book I will say it now: beware of partisanship, my mistakes of fact and the distortion inevitably caused by my having seen only one corner of events.'
GEORGE ORWELL[1]

We are all reasonable people, after all. As I speak on air, does it matter that my hair is dark or light? That I am right- or left-handed? That the only vestige of my Birmingham accent is how I say 'one'? (On that, incidentally, it does matter. Very much, to some people — a greater number than you might imagine. And they can lose their rag about it. Spend money on postage to spell it out, ballpointed in capitals.)

But the Jew-thing? Well it can matter, in a number of ways. I've touched on what might be decorously described as competing views over Jews broadcasting about Israel and the Palestinians. *Cogitant, ergo sum.* That is Pure Reason.

It can also matter in a more fundamental way. You could see how on an evening stroll in Beirut, as I wandered through the slender twilight into an independent bookshop. I had noticed in the window a large collection of English books. Behind the counter stood a middle-aged couple. It was clearly their shop, and they were proud. He had a cardigan and a moustache, I remember. We exchanged smiles and hellos. I scooched slowly around the shelves. Fiction, Classic Fiction, History, Food, Jewish Studies. That took up a central display, many books turned so that their covers were facing out into the shop. Some were academic inquiries into Zionism. Many were about the Holohoax. Many were about World Governments and the Jews. And there was a whole range of boutique editions of The Protocols of the Elders of Zion. I can't remember if I said goodbye to my smiling hosts. I think I did.

This is the realm where Everyone Knows. Like the amiable chap who helped run the diner we frequented in New Jersey. One lunchtime, as my colleague stepped into the restroom, I tuned into the conversation at the bar. The manager was trying to explain to the two regulars on the stools at the counter how the Jews control three banks that control all the others. Everyone knows.

A Jew in the media is even more alluring. The very fact of it just goes to show – as one of my fellow students from university insinuated, about me, as he posted on an early social media site for alumni. That was before emailing me, a few years later, to ask if I could help him get a job at the BBC. To be fair to the conspiracy theorists, it can, indeed, be useful to be Jewish in broadcast journalism. When, for example, I chaired a panel discussion for BBC radio on the role of the Orthodox Rabbinate in marriage in Israel, I had a working knowledge of how the system functioned. Just as it might, sometimes, be handy on my daily news show that I know something about classical music, or sport.

I am being coy, and therefore not particularly useful.

What of my prejudices?

There are two nostrums that BBC journalists like to say they hold dear. One is that we leave our baggage at the door. As we arrive for work, we shuck off our personal feelings – the ones which might interfere with our reporting. Assumptions and proclivities folded away, zipped, padlocked and ignored, until they can be unpacked back in our safe house.

Which leads to the second comforting proclamation: unblemished and unweighted, I can rely on the oldest of guardrails to keep me on track: if I'm getting it in the neck from both sides, then I'm probably getting it right. (See Brexit, the Middle East, puberty blockers, etc.)

I understand why we say those things. I'm not sure how much solace they should give us.

What about those pre-judgments, those predispositions you take to be inalienable truths? Some issues do not have rational or moral equivalence. That is obvious. But we were not always there. Man's baleful contribution to climate change is no longer 'on the one hand, on the other hand'. Nor is teachers beating pupils. We can tut and sigh over the solecisms of the past. A more useful reaction might be to adopt a certain questioning humility about what we think we know now. The chances are, we're continuing to get things slightly – even massively – wrong. In 350 years, assuming we're still around as a species, who will our descendants regard as we now regard Spinoza – a hugely important thinker seen in their time as unprintably dangerous?*

Skirting sinkholes and avoiding cul-de-sacs will be something I return to in the later section 'On Risk'. Understanding our distance from the most complete iteration of truth: that is a hint of where I may end up, when I suck up my courage in the final chapter, and attempt to foreground not journalism, but Judaism.

I do not mean to hector. It can be phenomenally difficult. I speak from continued experience: a dilettante, skating from one story to the other; the new maths teacher, trying to stay one page ahead in the textbook. There is not always time – at the time – to reflect adequately. So try to be aware of your own shortcomings. Hannah Arendt – she's back, cigarette in hand – is attempting to tell us *how* to think, not *what* to think, which is why, it seems, she has been so disparaged by the marble busts – generally male – of history and political philosophy. They appear to see her more as an observer, a journalist even.

Spotting the story is how we began. That is an easy enough concept. Prejudice is trickier. And the easiest prejudice to hold is to imagine that you harbour none.

~~~~

---

*"What greater evil can be imagined for the Republic than that honest men should be exiled as wicked because they hold different opinions and don't know how to pretend to be what they're not?"[2]

THE STUDENT (DENOUNCED 1725)

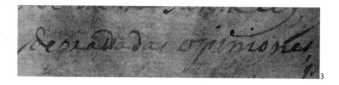

There are no crossings-out, no slip-ups. The neatness is ominous; the text is relentless. The paper may be a little mottled, the ink faded, but the letters blaze across the page. They spell out a denunciation, demanding that a fellow student be kicked out. Or, as it is expressed in the last of the petition's three pages: that the gentlemen governors of the synagogue's *mahamad* – its governing council – 'tear out this weed so wicked and harmful'.[4] It is 15th August 1725.[5] The signature high and central amid a crowd of 12 is as precise and careful as the text it affirms. Capped with a modest flourish, we meet great-great-great-great-great-great-grandfather Abraham Mendez Chumazero.

Abraham was 20, at most; maybe still a teenager. He was in the class of 'very advanced Talmudic scholars',[6] poring over hallowed words under the tutelage of David Nieto, the first *Haham* – senior rabbi – of Bevis Marks Synagogue in London.

Debate, even dialecticism, is at the root of traditional Jewish study. Should you be allowed today to peer from a balcony over a *yeshiva* hall of study, you will find desks facing each other in pairs; great volumes slabbed on slopes; young men bent and bobbing over paragraphs and then discussing, often disputing animatedly, the significance of text and commentary – and commentary upon commentary – ranging from the abstruse to the messianic, from the allegorical to the microscopic.

Into this timeless scene strode a student named by the petitioners as Ishac Baryentos. The class was immersed in the place it all begun, the explosion of creativity at the start of Genesis. Isaac, as we will more familiarly now spell him, asked his fellow students what they made of the sixth verse: 'And God said: Let there be a vault in the midst of the waters.'[7] Whatever they said, he challenged. The argument barrelled towards its dénouement. Traditional, Orthodox Judaism holds that the Torah was communicated directly to Moses by God, atop Mount Sinai. It cannot be, said Isaac. God has none of the human organs for speech. Moses must have been in a trance, in which God *appeared* to speak.* At least that is how the indictment against Isaac reads: he of the 'scandalous beliefs' and 'depraved opinions'.†

The charge of apostasy could barely have been more serious. Isaac, 'fluctuating between hope and fear', wrote an impassioned letter of defence against these 'criminal accusations'. He cited, in justification, passages from Maimonedes, among other medieval greats.‡

There is no record in the archives for what judgment was handed down. But what there is, is far more dread. A total absence. Isaac disappears. No record of marriage, nor burial. Neither in London, nor Amsterdam. He is not catalogued among those who head to the territories of the New World. Perhaps Isaac walked away. Much more likely is that he was cast off, the weed ripped out.§

And so I had my portrait of Abraham Mendez Chumazero, as he spelled himself: the uncompromising upholder of Orthodoxy, fired by righteousness to the point that he would sign the most wounding indictment. He might even have been the lead author. Three years later, when the Haham died, Abraham — by now not

---

*'Es a modo de un letargo en que Mosseh contemplaua y le pareda que Dios Ablaua'
†See image above
‡The third of Maimonedes' 13 Articles of Jewish Faith proclaims God's non-corporeality. Previous generations of theologians had, it seems, allowed the possibility of prophecy being revealed through dreams or chances. But emphatically not in the case of Moses: what sets him apart, they said, was that he encountered God directly.
§Compare the language of Yitzhak Rabin in the Knesset, after the Baruch Goldstein massacre of Palestinian worshippers in Hebron (quoted by the *New York Times* 01-03-1994): 'In words both lacerating and relentless, Mr. Rabin declared murderous settlers to be outcasts, alien to Israel and to Judaism. "I am shamed over the disgrace imposed upon us by a degenerate murderer," he said. "You are not part of the community of Israel," he continued, addressing the most militant settlers. "You are not part of the national democratic camp which we all belong to in this house, and many of the people despise you. You are not partners in the Zionist enterprise. You are a foreign implant. You are an errant weed. Sensible Judaism spits you out. You placed yourself outside the wall of Jewish law."' As for those 'most militant settlers' — for many years, Itamar Ben-Gvir hung a portrait of Goldstein in his home. In 2022, in the 37th Government of Israel, Ben-Gvir was appointed Minister of National Security.

just a pupil but a 'friend' of the rabbi,[8] was one of several called on to deliver obsequies. Abraham spoke in Spanish that day; others used Portuguese. The letter to *mahamad* accusing Isaac Baryentos had been written in Spanish.

Others may have ancestors who were cattle-rustlers or gun-runners; in my circles, having a fundamentalist in your family is just about as outré.

Abraham may not thank me, much less need me. But let me offer some context – political and then pseudo-psychological.

Bevis Marks Synagogue would, in time, become one of the imposing pillars of the Anglo-Jewish establishment. So establishment, indeed, that at its bi-centenary in 1901, its then *Haham* called it 'The *Cathedral* Synagogue of the Jews of England.' But when the building had first opened for prayers, it was just 45 years after Cromwell's *de facto* permission for the Jews to practise their faith openly for the first time in almost four centuries.[9] This was not, in Abraham's time, a privilege yet to be taken for granted.

The first *Haham* had been an inspired choice: Venetian-born David Nieto – a polyglot and a polymath, 'equally distinguished as philosopher, physician, poet, mathematician, astronomer and theologian',[10] and who centuries after his death would still be regarded as 'one of the most eminent of the Rabbis who have ministered to a Jewish Congregation in this country'.[11] Nieto was the rabbi leading that class at which Abraham and Isaac clashed.

And around the *Haham*, the congregation thrived, at least intellectually: 'a far greater number of men of science and of letters gathering around…or within the walls of the Synagogue than at any time afterwards.'[12]

So those early years may have been gilded by brilliance. But around and beyond the synagogue's handsome arches angry waters churned.

Nieto had arrived in England late in 1701, understanding that what the country's authorities granted, they could dilute or even remove. And so as the rabbi wove Judaism and the sciences, as he inveighed against certain mystics, as he poured himself into literature, he was underpinning his belief that the very survival of the

Jews, as Jews, in England depended on 'appropriating the conceptual language and ideological underpinnings of (the English) religious establishment'.[13]

That clarity of tactics and purpose was further sharpened by the lingering effects of two phenomenally controversial episodes from the middle of the previous century. Great swathes of the Jewish world had swooned at the feet of a self-proclaimed messiah, the exotic, unstable and for a time irrepressible Shabbetai Ts'vi – a travelling mystic whose outrageous visions, interpreted and propagated by his brilliant evangelist Nathan of Gaza, captivated an audience immersed in *kabbalah* and touched by the broader vogue for millenarianism. Even now, decades after his death, the fear remained that the contagion had yet fully to be controlled.

Baruch Spinoza had been a far more sober figure, but whose seeming subversion of the conventional order posed its own great danger. He posited the idea that God and Nature are inextricable, and that God's power is the causality we experience. As we become more rational, so we integrate ourselves further into this system and become tinged with the divine. But we shouldn't kid ourselves there is a grand purpose or a moral Godhead. Even before publication, Spinoza had been banished, threatened, and extravagantly cursed by Amsterdam's Jewish authorities.[14] But the shadow – or illumination – from his writings endured.

It was for that reason that a *Shabbat* sermon *Haham* Nieto delivered on 20th November 1703 prompted, in the historian Albert Hyamson's winsome phrase, 'considerable excitement'. Some of the rabbi's listeners detected in his words 'heretical tendencies, inspired by the pantheistic teachings of Spinoza'.[15]

Nieto doubled down. '*Es lo que dixe* – As I said,' he wrote in 1704, '*que Dios y Naturaleza, y Naturaleza y Dios, es todo uno.*'[16] If his opponents thought this was a confession, the rabbi was about to elude their grasp. Spinoza, he said, had not invented the idea that Nature and God were 'all one'. Earlier scholars and mystics had said the same. What was key was the *reason*: and it stood in contrast to Spinoza's view of traditional teleology as illogical and superstitious. For Nieto, tradition was the reference point: God had a plan and we are God's instruments.[17] It fit with the *Haham*'s Olympian view that the arts and sciences and currents of philosophy were all fascinating, worthy of study, but cacophonous and often contradictory: the only solution was to rely on the ultimate Truth.*

The argument burned on. 'Independence of thought is...so widespread among Jews, and a tendency towards criticism so strong,' Hyamson timelessly observed, before delivering another of his soft-shoed shin-stingers: 'There was a group of critics, with a capacity for respect and admiration inadequately developed, who seemed to believe that in most, if not in all, matters their opinion was as justified as that of anyone else, if not more so.'

No one backed down. There were expulsions, appeals; the communities of Amsterdam and Altona were drawn in to adjudicate. Nieto survived and generously supported the rehabilitation of his accusers.

It was an episode which tested the patience and comprehension of even philo-semites: not so much the substance of the dispute as the fury with which it had been pursued. The contemporary philosopher Jean-Baptiste de Boyer wrote of it through an imagined Portuguese New Christian. The fictional refugee had only recently arrived in London. He'd gained respite from persecution, but not from trouble. Around him in London '*La discorde alloit à la fureur, on ne vouloit plus se voir ni se parler* – Discord grew into rage; people no longer wanted to see each other or speak to each other.'[18] So buffeted was the poor *converso* immigrant by the disagreements that we're told he wished himself back in Lisbon, God help him.

Alongside the competing -ologies and -osophies, there were also the perpetual tussles over ritual and rules. London's older

---

*There is a contemporary view that there is more to unite Spinoza with classical Jewish thought. We should think of him less through pantheism than *panentheism* – the belief that 'all bodies (and thoughts) are in God, yet do not exhaust God – i.e. there are some aspects or elements of God that are beyond physical (and mental) nature'.[19]

sister congregation in Amsterdam was soon in turmoil as members of the community began to chafe against rabbinic authority and tradition, in pursuit of a 'purer' faith.

In London, the tensions over observance came from a different urge – a reflection, maybe a prefiguring, of looser Hanoverian mores.[20] It reached the point where 'the London Sephardi* communal elders felt obliged to tolerate the new, more casual attitude in matters of *kashrut*, Sabbath observance, sexual conduct, and other matters of communal discipline and observance, in order to avoid having constantly to reprimand prominent and affluent persons with the attendant risk of such friction driving too many away.'[21] *Haham* Nieto was appalled by such laxity.†

Such, then, was the religious and intellectual ferment[22] in which Abraham was studying. What of the young man himself?

~~~~

Abraham's parents had wed in Amsterdam in 1704.[23] Rachel Cohen had come north from Antwerp; Jacob Mendes Chumazero, as he signed himself, from Seville.

It might seem odd that, nearly two centuries after the start of the Inquisition, Jews were still living in southern Spain. Those who did stay on the Iberian peninsula were either *conversos* – New Christians – or labelled as *marranos*: the term that conveyed the idea, pejoratively by the local population at the time, romantically later by émigré Jews, of crypto-Jews, or more perniciously and dangerously, crypto-Judaisers.

---

*For centuries, Jews grouped themselves into two broad categories. The *Sephardim* are the diaspora who before 1492 had settled on the Iberian Peninsula. (*S'farad* is the Hebrew for Spain.) The *Sephardim* became the catch-all for Jews from not just Iberia, but those who began at the end of the fifteenth century to re-settle in North Africa, the Balkans, the Middle East. The *Ashkenazim* are the diaspora who coalesced initially in what's now Germany and France, and then moved east and north.
†We'll enter these louche premises at the end of the book, via the woman who will marry Abraham Mendez Chumazero's son. Her half-brother is there, drunkenly hammering on the bedroom door in an English stately home, as his wife spends the night with one of the eighteenth century's most renowned portraitists.

It would be useful now to generalise, and to abbreviate. But historians disagree on the subjects and objects of the Inquisition: over the Holy Officers' primary motivation, and to what extent they – the class of 1492 and their heirs – were, in the rich and diverse field of Jewish persecutors, outstanding;[24] they disagree too over how far *conversos* cleaved to the old faith, how far they embraced assimilation, or – in some cases – a full-throated and ardent re-birth. Even a historian as sure-footed as Simon Schama points out, 'just what percentage of the *conversos* were authentically true believers in their new faith we shall never know'.[25]

I can add nothing other to the generalisations than a journalist's guess. Having seen other minorities routinely disparaged or despised, some – gladly or reluctantly – do forego their identity; many others just keep their head down, and try to carry on living in their homeland (especially if they cannot emigrate*) by not drawing attention to themselves. And there is the gnawing knowledge that when the next casual denunciation is tossed your way,† the presumption will be of guilt, not innocence. But it is also true that not all discrimination is the same. In that epoch, the waves of dispossession, the expulsions, the bloodshed and – a theme down the centuries, this – the fastidious bureaucracy devastated the Sephardi community. Part of the trepidation and the suffocation was not knowing when the next surge of persecutions would crash through the door. And when it did, whether with wild-eyed fervour or cynical opportunism, the charges were, at root, serious: you had killed the Messiah and you were standing in the way of salvation.

As for my opening question: 'Chumaceiro'? It is possible that the family had moved from Portugal to Spain in the early seventeenth century. The border had re-opened to Portuguese *conversos* in 1580, when Portugal had been annexed by Spain. Many moved to the economic power-houses of Seville, Cadiz and Madrid to seek

---

*As many *conversos* couldn't.
†Think of the charge of blasphemy in present-day Pakistan.

work,²⁶ or to escape the Inquisition, which was increasingly ferocious in Portugal.²⁷

The mood soured sharply in 1643, the year that Abraham's grandfather – also Abraham – was born in Cadiz.²⁸ The man who more than anyone had encouraged the migration of the Portuguese *conversos* to Spain, Count-Duke of Olivares, left the Alcázar Palace in Madrid. Philip IV may have been king, but Olivares, his long-serving Prime Minister, had been running the country.²⁹ He had encouraged Portuguese *converso* financiers to help fill the increasingly large gaps in state coffers. With his retirement – or enforced departure – the wider *converso* community lost their protector. The wheels of the Inquisition began to grind faster.

A footnote, which I can't quite relegate to the footnotes. Replacing Olivares as the new power at court was one of the count-duke's great antagonists: indeed Olivares had forced him to spend the previous ten years in exile in Rome. Now though, don Juan *Chumacero* was back in Madrid, and the new president of the Council of Castile. His driving purpose was borne of a parched, ascetic morality.³⁰ Under his leadership, possibly at his instigation, don Diego de Arce y Reinoso was also recalled from Rome to court in Madrid, and made Inquisitor General, 'with a mandate to revitalize the authority and credibility of the Holy Office'.³¹ Under his supervision, the great Seville *auto-da-fé** of 1660 was held: 'a throng estimated at no less than 100,000 persons is said to have witnessed it. Forty-seven Judaizers (mostly Portuguese³²) figured in it, of whom seven were burned – three of them alive.'³³ The memory would have been seared on the family of Jacob Mendes Chumazero, born in Seville in 1680.

There is no evidence³⁴ that don Juan Chumacero was himself of *converso* stock, let alone a relative of ours. But Chumacero/sero/ceiro/seiro/zero does not appear to be a common name. And if you had political, professional, institutional or even just educational ambition, you would have done all you could to sterilise your back-story because, through the sixteenth and seventeenth

---

*'Act of faith', let's not forget. For Heaven's sake.

centuries, to get on meant first to prove – or at least persuade the authorities of – your limpieza de sangre (purity of blood).³⁵

It was towards the end of the seventeenth century that Abraham's Seville-born father and Cadiz-born grandfather at last took this Chumazero family out of Iberia, and the maw of the Inquisition. For those who had already left, Amsterdam was not their only sanctuary. But it became the greatest. In the mid-1600s, the push from Spain coincided with a pull from the Netherlands. As the energies and malevolence of the Inquisition again swelled, across the water there was a resurgence in Spanish–Dutch trade (after the crazed, ruinous patchwork of wars across Europe in the preceding decades), and an increasingly settled community, amid the confidence and wealth of the Dutch Golden Age, which helped underpin the pragmatic, self-assured Calvinist view of these erroneous Jews. There was even a shmear of admiration in the Jewish love of text – particularly the 'Old' Testament – and the antipathy to the graven image.

The appreciation was mutual. 'The City of Amsterdam… resembles Jerusalem' wrote an immigrant Jewish historian towards the end of the seventeenth century.³⁶ (You'll meet him in the penultimate chapter, strumming a lute while sitting on a vanquished griffin.) As Yosef Kaplan neatly puts it: the New Christians could become the New Jews.³⁷

For many of these New Jews and their children, though, Amsterdam was but a way-station. Around the start of the eighteenth century, the Golden Age was fading, opportunity was shrinking, even as more immigrants came to this land – this city – of succour and safety. Dutch pre-eminence in trade was beginning to recede; add to that the 'crippling'³⁸ restrictions on jobs and guilds for Dutch Jews, and poverty among the majority of community climbed: 85 per cent of Sephardi Jews would end up on 'poor relief'.³⁹ The community welfare registers teemed with those granted money for 'emergencies'. Each year dozens were also given cash to head abroad.

On 18ᵗʰ July 1723, 'Ab'm Mendes' was given 30 guilders to go to London.⁴⁰ Maybe it was hardship that pushed him; maybe it was London that attracted him. The Sephardi community there was growing rapidly enough to need and be able to build a new synagogue. By the time the young Amsterdammer arrived, Bevis Marks was already fizzing with energy and inquiry and argument.

~~~~

So, great-great-great-great-great-great-grandfather Abraham may have been rigid and a bit of a grass – but:

Excuse 1: Given what we know about the enormous rows the *Haham*, David Nieto, had had to survive over accusations of heterodoxy, if not outright heresy, and the rabbi's own concern about giving the British ecclesiastical authorities no reason to doubt the sincerity of these Jews' biblical beliefs, then perhaps Abraham was less a slavering denouncer, than one of those prevailed upon to provide a witness statement.

Excuse 2: Add to that possibility, the much higher probability that he would have known what a privilege it was to be able, at all, to devote oneself to classes such as these. Abraham was from a family which had just escaped the strain, if not outright terror, of the Inquisition. Who knows what privations and pain his forebears, recent and receding into history, had had to endure to tend the roots of their Jewish identity, to protect them from extinction? And here was someone airily attempting to kick from under him a fundamental tenet of that faith (however tempting it is for me, now, to think that Isaac Baryentos' view of Moses and the writing of the *Torah* might be closer to my own guesswork). The blows, the scarring inflicted, even subconsciously or epigenetically, on the immigrant and their world-view: that will return in the stories to come.

Excuse 3: Add to all the above, the certainty that Abraham was still, just a young man, perhaps in his teens. A raw student.

And yet all these potential mitigations were only that. They did not alter the fact that the only firm evidence I had to assemble my picture of him suggested a hardcore follower of Orthodoxy, fired by righteousness.

Until I happened across other documents – one in particular – whose pages sketched the possibility of a different figure. They challenged, if not my prejudices, my pre-judging, then at least my comfortable judgment of Abraham.

~~~~

Abraham was back in Amsterdam by 1738.

He had had the equivalent of an academic promotion, selected with two other scholars to become members of probably the most prestigious *yeshivot* in Amsterdam.[41]

For each of the next two years, Abraham had a sermon transcribed and preserved in the collection of Ets Haim – the magnificent wood-panelled library which sits within the grounds of Amsterdam's great Spanish and Portuguese Synagogue. He topped the achievement in May 1740: a sermon on *Shabbat Emor* which merited *three* manuscripts[42] in Ets Haim. The words even crossed the North Sea. They pour across 63 beautifully transcribed pages, bound in leather, and held in the Bevis Marks archives.

Above the title page of that copy, in small Hebrew script, which someone has been thoughtful enough to translate, is this: 'I have heard from my relation the *Haham*, Abraham, the son of the *Haham*, David Meldola, when I was in the city of London that this sermon was one of the best of those preached concerning the virtues of Moses Hayim Luzzatto of blessed memory. May his worthiness be with us.'

Which prompts two thoughts. That this must have been a cracking speech: quite apart from the three copies held in Ets Haim, whoever had heard about it from 'the *Haham* Abraham' had done so many decades after it was delivered – possibly a century or more. Abraham Meldola was the senior rabbi of Bevis Marks between 1828 and 1853.[43]

And that our Abraham – now Rabbi Abraham – had a depth and a range and maybe even an open-mindedness not hinted at by the Baryentos incident. The *parasha* itself (the section of the *Torah* which was read that *Shabbat*) was from the more unforgiving pages of Leviticus. It sets out rules for the *kohenim*, the priests – down to their choice of spouse, and their appearance – and the divinely commanded punishment for a blasphemer: a communal stoning. There are other, less harsh matters to reflect on: the timetable of the year; the maintenance of the everlasting light and the shew-bread inside the Tent of Meeting; the importance of speech and of instruction.

However Abraham approached the text – and, doubtless, little daunted a man of his scholarship – he used it, we are told, to eulogise a brilliant and, at times, controversial mystic, poet, playwright, and philosopher. Rabbi Moses Haim Luzzatto (as it is more commonly spelled) was born in Padua in 1707. He died in Acre in 1747. He had been harried from the Republic of Venice, the rabbinical authorities increasingly incensed by reports of his visions and his writings.[44]

Amsterdam welcomed Luzzatto, where he became one of those three scholars – along with Abraham – to reach the highest ranks of the most elite *yeshivot*. He was such a rich character, so talented and versatile, so charismatic, so unorthodoxically Orthodox ('he had long relegated *halakhic* study to a mere two hours a day'),[45] that I cannot quite imagine that Abraham, had he been – or remained – a desiccated fundamentalist, would have found the itinerant[46] rabbi as attractive.

And then there is also the other circle that Abraham would have been close to, if not a full part of, in Amsterdam. We will join it in our final chapter. Enough to say now that this was not the realm of Amos Elon's ultra-Orthodox Jerusalem *yeshivot*, where 'over the centuries, the words have been pounded so fine they have long ago fallen to dust.'[47] It may, again, be my prejudice and my lack of textual insight; it is certainly a fond imagining – but I see Abraham, in London, deep into that summer night of 1725, copying out that letter of denunciation, a chiaroscuro clutch of equally outraged young men at his shoulder, the desk barely illuminated by a guttering candle. More than a decade later, the setting is Amsterdam, and this radiant company is sketched in sunlight and delight. It was when a poem of Luzzatto's, arranged by the composer Abraham

Caceres and sung as a duet on the happiest festival of them all, *Simchat Torah*, drew, in the words of a contemporary historian, 'an innumerable crowd, utter silence, and then indescribable joy'.[48]

Abraham did not have long to enjoy the glow. He could have been no older than 35 when he delivered his tribute to Luzzatto. Six weeks later, he was dead. He was buried in the Beth Haim cemetery, to the south of Amsterdam, on 29th June 1740.[49] It is a peaceful plot, a few paces from the Amstel, the field bounded by a bed of reeds.

His widow, Leah,[50] lived another 35 years — long enough to see her and Abraham's 25-year-old second son, Aron,[51] marry in Amsterdam in 1764. His bride: Ester, daughter of our Portuguese refugee Ester Orobio Furtado and the poet Joseph Siprut de Gabay. Joseph's own work will be set to music by Abraham Caceres and sung in the synagogue. The branches weave and braid.

THREE

On Risk; The Risk-takers

'Unless you can get beyond yourself, you were never there.'
CLIVE JAMES[1]

I have long and fondly fantasised about a second career as a professor of journalism at a handsome North American university. A sabbatical would also do. There is one insurmountable problem, before we get on to all the others. The brevity of my instruction.

Be curious.
Tell the truth.
Write well.

There is nothing else. Everything I have said up to this point and will say in the rest of the book about the practice of journalism bloviates from these three primary-coloured balloons.

Think, for example, of that crayoned platitude at the start of Chapter Two, about 'avoiding prejudice'. How useful was that? 'Embrace prejudice' would have been, well, more bracing.

I suggested that one way to avoid pre-judgment was to question not just how we are covering a story, but what we are covering. That a suspicion of sweeping generalisations might be a useful instinct. And to remember that today's statement of the obvious may be just that: today's. It was not unreasonable for us to see nothing particularly remarkable about the sun tracking across our sky, until a sixteenth-century Prussian mathematician showed that it was we who were on the move. A few decades later, Michel de Montaigne brought us back to earth, and then flung us out again. The great Ptolemy had 'established the boundaries of the known world...it used to be heresy to allow the existence of the Antipodes! But now...geographers today proceed to assure us that everything has really been seen and discovered this time... Since Ptolemy was once mistaken over his basic tenets, would it not be foolish to trust what moderns are saying now? Is it not more likely that this huge body which we call the Universe is very different from what we think?'[2]

So what to do? Discard the lens? Let the light pour straight through the socket to the back of the brain?

We need those filters, those frames of reference. Otherwise nothing will make sense. Perhaps it is better not to spend too much time trying to avoid the hard-edged prejudice, so we can invest more time navigating the far greater surface-area of space around it. Like a traditional Chinese ink drawing, the clearly delineated figure occupies only a small part of the canvas. The rest – the negative space, the background – is the territory of conventional wisdom.

It sounds pejorative. It may not be. These days most conform to the view that the electorate should extend beyond propertied men. But it may be worth recalling how recently that axiom has prevailed. In France, it was 1944 before women were granted the privilege.

What about the tougher ones? When does self-determination stray from liberating to exclusionary? How do we balance the right to offend sensitivities against the need to defend sensibilities? Is democracy the ultimate form of political organisation? If so, is our job simply to refine, to tweak? How long should the international consensus remain that the only viable solution to the Israeli–Palestinian conflict is the one that has been decades in the not-happening?

The job of the journalist is not to provide the answers, but to know what questions to ask, and when. Perhaps another Prussian provides a framework: that our understanding of the world lies somewhere between reason and experience. So much, so sort of fortune cookie Kantian. That we are guided by argument – or deduction – and fact. By being alert and open to both, we can test them. But importantly, what others say as well as what we can see, can change our position. That is our Copernican Revolution.* Our scepticism should not just be directed out there. It should be turned inwards. Are we sure we are always getting it right? Almost certainly not. But that is fine. Our reason and experience have value precisely because we are willing to challenge them, and allow them to develop and change.

Frederick Douglass deserves his place in the pantheon for many reasons: his journey from orphaned, monstrous enslavement to freedom to campaigner; his mental, physical, moral uprightness – unbending, despite lifelong assault. His eloquence and clarity; his empathy and righteous anger. And – utterly secondary to those achievements, but useful here – this brief recollection.

It is 1855. He is in the final chapter of his memoir, *My Bondage and My Freedom*. For years, he writes, 'I held it to be the first duty of the non-slaveholding states to dissolve the union with the slaveholders.' For years, this was his campaign, in person and in pen. And then, 'upon a reconsideration of the whole subject', he became convinced he had been wrong to advocate dissolution; that the constitution of the United States could be read as 'demanding the abolition of slavery as a condition of its own existence, as the supreme law of the land. Here was a radical change in my opinions... To those with whom I had been in agreement and in sympathy, I was now in opposition. What they held to be a great and important truth, I now looked upon as a dangerous error. A very painful, and yet a very natural, thing now happened. Those who could not see any honest reasons for changing their views, as I had done, could not easily

---

*I use this as a convenient shorthand, but hesitantly: I would be the first to admit how superficially I understand the work of Immanuel Kant. But my imperfect, possibly wrong-headed comprehension of his metaphysics has, at least, helped me order my thinking. I think.

see any such reasons for my change, and the common punishment of apostates was mine.'[3]

This is not to suggest we might be cast in the mould of Douglass. We are journalists, not heroes. And in the breathlessness of the day job, we have to make some assumptions, perform some shortcuts, otherwise every report would be freighted with footnotes. Yet we should still encourage our inner child to sing the four-year-old's refrain: why? but why? And we should let that child gambol, unchaperoned, around the Garden of Received Opinion. Some of the flowers may be harmless, some beneficial, some may be sedatives, some poison. But how dreary – maybe how pernicious – to stay cautious and cocooned. We have to permit ourselves not to flinch. And the best place to begin is inside our heads.

So perhaps I can extend my academic tenure with an eighth and a ninth word:

Take risks.

~~~~

For the reporter, the risk may not just lie in the conceptual. We are drawn to those places where things are going wrong. At which point, there is a simple calculus. Am I putting myself or others at too great a danger? The problem is that the factors are so imprecise. And that even afterwards, you may not have a clear answer. Yes – you are alive, and largely unscathed; that does not necessarily mean you made the right decision.

I am sure I have miscalculated many times. But that is guesswork. Far more unusual to know for certain what an idiot you have just been. Nor was this anything to do with the trajectory of a missile, the proximity of a bullet, the company of militants, the chaos of a riot, the promise of a beating. All those I have known. No, this was me being a twat all by myself.

The trip to Venezuela had been unlike any other. I had seen plenty of poverty and instability and repression and dysfunction. But I could not think of another country so awash with treasure

– oil – which had fallen into such appalling disrepair. The scale of the shortages, the corruption, the criminality was almost inconceivable, and all too conceivable in its human cost.

It was also one of those rare places where, not for linguistic or sectarian reasons, we needed two fixers in the same city. One for pretty much everything. The other for the tough barrios.

Antímano was the toughest of the lot. It was the neighbourhood that Eduardo – not his real name, as this is on me – was from. We had already had one slightly unnerving morning when he had shown us around, got us some decent voices, and persistently encouraged us not to stand out even more than we were, certainly not to use our smartphones, and to keep moving when on the streets, especially the higher we went, as climbing the hillside meant plumbing the deprivation. Otherwise, Eduardo said, we would be shot first, robbed later. To put this in some context: even in the middle-class area of Caracas where we were staying, we were told not to risk walking more than a couple of streets to a restaurant after dark; on our first night, over dinner, a local BBC colleague said that his girlfriend had been robbed that morning at gunpoint, but they both felt grateful that it had been 15 months into his posting before this had happened.

Antímano was not a middle-class part of the city. It was one of the poorest. It was also avowedly Chavista. And so it was a key part of the story, ahead of the parliamentary elections. Our last chance to gather some good sounds, some good colour was a rally that evening in Antímano. Maduro himself might turn up.

The time ticked on. Eduardo – still not his real name – had not arrived to collect us from close to our hotel. Part of our cover for going to some of the harder-bitten neighbourhoods was that we travelled in Eduardo's friend's car. This was standard practice around the world. I am very happy to take local guidance on when to ditch the armoured SUV, leave at base the six-foot-four pink-skinned safety advisor, and head out in a dented hatchback with spongy suspension. Antímano was a prime case of not advertising your arrival. So no taxi.

The problem was that Eduardo's friend's car had slipped from un-showy to non-working. This was not mere carelessness. Shortages were so acute that even if you could find a reconditioned fan belt, you might not then have ready access to the requisite carrier-bagfuls of banknotes.

Eventually, Eduardo arrived, on his own. We could try to go by public transport, but the chances were, we would arrive too late. There was only one surer way for us to get to Antímano in time: by mototaxi.

Days before, on the drive in from the airport, these bikers had provided my first sense of how Caracas did things differently. Bug-eyed, I had watched them careen and cut their way through, around and against the traffic. They moved in a way which would have felt glitchy in an eighties video game: all right-angles and full-rev acceleration and ripcord brake. Priority, traffic flow, size of enemy vehicle were immaterial. The riders' helmets were hard-hats with a chin strap.

You may know where this story is heading, but believe me, I am the most un-cavalier horseman. I have, elsewhere, worn the scorn of colleagues and the full tunnel-boring disgust of the local driver when I have announced that whatever car we take on tomorrow's long journey through the conflict-ridden Caucasus will have to have seatbelts in the back. The driver may have a gun in his glove compartment, and I may be spitting on his honour, but on this, I will win. And I did.

Eduardo said our only chance was to hail two mototaxis. We decided that Leana, the producer with me on the trip, would stay behind. I would go alone with the fixer. I set the tone by then saying to Eduardo two things of surpassing stupidity. 'On a scale of one to a hundred, what are my chances?' Eduardo: 'Fifty.' Whatever I was supposed to do with that information, I didn't. Eduardo then gave what I presume was a rough address to the impatient man revving his – my – motorcycle. I climbed on the back, took the hard-hat he was offering, attempted to tighten the chin strap, and addressed Eduardo's back: 'let's make sure we stay together.' I may as well have been ordering a sparrow and a squirrel to proceed in convoy.

Never have I been more aware that time is money. Nor that everyone else on the road is in the way. That traffic lights are an affront. That roundabouts make no sense. That I may have thought I was clambering on to the back of a bike; it was actually a tank with the torque of a fighter jet. How else to explain the calculations being made, as we dodged and feinted and bucked and roared, and lorries, buses and cars bore down on us and screamed.

Eventually, we made it on to the highway west. The sun had set. My driver ripped the throttle. Unfortunately, I only had two hands. One was gripping my heavy, bulging backpack filled with recording gear, notebooks, phone, passport, wallet; the shoulder straps had been loosened by the whipsawing journey and, in the bag's understandable bid for freedom, it was further unbalancing me. My other hand was gripping, as far as it sweatily could, a bar on the side of the bike. So although I realised that my chin strap was beginning to swing free, and my helmet was beginning to tilt, I would just have to trust my head to remain snug.

It may have done, had cars veering for exit ramps not made us swerve once more. My helmet flew off. I am not entirely sure why, given the marginal benefit there might have been in my driver keeping his eyes on the road ahead, but I tapped him on his shoulder. He glanced round; didn't brake, but glanced round, and saw my uncrowned head. He said something which I did not altogether catch, but I think connoted displeasure. And in one smooth movement – we still hadn't braked – he skid-arced the bike from the outside lane to the hard shoulder and then back into the raging tide of traffic of the lanes of highway, *against* the direction of travel. In a way, there was an irrefutable logic. He wanted his spare helmet back.

I wish I could tell you what I could see through the windscreens of the traffic approaching at a net speed of very fast. I can't. I was concentrating on four things. Holding on. Reciting the Sh'ma — one of the key prayers. Apologising to my family. And chafing at the prospect of being an object lesson at Hostile Environment Refresher Courses forever more, as tooth-sucking ex-soldiers led discussions in what an abject fuckwit I had been from soup to nuts. I am not sure how they would get to know about the details, given that I knew that I would be too dead to own up, but somehow they would know, and I found my imminent and permanent reduction to a learning experience galling.

I did not die. But nor did my mototaxi man find his helmet. I tried, once more, to communicate that I would pay him for his costs.

My relief at us eventually driving again in the same direction as the rest of the tearing highway traffic waned by my man signalling that he did not know which of the several exits for Antímano to take. He decided — it seemed at random — on a ramp which, even by this barrio's hard-boiled reputation, seemed to sing of dark desolation. There was no sign of crowds, or a rally. At least this way, I thought, I will know if Eduardo was right: whether it is indeed shoot first, rob later.

My driver invited me to dismount. I gave him money. And there was Eduardo. Before I had a chance to fall sobbing into his arms or to yell in fury, my driver had recognised him and yelled in his own fury about the helmet. I gave him more money. And then Eduardo and I went to the rally, did our evening's work, and got the metro back.

~~~~

We will visit Venezuela and the Caribbean again in the company of the relatives you are about to meet. But that is not the only connection. Some of them also took risks: they tangled with the barriers of tradition, challenged conformity, cut new paths. Was it always laudable? Please: I work for the BBC.

~~~~

THE RISK-TAKERS (DISEMBARKED 1855)

Haham Aron Mendes Chumaceiro

4

The founding solipsism of this book – I am a Jew and I am a journalist – was the basis of my valedictory *From Our Own Correspondent* as BBC Middle East correspondent. For that, the then editor of FOOC gave me the radio equivalent of a peerage. I was allowed to double up. Normal-length FOOCs are already an indulgence for a broadcast journalist: five minutes, unbroken, of you telling the story. Five minutes; 800 words. I was granted 1,500.

The sermon that made Aron Mendes Chumaceiro's name was well over 8,000. It would have taken more than 50 minutes to deliver. And it is an address to a Bar Mitzvah. A 13-year-old boy, standing below the *bimah*, neck cricked, cheeks flushed, mind wandering.

It is a relief then – and particularly for that boy in 1839 – to learn that this was a sermon to an *imaginary* Bar Mitzvah.[5] It was written to be read, not read out.

Aron was the great-grandson of Ester Orobio Furtado, whose escape from Lisbon to Amsterdam began this story. He was also the great-grandson of that differently spelled, differently cast Abraham

Mendez Chumazero – the student whose views were forged in the white heat of religious righteousness, and perhaps in his own family's recent trauma and exile from the Inquisition, and – before they reached Amsterdam – their inability, in southern Spain, to practise their Judaism.

A century later, in Amsterdam, Aron was living in more confident times. He seemed set for success. He was energetic, award-winning, assured. But when he should have been reaching his clerical prime, in his forties, he did not fill the long-vacant position of *Haham* (Senior Rabbi) in Amsterdam. 'On account of his liberal-conservative views Chumaceiro was strongly opposed by the ultra-Orthodox party,' his son wrote, after his father's death. 'He therefore accepted in 1855 from King William III the appointment of chief rabbi of the colony of Curaçao.'[6]

It would be a journey to open new continents to the family – America, North and South. The spur sounds simple enough: Aron was stymied by the old guard. But is that the whole story? And what of that mystifying description – 'liberal-conservative'?

~~~~

Perhaps it is better to start not with the man but the milieu. They were 'more confident times', I wrote. *Changing times* may be safer, if rather more yawningly vague. The Netherlands had long offered Jews freedom of confession. But it took Napoleon's revolution to extend those rights. Jews were swept up in the general inclusion across conquered lands of all religious groups which had previously been proscribed from swathes of polite and public life. At least, they were in principle. The authorities in the new Batavian Republic didn't move quickly to emancipate Jews. And – crucially, and counter-intuitively – the authorities in the Jewish community didn't rush to embrace the offer. We'll come back to that.

It's also worth remembering that come the end of the eighteenth century, the large majority of Dutch Jews were living in penury and on the margins. The governing structures of the community, and the rights to and restrictions on municipal office may not have much affected the daily grind. Rather, those hard-grafting Jews would have been more caught in the recessionary backwash of Napoleon's grand scheme to immiserate Britain. Dutch maritime trade had already been beaten into submission by the British. Napoleon's 'Continental System' administered the coup-de-grâce.

Aron was born in 1810, the year that Napoleon annexed Holland, having finally lost patience with his Dutchophile younger brother Louis, whom he'd installed as king four years before. Our toddler would have barely got to know the Emperor, though, before there was further change at the top: the French retreated, the House of Orange returned, and with the backing of the Great Powers, Willem I proclaimed himself King of the newly united Low Countries.

In some important ways – important, at least, for the future of young Aron – the essence of the Napoleonic reforms remained: a centralisation and bureaucratisation of community in the 1814 establishment of The General Committee for Israelite Affairs (*Hoofdcommissie tot de Zaken der Israelieten*); three years later, a royal decree endorsing Louis Napoleon's move, during his reign, to embed Dutch into synagogue services. (That was aimed principally at the Ashkenazi immigrants and their reliance on Yiddish, and sat within a broader push to standardise Dutch throughout the newly unified Netherlands.)

Poor Aron. We're barely giving the boy time to play before assessing his chances in the light of consistories and acculturation.

And other avenues, other opportunities would have been opening to him. The reforms at the start of the century had also broken the power of the guilds: Jews could now move into new occupations. But perhaps Aron had letters in his blood. One scholarly great-grandfather of his – Abraham – we've already met. I've wafted the promise of his literary great-grandfather – Joseph – in the penultimate chapter.

Home for Aron was number 6, Rapenburgerstraat – down the same road from the great synagogue and seminary where he would make his name. The street was at the heart of a Jewish quarter which was, even by the standards of early nineteenth century not-posh urban living, frequently squalid and utterly crammed. An attempt was made in 1795 to count the number of Jews occupying the two islands – Marken and Uilenburg – which hemmed Rapenburgerstraat in. The municipal officials admitted their estimates were rough; so packed were the houses 'even up to the attics' that there could be no guarantee that some people, 'especially children', had been overlooked.[7]

Perhaps, for that reason, Aron was drawn by the light and the calm of the synagogue and seminary reading rooms at the other end of his street, as much as by the texts and his talent. Those spaces would have been a contrast to, if not a relief from, the dirt and crush.

For most Jews, then, these were hard-scrabble times under the weight of recession. But for our future rabbi? The waters might have seemed rather more placid: a long-settled and patriotic community; an end to the great wars and power struggles; and a tradition of learning that was deep and highly regarded. But there was an undertow that tugged, naggingly, at one of Aron's singular talents: speaking.

In 1827, the *Hoofdcommissie* – that newly established link between the State and the Community – had a silver medal struck, for notable sermons in Dutch. The award carried a royal imprimatur. The obverse displayed a flaming altar; to its right leaned the tablets of the ten commandments; to its left, an anchor – a tribute to Dutch naval history.

Nothing could be less controversial, you might imagine, than the use of the national language to deliver sermons. Indeed, the only surprise might be that it was not already common practice; after all, the congregation has been in-country for decades, centuries even. But in the Sephardi synagogues across the Netherlands, the tradition remained for sermons to be delivered in Portuguese. Increasingly, heads would slump and benches empty.[8]

So conditions were ripe for change – the push to reform language sitting within a broader attempt to reform culture. The *Hoofdcommissie* stipulated that the medal would be presented not just for a sermon in Dutch, but one which had to 'stimulate general morals and a sense of social obligation, inspire religious feeling, patriotism and loyalty to the king, have a civilising influence on the young, encourage decent trades, and condemn begging and laziness.'[9]

By his twenties, Aron was already imbued with learning – he had attained the rank of Talmudic scholar.[10] His expertise in the intricate anatomy of Jewish law would lead him, later, to become president of the rabbinical court in Amsterdam. He was also a gifted speaker – although the official recognition of that came for the undelivered sermon he wrote for that imaginary Bar Mitzvah. This was a speech for publication rather than oration, and – for the publishers and the *Hoofdcommissie* – with a wider audience in mind: it was intended to be read by Christians as well as Jews.

And that may well have stirred another force – what one of the great historians of Dutch Jewry, R. G. Fuks-Mansfeld, called the 'insidious spread of a form of rigidity'.[11] This was not initially driven by the fear of the nascent Reform movement, which had been gathering momentum in neighbouring Germany since the start of the century. There, the use of the vernacular was seen as a useful tool for constructing wider change to Orthodox religious practice and the place of Jews in a non-Jewish land. Perhaps some in the Netherlands did see the promotion of virtues such as 'tolerance' which, while not un-Jewish were not seen as *specifically* Jewish, and therefore dangerously assimilating. But the bigger issue seemed to be about power.

The *mahamad* – that gentlemanly body of the great and the good – had governed Sephardi communities since their establishment at the end of the sixteenth century.* These men, drawn from the elite, 'would defer to no one but the mayors of the city'. Their sons did not train for 'the socially inferior post of

---

*At the beginning of the twentieth century, the *Jewish Encyclopedia* entry for '*mahamad*' defined it as a 'board of directors of a Spanish–Portuguese congregation...(who) exercise over the members of the congregation a despotic control which degenerated into a sort of police supervision'. (The entry was written by the emphatically non-Sephardi-sounding duo of Gotthard Deutsch and Max Schloessinger.)

rabbi...instruction was confined to the talented sons of poor local families' who were given a bursary. Rabbis were 'generally held in great honour', but they were also expected to know their place, to the point of 'subservience and obedience'. The creation of the *Hoofdcommissie* and the extension of civil rights to Jews was not, as Fuks-Mansfeld delicately puts it, 'met with unqualified enthusiasm'. It meant that the grip of the *mahamad* was being loosened.[12]

And the numbers of Sephardim were dwindling – especially compared to the immigrating Ashkenazim. For some, that was a spur to cling ever more tenaciously to the old way of doing things. Not all eminent members of the community would have been that profoundly observant themselves; maybe they were ever less so. But that may only have encouraged them to demand of their clergy that they be unbending in their traditions, and antipathetic to change. Hannah Arendt saw a similar double-standard in Germany: as the bigwigs moved away from the full rigours of *halakhic* observance, they 'demanded all the more orthodoxy from the Jewish masses'.[13] You can, dare I say, observe similar apparent contradictions today among some quarters of Anglo-Jewry.

In the meantime, we've been dancing around my lack of Dutch. What was it that Aron was saying in the words of his home nation? Did the message change with the language? Was he some cassocked revolutionary?

Even through the word-mincer of internet translation, I can see that Aron's style was confident, assertive and exhortatory. He placed the use of Dutch at the centre of the content, returning repeatedly to the question of what the role of the preacher should be. In the collection of sermons published in 1843, one starting point was Malachi Chapter 2, Verse 7: 'For the lips of a priest ought to preserve knowledge, because he is the messenger of the Lord Almighty and people seek instruction from his mouth.' He told his 'brothers and sisters' that others may have recoiled from the thought of allowing sermons in the vernacular, but not they. 'This deed deserves to be heralded in golden letters in the history of your community. Even better, it will be emulated.

You have forged the path in genuine religious civilisation and true enlightenment.'[14]

Aron was not alone in preaching in the vernacular. He was not, even, the pioneer. But he was in the vanguard. For him, there was no contradiction; rather there was mutual reinforcement. The rabbi's duty was to admonish, cajole and improve his community; it was also to make the Bible – the font of moral guidance – comprehensible; if in the pursuit of that, the sermons became more outward-facing, less of a club for initiates, with fewer recherché references, then that could only be a good thing.

To put it another way, Judaism still worked at other levels: the nanoscopic textual analysis of the rabbinic commentaries and the mystical astronomy of the *Kabbalah*. But those words used by Aron – *beschaving* (civilisation) and *verlichting* (enlightenment) – were no accidents. Fuks-Mansfeld writes that, during the reign of Willem I, it became clear that 'emancipation (was) a gift bestowed and accepted with equal reluctance'.[15] In contrast, for Aron and his fellow rabbinic riders, there was no inconsistency in a Judaism thriving and faithful, and one that was propagated in the wider polity.

So these sermons could, quite possibly, be seen as reforming. But Reform with a capital R? No. Take one of the more fearsomely saw-toothed lines of division – over the authorship of the Bible. We've seen where that could lead, with Aron's great-grandfather Abraham in London early the previous century extirpating a fellow student over the issue. As the historian Bart Wallet puts it: 'Chumaceiro was particularly strident against the new ideas about *Tanakh* (the Bible).'[16] Quite how strident, you can see just before his rallying cry to 'civilisation' and 'enlightenment', in that 1843-published sermon. Aron stopped to do battle with 'unbelievers', those who cast doubt on the laws and rules being anything other than the direct work of the Almighty. The law is immutable and eternal. And – crucially – do not even *attempt* to eff the ineffable: the very act of exploration is destructive. To try to investigate that which is beyond our comprehension, 'stabs godliness in the coronary artery' ('*dat steekt alle godsvrucht de hartader af*').[17] He concluded, slightly tautologically: 'that brings death to our doors.'

And yet, I can't quite let the case close. Not about the authorship of the Bible, and the question of the Divine; that is beyond me, in many ways. Nor am I trying to query Aron's religiosity. He was a profoundly Orthodox rabbi, a judgment I'm sure he would be relieved to be granted, coming as it does from a scantily-read Reform Jew. But his adamantine – even gory – declaration of Orthodoxy surely has to be read in the context of those in the community who *were* doubting where he was coming from.

As he approached 40, there's further documentary evidence of his broad-mindedness. He was the first editor of the first Dutch Jewish weekly, the *Nederlandsch-Israëlietische Nieuws-en Advertentie-Blad*. According to Fuks-Mansfeld, in its opening issue, in 1849, Aron explained its founding purpose was 'to serve as a forum for all sections of Dutch Jewry. Through the public airing of current disputes, he hoped to effect a general reconciliation. The able and dynamic Chumaceiro...was the ideal arbiter between the factions. He was progressive and open to European cultural currents, but conservative in the religious field.'[18]

And look at the man: that lithograph at the start of this chapter. This was a rabbi without a flowing beard. That carried a certain meaning.[19]

~~~~

We may be closer to understanding his son's description of him as 'liberal-conservative'. But how hostile was the community to the changes that he espoused? Or, more importantly, how significant was the hostile faction, the 'ultra-Orthodox party' that his son says opposed him, to the point where Aron chose to uproot and make the 5,000-mile voyage to Curaçao?

It seems unlikely that the chunterers, however loud and persistent, *were* dominant, or at least completely inimical to Aron. Because just a couple of years before Aron took the job in the

New World, the synagogue authorities had given him a singularly sensitive and top-order mission. An account was written decades later by one of his sons.[20] It appeared in *The Jewish Chronicle* of 26th November 1875.

'A ROYAL VISIT. We lately referred to a visit paid by the deceased King of Portugal to the Portuguese Synagogue of Amsterdam. The *Jewish Record* contains the following account of this occurrence, written by an eye-witness: "In the year 1852 or 1853,[21] the young King Pedro of Portugal,[22] then under the guardianship of his uncle, visited Holland *incognito*, and our illustrious King William advised him when visiting Amsterdam, not to neglect seeing the Portuguese Synagogue. A dispatch was received, that Don Pedro V, with attendants, would pay a visit to the synagogue at 3pm of the same day. None were permitted to attend but the Mahamad or Kerkeraad, the clergy, and a few invited guests. Being quite a boy at that time, curiosity led me to witness 'the grand show' and through the back door of the residence of my uncle, Hazan Joost Chumaceiro,[23] I got entrance to the women's gallery of the synagogue... When everything was shown to the illustrious visitors, they were conducted to the Mahamad or meeting-room of the congregation. There, my father, Rev. A.M. Chumaceiro, solicited by the president,[24] addressed the king in the Portuguese language. From there they went to the Beit Hammeddrash,[25] and after reading the names of the donors to the institution for the last two hundred and fifty years, which names are painted on large boards on the side walls, the king...imagine(d) himself that moment to be in the large halls of learning in Portugal. He spoke of the tolerance our people enjoyed in Amsterdam, of the wealth and industry they had brought to that city, and of which Portugal was now deprived. He promised that on his return to his country, he would make proper use of these impressions, so that on an early day the Jews might return to that country which had suffered so much from their expulsion. The king's brother, Alphonso,[26] was among the visitors. On their return to Portugal, he honestly carried out his liberal intentions, but unfortunately died after a short reign, with other members of his family, from a malignant disease that prevailed in the royal palace. His brother Alphonso succeeded him to the throne... Alphonso, present king of Portugal, has faithfully complied with the desire of his lamented brother, and nowhere in Europe do the Jews at present enjoy greater protection than in Portugal. My father still considers that event as one of the happy moments of his life, and often spoke to his children of these remarks as they have been related to you by his son."'

It is a glorious story: Aron, the descendant of Portuguese émigrés,[27] of refugees, conversing with the royals from the dynasty that had once overseen the imprisonment, the torture, the garrotting, the burning, the confiscation from, the prohibition from being, the full-panoplied persecution of the Jews; and he was conversing in their language. The Inquisition from which his ancestors had left – in most cases, fled – had only been formally ended three decades before: 1821. Aron – was it his idea? – had brought his visitors to the white-washed, black-lettered panels that bordered the synagogue seminary, inscribed with the indisputably Portuguese names of benefactors – Gutierres, Pessoa, Caminha, Coutinho, Brandão, Morão, Peixotto, Veiga, Teixeira, de Leão. A moment of silence was perhaps left, the question unspoken: does the House of Braganza see what it has lost? The teenaged regent is moved; he vows to right the ancient wrong. In 1868, his brother completes the task: 'King Dom Luiz I granted to the Jews of Lisbon permission to construct a cemetery for the burial of their co-religionists.'[28]

The incident also shows that Aron was no outcast among the *mahamad*. What he was, though, as the passage reminds us, was that he still held the rank of 'Rev.'. He was senior; by now he was the *av beit din*, the president of the rabbinic court. But still the synagogue itself, the 'Esnoga', did not fill the vacancy that had existed since 1822 for *Haham*. Nor would it until 1900. At one point, the synagogue did, in fact, ask Aron to become its senior rabbi. But only later. And he would say no.

Two years after the royal visit, whether from thwarted ambition, weariness with the linguistic stick-in-the-muds, or just a desire for new vistas, Aron accepted the job of *Haham* to the community of Curaçao – a Dutch colony. He fulfilled the criteria for the job, which beyond the 'regulation requirements', stipulated that the rabbi have 'a good appearance, modesty, tolerance, and eloquence'.[29] It was a significant appointment, made with the approval of King Willem III, on the recommendation of the *Hoofdcommissie*.

On 24th November 1855, Aron delivered his farewell sermon to the community. It was, as tradition demands, based on that week's *parasha*, or section of the *Torah*. For Aron, doubtless the occasionally rockier uplands of Leviticus and Numbers would have held no terrors. But the cycle of the year offered an easy picking, from the fertile gardens of Genesis: the *parasha VaYishlach* spanned chapters 32 to 36, out of which Aron chose one short, heavily pregnant exchange – 32:27. Jacob, the man who would become known as Israel, has spent the night wrestling with a stranger, a divine emissary – maybe an angel, maybe God himself. The stranger has dislocated the young man's hip. Still Jacob clutches him. The verse begins with a plea from the stranger, and a response from Jacob: 'Let me leave! Dawn is breaking.' 'I will not let you leave unless you bless me.'

Aron could have read the words, cocked his eyebrow, and left it there. But with a theme of such fecundity, he gave it the full Verdi: it was an operatic tour de force, a great aria of farewell. Ahead lies deep danger and a heavy task. I must forsake my father's house, my land, my birthplace; leave my country, my king, friends and relatives. I am grateful that several attempts have been made to keep me here. Don't blame me. I go in sadness. But I go called by God. Be good, be a light unto others. May God bless you and keep watch over you. May God enlighten you and grant you grace. May God turn his face towards you and grant you peace. Amen, amen.[30]

Four days later, Aron, his wife Abigail Lopez Cardoso, and their children – 19-year-old Simcha, 14-year-old Abraham, and

11-year-old Joseph Hayyim embarked for the New World, aboard the *Pegasus*.[31] It took them 53 days to reach Curaçao.

~~~~

It was 1634 when Samuel Coheño had stepped ashore with other members of the Dutch West India Company, and Spanish rule ended. Coheño's own attempts at gold-mining failed and he left.[32] Sixteen years later, twelve Dutch Jewish families were given free passage to Curaçao, 'in order to cultivate the land'.[33] It did not go well. There was ill-will towards the 'usurious and covetous'[34] Jewish settlers, led by the governor of New Netherland and Curaçao, Peter Stuyvesant. But with trade growing between the old country and South America, with the short-lived colony of Dutch Brazil ceded to the Portuguese in the middle of the seventeenth century, with Jews proficient not just in Dutch but the languages of the Iberian colonisers, and with those 1,500 Jews of Netherlands Brazil dispersing across the Caribbean, 'Curaçao...was shortly to become the most important of all the Jewish communities in the New World.'[35]

The magnificent, Dutch-gabled synagogue, *Mikvé Israel*, was finished in 1732. 'A sober, fortress-like yet graceful building painted yellow and white, its floor was covered in sand. The four principal pillars supporting the main hall are named after the four matriarchs – Sarah, Rebecca, Rachel and Leah.'[36]

It may have been one of the – if not the single – oldest communities in the western hemisphere, and it may still have been active and observant, but the 1000-strong Jews of Curaçao had been without a rabbi for more than 40 years. So the island community was delighted to land a leader of Aron's calibre. One of his twentieth-century successors, Isaac Emmanuel, ladled praise on Aron's head: 'both enlightened and orthodox'; indeed, wrote Rabbi Emmanuel, 'in spite of (my emphasis) his profound Talmudic erudition, he was liberal for his time'.[37]

Aron's preaching drew a non-Jewish crowd: his first sermon, on 26th January 1856, 'was received with a great deal of approbation by all the audience including the ministers of the Protestant Church of Curacoa (sic)'.[38] This was no one-off. During the high holy days of 1858, 'Haham Chumaceiro delivered six instructive sermons, which were admired by all present, Christians no less than Israelites.'[39]

But he was much more than a preacher, a leader of services. A month after his arrival, he founded and ran a school, recruiting locals and young teachers from Amsterdam – Joseph Bueno de Mesquita and Joseph Oëb Brandon. Shortly after their arrival, the two young men succumbed to yellow fever. Aron gave a home to Lea Brandon, the widow, and her daughter; three months later he and his wife Abigail were in sole charge of the orphan: the virus had killed the mother, too.

There was adult education, a *Beth Din*, and a new Hebrew teacher (a young rabbi from Amsterdam with an obdurately New Christian-rooted surname: he was Haim Judah Santcroos; he married Aron's daughter Simcha on arrival). Aron supervised the exhausting intricacies of *kashrut* – 'In 1867 when certain Jews refused to eat French bread on the ground that it contained forbidden ingredients, Chumaceiro made the necessary investigations and then sanctioned its consumption.'[40] A decades-long rift in the community over what appears to be a dividing wall, he resolved on the irrefutable grounds that most of the original complainants were dead. He visited, nurtured and campaigned for the neglected communities on other Caribbean islands, in Venezuela and Colombia.

He organised a huge 'exposition of manual art by women',[41] which raised money split equally between Catholic, Protestant and Jewish communities. As news arrived from Syria of a Druze massacre of 20,000 Christians, Aron collected 875 florins: 'this sum was collected entirely among Israelites, without a single cent from Christians,' huffed the journal of record for American Jewry, *The Occident*.[42] 'What a commentary this is on the slanders heaped upon our people.'

But the work and the tropical climate were leaching Aron of his energy and health. Curaçao is rarely, if ever, anything other than hot: between October to December it is also wet and even more humid. Ahead of another sweltering Caribbean summer, Aron returned for a refreshingly bleak few months in Amsterdam. There, a large delegation of *parnasim* pleaded that he remain, and become the *Haham* of the great Esnoga. Aron declined, saying Curaçao needed him more.

The following year provided proof. A smallpox epidemic swept the island. 'Rabbi Chumaceiro...visited sufferers of all colors and persuasions, praying at the bedsides of the non-Israelites if they desired it. Many ministers of other religions fled; but this heroic son of Israel braved the assaults of a disease which appals the stoutest heart.'[43]

He was thanked by the governor, and won praise abroad. His reputation could not have been higher. He was about to stumble.

~~~~

As Aron was growing up, over the border in Germany the Reform movement had begun to buffet the tenets of Orthodoxy. From middle Europe, the ructions spread westwards. Before Aron landed in Curaçao, 'there was friction (on the island) between a group demanding a series of reforms and an Orthodox group opposing them. Each group believed that the *Haham* would support it.'[44] When it came, though, the fissure did not at first tear open over difference of religious interpretation or practice, but rather over formalities and perceived impoliteness: over who had been consulted on what, when. 'Each party accused the other of being at fault... Lamentably the spirit of antagonism, exaggerated pride and ambition to lead the community dominated both parties,' wrote Emmanuel.[45] The leading figures who could have defused the tension only wound it and themselves up: 'this schism was due mainly to the unusual sensitivity of the illustrious Dr. Sol Cohen Henriques (later, Attorney-General and as such ranking second to the Governor) and to the lack of subtlety in that instance displayed by brilliant Hakham Aron Mendes Chumaceiro.'[46]

Certainly, by September 1864, 'subtlety' has been chained to a boulder, rowed towards the horizon, and heaved into the turquoise sea. Aron had a 'pastoral letter' published in *The Occident*.[47] 'We have suffered in silence all insults.' We've treated compassionately 'free-thinkers, no-thinkers and profound thinkers'. Others preached war, we presented the olive branch. We were kind, magnanimous.

It was the fourth pamphlet of the Reformers' El Porvenir (The Future) society that had blown it. It appeared — although it was not made explicit — that the pamphlet had argued that a paragraph from the central prayer of the daily liturgy, the *Amidah*, was in effect a curse on Christians.[48] Nonsense said the rabbi: the text, railing against slander, wickedness and arrogance, was written centuries before Christianity was even a thing. But worse, far worse: 'You men of El Porvenir! you have caused a heavy responsibility to fall on your shoulders.' Because you could not have written a more dangerously anti-Semitic tract had you tried. What if it fell into the hands of an enemy (not here, as the Christians are 'sufficiently enlightened')? Should a Jew then be slaughtered, 'on whose soul will such a murder devolve?'.

'We do not curse you, because you are fellow-creatures, but you have cursed yourselves... If you do not yield and repent before your God, you will be morally dead to our religion, in spite of the honorable position you may occupy in society.'

No one backed down. The separate Reform community was set up. And the pain would sharpen for Aron. 'Without wanting to,' Emmanuel says, 'Chumaceiro was obliged to introduce certain reforms — some very daring for that age — in order to hold the liberal element of Mikvé Israel from veering to the Reform Congregation. These changes certainly affected him deeply.'[49]

Those 'reforms' may have had a lower-case 'r', but Rabbi Emmanuel is bang on. They were set out across three sensational pages in the January 1865 edition of *The Occident*.[50] Among the changes in synagogue — an organ was to be used, albeit 'not played by Israelites'. The correspondent wrote that 'Rabbi Chumaceiro manifested in very strong terms his reluctance in deviating, at his age, from the course he was so used to; but seeing that it was the clamor of the Community in general and not being able to find anything against it in any of our religious law books or *Dinim*, he was obliged to allow it for the sake of our Community.' Services were to be shortened: '*Kol Nidre* only said *once* instead of *thrice*'; 'no repetition of the order of *Hamida*'.*

These were astounding, arresting decisions. And they were set out in no drily recorded minutes: 'By our reform we have established an insurmountable dyke...to protect us from the destructive flood of falsehood and slander disguised by enticing show, and hidden beneath the deceitful mantle of *bettering our creed*.' The report concluded that despite the 'poisonous arrows' and 'ardent solicitations' of 'the so-called *Reformed Community*', their number remained a puny 100-plus, compared to the 800–900 of the *Mikvé Israel* congregation.

The correspondent was not identified, save for a 'C' in the bottom right-hand margin. Perhaps this was son Abraham – still in his early twenties, but already beginning to build a reputation as a polemicist; he would later be lionised and disparaged as a political liberal.

If it were Abraham, he may have been doing his best to defend his father's honour and ease his discomfort. But from the Orthodox North American mainland, the shrift was short. The January 1865 edition of *The Occident* had a terse paragraph on the 'doings in Curaçao'. 'We can only say that we deeply regret that the Rabbi should have felt himself compelled to yield to the introduction of instrumental music in *his* synagogue.' Such a thing is explicitly proscribed, and will only lead to further change.

The pity of it. That there be such strife, such a sundering.† It feels – and I have nothing on which to base this other than a hunch – that this was a spasm from the time and place we began the chapter: the Old World and old world, where the mighty and high-table of the *mahamad* took their secular standing and sense of

---

*i.e. *Amidah*
†The schism was repaired exactly 100 years later, when the communities voted overwhelmingly to merge.[51]

entitlement into the synagogue. The rabbi was to be treated with respect — but ultimately, he was a functionary. For his part, Aron never comes across as egoistic or bombastic, a cleric ripe for Jane Austen's skewer. Indeed, after an earlier health scare, he had left detailed instructions for how his funeral and mourning period should be pared back and abbreviated, even down to the humble honorifics by which he should be known.

But nor does the rabbi appear — from his days in Amsterdam onwards — as short of self-confidence. Curaçao may have been a plum posting, and the community may have had a grand history. But it had gone through lean decades, and he had invigorated it, nurtured it; he had later turned down the highest honour in Amsterdam for it, and — for those who did care about these things — well, he was paid and treated by the island authorities on exactly the same terms as the Christian clergy, and that was not a given. And so, an act of impolitesse and hauteur — whether calculated or simply misjudged — was catalyst enough to cause a violent reaction between the forces of Orthodoxy and Reform.

And Aron was no orthodox member of the Orthodoxy. He was — said his Orthodox successor, Isaac Emmanuel, 'exceptionally liberal for his day'.[52] He had stood up to the fierce opposition from the Orthodox (and Sephardi) rabbis of Turkey to the establishment of the *Alliance Israélite Universelle* in Paris. They apparently saw this brand new entity — a global advocacy and relief group for Jews, particularly those deprived or persecuted — as a danger to the practice and primacy of Orthodoxy. Aron declared himself 'devoted to the (*Alliance*) and disposed to lend his cordial co-operation'.[53]

That had been in 1863, before the schism, and the same year that he had marked the emancipation — at last — of slaves in the Dutch West Indies. The rabbi 'conducted a solemn service in the synagogue and distinguished himself with a brilliant sermon'.[54]

But the *Haham* was beginning to run low. Whether exhausted and deflated from the rupture in the community,[55] whether just getting on a bit, or whether he himself had been touched by the latest smallpox epidemic.[56] in 1868 Aron departed for the Netherlands to recuperate. He sailed with his wife Abigail and their adopted daughter, the orphan of Joseph and Lea Brandon. Abigail died in 1870, in Amsterdam, and Aron never returned to the Caribbean, although it was almost three years before the *mahamad* on Curaçao received his formal letter of resignation.

He died on 18th September 1882, in the days between *Rosh Hashanah* and *Yom Kippur*.

Aron's death made page 5 of *The American Israelite*.[57] It was not an obituary, but a recollection of a Dutch native now living in the US. He (I presume he's a he) had only encountered the rabbi after his return to Amsterdam from Curaçao. 'Haham Chumaceiro was a man of royal appearance, towering from the head upward among men, and must have been, in his younger days, of exceedingly beautiful countenance. I heard him preach once, upon his return from the West Indies, and I shall never forget the occasion. Not alone that the venerable preacher held his audience spellbound, speaking in a voice whose every whisper could be heard in the immense synagogue, but to see the hundreds of men file past the (*Parnasim*) bench, in which the reverend guest was seated, to press his hand or kiss his face... was a picture so vividly impressed upon my mind that, had I the power, I could produce it on canvas.'

Rabbi Isaac Emmanuel, whose monumental history of Jewish Curaçao was written in 1950, had a final reflection on his predecessor. It was simple, but striking — given that Emmanuel was writing in 1950, more than 80 years after Aron had sailed away. 'Elderly members of Congregation Mikvé Israel still speak of him with love and reverence.'[58]

~~~~

Abraham Mendes Chumaceiro
There is a punchline, which like most punchlines, was probably funny once. And like most punchlines, and croissants, doesn't bear prolonged exposure.

'*But is it good for the Jews?*' could have been a zinger in the age of Lenny Bruce.* That era – roughly between Abraham Mendes Chumaceiro and now – when Jews in the *goldene medina* were beginning to rise from the expectation, from others and from themselves, that they might be better off downplaying the Jew-thing, at least in mixed company. *BiigftJ* would have been a self-ironising tilt at the trope that Jews cared about their own more than any other; that they were of a single mind as to what that group self-interest was; and, by inference, what loyalty they had to their host societies was a mask behind which their parasitical work could be done. But along with the irony came a layer of self-fulfilment, with some Jews arguing – indeed to this day – even if they *do* ask the question then you can't blame them, given they've endured millennia of persecution.

Why the rant? Perhaps because I rarely get to vent in my day job.[59] But more, that Abraham's most famous piece of writing slices through the corkscrewed reasoning.

~~~~

Abraham – the second son of Rabbi Aron Mendes Chumaceiro – was not just a polemicist and a pamphleteer. There were, after all, nine children for him and his wife Abigail[60] to support. In his early thirties, he became a lawyer. He had no legal training;[61] indeed his education ended at school. But 'autodidact, he managed to work himself up and form himself into a man who commanded reverence and admiration (for) his astute intellect.'[62]

He had walked unsteadily on to Curaçao after more than seven weeks at sea, disembarking on an exotically hot day in January, 1856. He was his father's son – religiously observant[63] and fiercely loyal; for some, too fiercely. The year of the schism between Mikvé Israel and the nascent Reformers, 23-year-old Abraham catalogued

---

*Take his 'Jewish/Goyish' routine, first given the run-out in 1961. 'Count Basie's Jewish. Ray Charles is Jewish. Eddie Cantor's goyish.' (At the risk of explaining the joke: Eddie Cantor was a talented, middle-of-the-road, all-round entertainer, born Isidore Itzkowitz.)

the Reform community's lay-preachers as 'doctor, lawyer, poet, consul, translator, planter, navigator, lieutenant and...gambler'.[64] The targets of the ridicule considered proceedings for libel, but decided against.

Six years later, though, Abraham *would* be sued for defamation, and he would lose. His achievement – his crime – was to libel the governing party in Venezuela. Curaçao's economy was on its uppers, and the belated emancipation of the island's slaves in 1863 had left it ever more reliant on subventions from the Netherlands. In 1868, some members of parliament in The Hague suggested selling the island dependencies: they were too much of a drain.[65] Dutch ministers rebuffed the idea, but the islanders were not entirely reassured.

Just to the south, the vast expanses of Venezuela had a new, ambitious leader. Antonio Guzmán Blanco had shortly before been sheltering on Curaçao, among the quiet streets of Willemstad. That was, until the Dutch Minister for the Colonies, acting 'not solely on ignorance but also on minimal interest',[66] had decided otherwise. On the orders of the minister, the Governor of Curaçao had reluctantly informed Guzmán he was to be expelled, for plotting against the government of Venezuela.

That was February 1870. Ten weeks later, Guzmán swept into Caracas. But assuming and consolidating power in Venezuela had rarely been placid. And Guzmán didn't just have reason to resent Curaçao, he more importantly saw it as a threat – a source of smuggled materiel to his opponents in-country. The key conduit was the Jewish shipping merchant, Abraham Jesurun. Up against him, on Curaçao, a shipyard competitor, Jacob Rois Mendes, positioned himself as the new Venezuelan government's representative on the island.

Mendes energetically campaigned against and complained about the fresh batch of Venezuelan émigrés on the island, drawn from the previous administration. Most of Mendes' arrows fell short. But he had more success in suing Abraham (Chumaceiro), who'd published an anti-Guzmán pamphlet in 1871, entitled *What They Call in Venezuela the Liberal Party Judged by Itself*.

Proceedings were delayed, initially, by an outbreak of tact. The judge who had been in charge of the case, like Mendes, and like Abraham, was Jewish. And not only that, he was Sol Cohen Henriques – the Reformer whose dispute with Abraham's father had led to the schism. Dr Henriques asked the governor that he be recused, for fear of exacerbating division within the community.

The governor assented. The new judge, a Protestant, still found for the plaintiff: he fined the defendant 200 guilders, plus 50 guilders in costs.[67]

Abraham appeared undaunted. He continued to publish the magazine he had co-founded in 1870, and which ran until 1874. *De Onpartijdige* ('The Impartial') may have had a Dutch title, but it 'included a considerable amount of literary writing and poetry in Spanish'.[68] That fit with its main aim: to oppose Guzmán's increasingly iron rule. And despite being at the wrong end of court action – perhaps because of it – Abraham spent the next three decades as one of Curaçao's most prominent and respected lawyers.

It was a reputation he burnished in 1877 outside the courtroom, after the island had been devastated by a hurricane. 'The lawyer Chumaceiro distinguished himself on this occasion by carrying the wounded on his shoulders from the danger zone.'[69]

Two years later, he was back in battle against Guzmán. And not just him – but the increasing diplomatic muscle of the US. The Monroe Doctrine dictated that the old world be cleaved from the new; that the Europeans clear off. The American consul in Amsterdam was given his instructions: persuade the Netherlands to sell its Caribbean islands to Venezuela.[70]

It was in this stormy context that Abraham wrote one of his signature pamphlets. *Is Curaçao Te Koop?* (*'Is Curaçao For Sale?'*) was published in The Hague in 1879. Abraham made extensive, lawyerly arguments against the false convenience of his island's disposal, and suggested ways in which Curaçao could become more self-reliant and less of a drain on the exchequer. He bookended his case with an appeal to Dutch honour. Guzmán, the military veteran, will wage a campaign of attrition, trying to squeeze us into submission. But he knows the Dutch are too noble-hearted, have too proud a history to let such a stain (vlek) adhere, to let the deed go unpunished. Curaçao, the Netherlands and the House of Orange will remain united. 'Curaçao *will not* (his italics) be sold!'

Nor was it. Abraham, though, did not have an unquestioning loyalty to all things Dutch. Or rather, all contemporary opinions Dutch. His greatest contribution came out of a very public scrap with a prominent member of the colonial establishment. The episode would lead, posthumously, to a statue, a stamp and a street: A. M. Chumaceirokade.

~~~~

About 200 years before Abraham arrived on Curaçao, in the mid-1600s, the first ship carrying Africans reached the island.[71] Those, that is, who survived the brutal, brutalising passage. Capture thousands of miles away, in a village or a homestead, was but the start of the deliberate, dehumanising terror. Then incarceration. A forced march to the coast. Further imprisonment. Fetters, branding, dysentery. A two-month passage of unrelenting stench and degradation, where survival was uncertain and not necessarily welcome. These were not people: they were chattels. On arrival they were assessed, auctioned, and — largely — shipped on elsewhere. Their reward for getting this far: a half-life ravaged by exploitation and cruelty. Curaçao was a staging post: the soil was too poor for plantations of cash crops. Although the last slave ship docked in Curaçao in 1788, it was not until 1863 that the Dutch abolished slavery in their Caribbean possessions.

Blacks and those of mixed race had long been the overwhelming majority on the island. A growing proportion were 'freed'. But this was often because the slave-owner just didn't want to pay for their food and shelter: 'a Curaçaoan slave was less a capital good than in Suriname and more of a luxury servant, sometimes even a form of conspicuous consumption.'[72] And 'freed' did not, of course, mean 'free'. They were pauperised and discriminated against, in livelihoods and the law.[73]

So the formal end of slavery in Curaçao was, as in much of the western hemisphere, not a moment of transformational liberation for the enslaved or their descendants. Nor was it a moment of universal illumination for the white population.

J.H.J. Hamelberg was a 'pioneering', 'well-known'[74] historian and archivist; he was a man of God, a pastor; he was a knight of the newly created 'Order of Orange-Nassau'. In 1894, as he looked down from his double-bagged eyes, past the thick, clipped chevron of his moustache at the words he had just penned, he knew they would carry heft and reach. They were a forceful rebuttal of the ill-considered agitation on Curaçao for the Island Council to be elected rather than appointed. What is more, some radicals were even talking of 'universal suffrage'.

Hamelberg's assertion, which he shared with readers of the magazine *Questions of the Day*, was that the right to vote would lead to separation from the motherland, perhaps even secession. And he had, literally, a killer follow-up: inviting readers to gaze northwards across the Caribbean Sea, he reasoned that with suffrage, Curaçao would become a '*negerrepubliek*'. With blacks able to vote, 'Then it is Troy. No, then Curaçao will become a second Haiti, where human sacrifice, animal behaviour and cannibalism will occur.'[75]

This was not the pathetic hysteria of a foul racist. Well, yes it was – but it had elevated company. Almost three decades before, President Andrew Johnson had patiently laid out the 'known facts' on this issue in his third State of the Union address to Congress. 'Negroes have shown less capacity for government than any other races of people...wherever they have been left to their own devices they have shown a constant tendency to relapse into barbarism.'[76]

It was time for Abraham to pose his defining question. '*Zal Het Kiesrecht Curaçao Tot Het Kannibalisme Voeren?*' ('*Will the Right to Vote in Curaçao Lead to Cannibalism?*') was a fine title for a pamphlet. Having hooked the reader, Abraham turned advocate – taking on Hamelberg point by point.[77]

The pastor had argued that universal suffrage was doubly wrong, on the grounds that it would mean not just blacks getting the vote, but Jews, who were only interested in trade and in themselves, and had no 'bonds of blood nor of history' with the colony or the Netherlands. Abraham spent ten pages patiently plucking, de-boning and mincing that canard, and garnishing it with examples of Dutch support for the Jews. He also drew attention to the ways in which the Jews of Curaçao had benefited the island, and thought deeply about its needs, beyond the ability of some to generate wealth: they also cared for education, sanitation, welfare and the common good. And were they to have the chance to vote, 'where is it written that all Jews think the same and would be the same in their actions?'[78] Now *that*, dear reader, is a question for the ages.

That aside, the argument was decent but unremarkable. What made the pamphlet stand out was its central line of attack – or more accurately, defence. Hamelberg's depiction of Afro-Curaçaoans (and Haitians), was way off-beam, said Abraham. The black population had made tremendous progress even before emancipation, despite all the disadvantages they still carried, and how little the authorities had done for them. It was *wonderbaar* how far they had come. Why not aid that process by giving them equal opportunities?

Abraham cited an example from his wide personal and professional experience on the island. Take schools across Curaçao, where sometimes he supervised exams. He had seen the lack of money and attention that went into the education of non-white children. Nonetheless, 'it was not rare that at such events our attention was drawn to a curly head, with pitch black skin, from whose eyes we could see spirit and intelligence glimmer, and who could give a good and correct answer to all the questions just like his lily-white fellow student.'

Hamelberg was wrong about Haiti, too. He exaggerated the instability. In any case, 'revolutions are the norm rather than the exception throughout Central and South America'. And what is to say that Curaçao should follow the excesses of Haiti? That only shows such bias against the island Hamelberg professes to love that 'we fear his sickness is not to be cured.' There is tremendous unity of spirit and purpose between blacks and whites, both Christian and Jews. And they are linguistically bound by their use of the local creole language, 'our beautiful' Papiamentu.

Abraham's full-throated advocacy of a black right to vote was extremely rare, if not altogether unique.[79] It was also unrequited. Indeed, he was forgotten after his death in 1902, writes his great-granddaughter, and it 'would be several decades before (his ideas) would be understood and realised'.[80]

In 1938, the Island Council was replaced by a legislative chamber, chosen by an electorate of property-holding men. At its opening session, the Governor paid tribute to Abraham. But it was only in 1948 that the suffrage which he had championed was extended to all men and women.

There followed a plaque, a bust and a street. Abraham Mendes Chumaceiro Boulevard is not Willemstad's most handsome drag, but it winds as long and sinuous as his whiskers, embracing the site of the National Library, and wrapping around a bay named *Waaigat* – 'Blowhole'.

The mutton chops were further celebrated in 1989:

~~~~

We can look back now and plot some terrible lines: tracks which, as we'll see, will take the Chumaceiros who stayed in the Netherlands into the twentieth century to their deaths. We can say, with reason, that that dehumanisation, that mechanisation of misery did not come from nowhere. Those methods had been tried, refined, institutionalised, accepted, ignored by Europeans abroad – and in the case of the United States, at home. Great schools of science had been built from theories of racism. Yes, the Holocaust sprang from a particular genocidal lust. But the engineering and the ideological underpinnings were not revolutionary.*

Still: I'm not giving Abraham the power of prophecy. That would be both to inflate and – strangely – to devalue what he did. It's more straightforward.

I began by saying that Abraham's most influential pamphlet, his visionary argument for universal suffrage, had prompted me, despite myself, to think of that question – perhaps once briefly amusing; now tired and falsely premised. So, given that we've got here, was *Zal het Kiesrecht...* 'good for the Jews'? That's simple. No. It was just good. Good for everyone. And so, actually, yes.

~~~~

Joseph Hayyim Mendes Chumaceiro

In the yet-to-be-published *I Spy Book of Rabbis*, there are the pastoral, the academic, the pedagogic (5 points each). There are the softly-spoken, the finger-jabbing, the incomprehensible (ditto) and the inspiring (15 points). Some rabbis can be more than one thing.

The immediate, single adjective which comes to mind – my mind, at least – for *Haham* Aron's third son Joseph Hayyim, is battle-hardened (10). His congregations were scattered across the *post-bellum* United States. Many had emerged from that convulsion to be consumed by another: the fight between tradition and reform. Joseph, reports suggest, was his father's son: 'on the one

---

*See W. E. B. Du Bois, *The World and Africa* (1946), et al.

hand, a liberal rabbi and, on the other, a representative of the traditional Spanish–Portuguese heritage'.[81]

He had been born in Amsterdam in 1844, and had studied for the ministry under his father while they were living in Curaçao. He was in his early twenties,[82] when the congregation of *Kahol Kadosh Beth Elohim* in Charleston, South Carolina, secured his services.

Joseph was no traditionalist. Charleston was the first of a series of clerical posts he held where the community was either en route to, or even close to arriving at, a full embrace of Reform mores. But even Joseph balked at some changes. In 1872, 'Beth Elohim's board voted to reinstall the congregation's infamous organ, which had been in storage since the Civil War. The organ's return coincided with the outbreak of a series of disagreeable controversies between Reverend Chumaceiro and the board. It is not clear whether or not a renewed enthusiasm for reform ultimately led to Chumaceiro's resignation in 1874.'[83]

Joseph took up a new position in New Orleans: a Sephardi congregation called *Nefutsot Hayehuda* – 'The Dispersed of Judah'. But barely had he made it through the vast portico, than he walked into another row over reform. Whatever changes to the liturgy and to services that Joseph was asked by the board to perform prompted him to write a courteous but lengthy list of objections,[84] although within a couple of years, he was reported to have shifted, and become a prime mover in the modernisation of services.[85]

In 1884, he was off again – to Philadelphia, to a community established 30 years before by the eminent Rev. Isaac Leeser, the founder and editorial force behind *The Occident* – the newspaper which had disparaged Joseph's father's concessions to the reform-minded of Curaçao. This congregation would have been staunchly traditional.

At some point during these two years in Pennsylvania, it seems that Joseph made a brief return to Curaçao. According to Emmanuel, Joseph threw himself into the cultural life and fundraising on the island. In 1890 he presented a farce for the benefit of the Poor Fund. The Governor attended and did not see the funny side, to the point where Joseph was 'severely criticised'. Chumaceiros may be thwarted; they tend not to be cowed. Joseph wrote to *The Home Journal*: 'we cannot censure in too strong terms, this common habit prevalent on this island of criticising all and everything (in) the actions of well meaning people... Sustain and support what you cannot deny.'[86]

The next move – from Pennsylvania to Indiana – appeared to bear out Emmanuel's account: Joseph 'declared that, like his father, he was for himself orthodox, for others liberal, and submitted to the will of the majority.'[87] Evansville was among a group of mid-west congregations which had sent delegates to the 1873 organising convention of the Union of American Hebrew Congregations – the proto-Reform assembly.[88] The penultimate move was back south, to Atlanta, before returning as rabbi of his father's congregation in Curaçao, in 1898.

And it was from there that came perhaps one of his most impressive achievements, in 1901 – one which suggested an unusual combination of forensic skill and tact.

A little context from slightly before: the foul bloom of anti-Semitism was recrudescing, if it ever particularly dispersed. In December 1898, Joseph wrote (from Curaçao) to *The Jewish Chronicle* (in London).

> 'The editor of *Pearson's Weekly*,[89] under the headline of "How Revolutions Are Bred in Venezuela", indulges on page 828, in the following harangue against the Jews of Curaçao: "the crowd of money-lending Jews who live and thrive there;" "the well-lined purses of the money-lenders are ever at the service of the revolution-breeder, whether Venezuela or any of the other South American republics, so that these countries are kept in a continual ferment of disorder, bloodshed and strife." "Of course the Jews demand an exorbitant interest, that the inhabitants of Curaçao fatten and grow rich at a frightful expense of both life and property; if the entire island was blotted out of existence humanity would lose nothing."'

Let's step away from the letter for one moment, consider that final sentiment from the editorial-writer, maybe shower and change our clothes, and re-join Joseph further into the letter. He regretted that the editor of *Pearson's Weekly* (Motto: *To Interest, To Elevate, to Amuse*) had refused to publish a refutation from two Curaçaoans, despite being asked in 'a dignified and polite manner'. Joseph then confronted the vile peroration, with an implicit nod to the Windward Islands Hurricane, which a few months before had rampaged across the Caribbean, trailing a swathe of death and havoc on the British colony of Barbados:

> 'This Satanic prayer has not been accomplished, which demonstrates that Providence is of a different opinion, for civilisation cannot dispense with the Jews of Curaçao, if for no other purpose than to relieve the sufferers of our neighbouring island of Barbados, which has hardly any Jews, but has lately been almost blotted out of existence. For not even the thorough-bred anti-Semite will accuse the Curaçao Jews of being uncharitable or unforgiving; they spend such wealth as they possess for suffering humanity, and have pity for the struggling anti-Semites, but they will never trust them, otherwise they may lose their reputation as honest and prudent bankers.'

That payoff is pitch-perfect. Subtle, soft-pedalled, but — were they to hear it — just mordant enough to cause the cigar-chuffers in their London clubs to pause and frown: Eh?

Joseph spoke, preached and wrote in Spanish, English and Dutch. And it was in his native language that he corralled all his skills, three years later.[90] Calvinism and Judaism had co-existed in the Netherlands, more or less happily, for several generations. Through the end of the nineteenth century, though, a missionary movement had grown. It wasn't just intrusive. It also clearly asserted that until Jews adopted the faith of the majority, they couldn't be considered true compatriots.

Defence is no Attack was the defensive title of the book. Its subtitle explained that this was 'An Exchange of Letters...a Reformed Pastor and a Jewish Rabbi about Jesus as the Messiah.'

Joseph explained his purpose in the foreword: a Protestant pastor had written to him, asking how he, a rabbi, a serious-minded scholar, could reject Jesus as the true Messiah; nothing could be more terrible (*verschrikkelijker*) to me, the pastor. It was, says, Joseph a question posed in earnest; it deserved an answer. So I do want to explain. But I don't want conflict. I certainly don't want to convert: indeed, 'as a Jew, it is strictly forbidden for me to proselytise.'[91]

Across 150-plus pages, Joseph offered close textual exegesis from the New and Old Testaments. I'm on safer territory with his unifying thought.

It was, in essence, that God is perfect and holy, and humans are not. Indeed they should not attempt to emulate God. What they do have is God-given free will. Their duty is to choose 'virtue, truth and love'.[92] For this they needed whole-heartedness, and not, in the case of the non-Christian, an intermediary named Jesus.[93]

Joseph had travelled thousands of miles; he had gone between tropical summers and frigid mid-west winters; he had crossed continents, languages and cultures; he had sometimes crossed liturgical and congregational swords. As he approached the end of his life,[94] he homed in on his central, abiding conviction. 'The Hindu who believes in Brahma, the Christian in Jesus, the Jew in God – they are all perfect and holy in that faith, in their truth, as long as they organise their lives and their behaviour accordingly... It makes no difference what others think and believe about their truth. Every righteous man must respect his fellow man. And for that, they must strictly comply with the single commandment proclaimed by all religions: "You will love *your* God and love your neighbour!"'[95]

The rabbi had perhaps sold himself short. He was, after all, a proselytiser. Just not a missionary.

~~~~

Alfredo Chumaceiro

For the first time, there's moving film footage of a Chumaceiro. Almost. It's a home movie, from 1976. The three minutes begin with a shaky pan across a slogan that runs one side of a stadium:

'O se salva Cuba, o que se hunda el mundo' – *Either Cuba is saved, or the world is sunk*. The film cuts to a podium, draped in national colours, flanked by flagstaffs, and with an honour guard at the base of the stage of two men in olive green paramilitary drab and beret, each next to a black pennant adorned with what appears to be a lightning bolt. The speakers address the crowd under a large hoarding: 'Cuba Sobre Todo', it proclaims – *Cuba Above All*. The slogan is atop photos of three men, captioned – Santana, Gomez, Chumaceiro.

~~~~

Pamphleteer Abraham and Abigail's first son, Josias – their fourth of nine children – was born not in Curaçao, but in Venezuela, in 1869. His parents had moved there – to the city of Coro, just 70 miles from Curaçao – in 1866. It's not clear what drew them to spend five years in Venezuela.[97] Abigail had been born there, but the small Jewish community had been expelled en masse in 1855, after a terrifying pogrom, the culmination of years of anti-Semitic incitement and extortion. It was only in 1859 that some Jewish families made a tentative return to the city.[98] Abraham himself wrote of his family's five years in Coro in the 1860s as a time 'when we tasted joys and sorrows'.[99]

The return to Curaçao would be the last stop for his son, Josias. He stayed for the rest of his life. But two of his children emigrated to Cuba, including his first-born, who took the name of his grandfather.

Abraham built a livelihood and a family in the Cuban hinterland, in the city of Camaguey, south-east of Havana. That's where Alfredo Senior was born in 1922. Cuba remained their home until the revolution of 1959 up-turned their lives, and they headed for Florida. The families had had a 'good business', Alfredo Senior's daughter-in-law, Eneada, told me,[100] but 'like most of the Cubans living in our country, had to leave because of the Communist regime'.[101]

One of those Cubans to leave and to settle in the US, after Fidel Castro and his paramilitary movement ousted the military dictatorship and established a revolutionary government in Havana, was Alfredo's young son. At the age of 22, on 25th July 1976, Alfredo Chumaceiro Jr appears on the front page of the *New York Times*.

3 CUBANS SEIZED WITH A PIPE BOMB

Police Say Anti-Castro Men Were Trying to Light Fuse at 14th Street Theater [102]

The 'arson-explosion' squad had been on a stake-out on the Lower East side, after a tip-off. Shortly after 3.15am, 'four officers brandishing guns were said to have closed in, shouting "Freeze!" as one suspect was about to touch a lighted cigarette to the pipe-bomb's four-inch fuse.'

Their target was the 3,000-seat movie theatre, which was hosting a sell-out music and dance performance that evening. It was billed 'In Concert with Cuba', celebrating the central date in the Cuban revolutionary calendar – 26th July.

'The three men seized outside the theater were described as Cuban aliens, living in New Jersey and followers of an anti-Castro group known as Omega 7.' 28-year-old George Gomez, 25-year-old Armando Santana, and Alfredo Chumaceiro Jr were alleged to have driven up to the kerb in a stolen car. One of them stayed behind the wheel. 'The two others got out with the bomb and a loaded .38-caliber automatic pistol.' A four-man team of officers leapt from doorways and a car where they'd been hiding. The bomb had an eight-inch length of pipe, contained more than a pound of 'high order' explosive powder. It had no timer: it was due to explode within seconds of being planted.

Although it would have detonated in the middle of the night, Captain Albert J. Sulzer said the bomb had 'tremendous potential' for injury and damage. Another officer said it 'would have blown out the whole front of the theater'.

The suspects were arrested without a struggle. The concert went ahead.

At their trial, a few months later, the defendants pleaded guilty.[103] On 14th January 1977, the Manhattan Supreme Court Justice Irvine Lang addressed the three men: 'The lesson must be loud and clear. Courts of this nation will not tolerate terrorism.'[104] Alfredo and his co-defendants faced up to 25 years in jail. They were sentenced to three, with the possibility of parole after one.

For years after his release from prison Alfredo said that he feared deportation to Cuba. The first attempt made by the US authorities was in 1983, but was, it seems, dropped. Four years later, as part of an immigration deal between Havana and Washington, a plan was renewed to deport Cuban-born convicts and undesirables. Union City, New Jersey 'grocery salesman Alfredo Chumaceiro said the prisoners "are being used like pinballs between Cuba and the United States... It's Christmas, right before these holidays, so how can the United States do this at this time?"'[105]

And what of this group, 'Omega 7', that Alfredo was accused of being a member of? Through the 1970s, *The Miami Herald* reports, the FBI and police had been 'on the trail of two anti-Castro Cuban exile terrorist organizations calling themselves Omega 7 and Cero (Zero) group'. There had so far been two assassinations, and several bombings – one of which caused horrific injuries. There had even been an attempted murder of a Chilean politician in Rome. Now though, in a 'major breakthrough...officials have evidence the two groups are a decoy name for the Cuban Nationalist Movement (CNM).'[106]

That evidence – according to Justice department officials – came in part, from what happened just weeks after Alfredo was arrested, in 1976, for the attempted movie theatre bombing in New York. The high-profile Chilean refugee, Orlando Letelier – a former member of the Allende government – was blown up, in his car, in Washington DC. Chilean secret police – working on orders from the Pinochet dictatorship – were blamed. But they hadn't been working alone. They had recruited, for the mission, members of the CNM. Indeed the boss of the New Jersey CNM branch was convicted of conspiracy and murder in the Letelier case. 'Investigators believe that (his) place as New Jersey leader of CNM has (now) been taken by Armando Santana.'[107] The same Armando Santana who had been convicted, earlier, alongside Alfredo.

A year after that intelligence 'breakthrough' was reported in *The Miami Herald*, 'Omega 7' were claiming to have been behind another brazen assassination. It was September 1980. Felix Garcia Rodriguez was an attaché to the Cuban mission at the UN. As he drove, early evening, through 'a heavily populated commercial area' of the New York borough of Queens, he was shot twice, once below the left ear, once above it. He died instantly. 'An anonymous male caller told the Associated Press that Omega 7, a terrorist group opposed to Cuban President Fidel Castro, had "executed a member of the Cuban delegation to the United Nations".'[108]

Newsweek followed up the story later that month. The magazine said that when its reporters spoke to the leader of the New Jersey branch of the CNM, Armando Santana, 'he refused to confirm or deny any connection with Omega 7, but last week CNM member Alfredo Chumaceiro insisted that "there is no connection" between the movement and Garcia's assassination.'[109] This *Newsweek* piece made it into the CIA's files – document no. CIA-RDP90-00806R000200840008-90. I know that because it's been accessible since 2010, marked as a 'Sanitized Copy Approved for Release'. Which might seem an unduly – even primly – bureaucratic procedure for a palpably open-source bit of intel. Except that a desk officer at the CIA had made it clear for us where their interest lay: halfway through the piece, one sentence was neatly underlined. 'Some of the (CNM) leaders are CIA-trained Bay of Pigs veterans who are still dedicated to the overthrow of the Castro regime.'

In time, Alfredo decamped to the centre of Cuban-émigré life, Florida. Still in his fifties, he had a stroke, and was able to communicate only with difficulty. So it is with Eneada that I exchange warm emails, about family history, family connections, and about the pandemic. I then ask about Alfredo's links to anti-Castro activity. I get no reply.

~~~~

Mordechai Ricardo

The threads which tie this family of Jews are stretching ever more thinly, ever more tenuously. Before they flutter entirely out of sight – I offer two unlikely ways to secure them. The first is weighty, absurdly so. The second is insubstantial, but perhaps rather more useful.

Mordechai Ricardo (b. 1771 the Netherlands, d. 1842 Curaçao), was, you see, my third cousin seven times removed.[110] We're approaching the boundaries of the known universe.

The events which led to a stamp – another cousinly stamp – being issued in Mordechai's honour begin in 1812. And so the great rock I am using to try to tether the n degrees of separation with Cousin M also covers the events of that year, albeit several thousand miles away. *War and Peace* is — believe me, I realise — on a different scale, a different canvas. But Tolstoy's repeated disavowal of the great man theory of history[111] at least opens the possibility that Mordechai's actions may have, through accident and compounding effect, come at an important time in the liberation of South America.

Far more plausibly (or rather, less delusionally), the second excuse for writing about Mordechai is that — to extend the tether metaphor — it is just a rather good yarn.

Colonel Simón Bolívar was 29. Within a year he would be proclaimed *El Libertador*. But for now, the outlook was bleak. The first Republic of Venezuela had collapsed. The Spanish had crushed Bolívar and his company at their last redoubt, Puerto Cabello. He fled, and then handed over to the royalists his defeated leader, Generalísimo Francisco de Miranda. Bolívar would insist, for the rest of his life, that Miranda had been the traitor in surrendering to the Spanish. Even his most sympathetic of biographers said Bolívar's betrayal of the old man, leading to a dungeon and death, was 'a monstrous act'.[112] It did though afford the young campaigner the chance to draw breath and regroup. On 27th August he set sail on a Spanish schooner for Curaçao. Within nine months, Bolívar would be greeted back in Venezuela as 'Liberator'.

He was brave, energetic, worldly, well-read and intensely charismatic. But in 1812, Bolívar's epic, continent-shaping journey had barely got going. So it was not a given that he would find succour and support in this quiet backwater, at that time under British occupation.

That he and two of his sisters did, was in large part thanks to the Jewish lawyer and merchant, Mordechai Ricardo. Bolívar had disembarked on the island, not just defeated by the Spanish, but stripped of all his property and money by the British.[113] He was 'humiliated and depressed', but Mordechai 'received him with open arms', and exhorted him to continue the struggle. He left, a few months later, a 'totally changed man'.[114] Depending on which history you read, it was either while still on Curaçao or shortly afterwards, that he distilled his call to revolution and his programme for reconstruction into The Cartagena Manifesto – 'one of the great documents of Latin American history'.[115]

Even after Bolívar had sailed for Venezuela, his two sisters, Juana and Maria Antonia, stayed for a further two years, first in Mordechai's own home, and then his mother-in-law's.[116]

In 1815, after one of the most bloody, vicious and brutal setbacks the Liberator and his supporters would endure, Bolívar washed up on the British colony of Jamaica. 'Seeing the black eyes glitter from an unnaturally gaunt face, the governor remarked that the oil had consumed the flame.'[117] And yet Bolívar still felt the urge to write to Mordechai. He had sent several letters before to 'his esteemed and long-standing friend',[118] which he understood Mordechai had not received, as they must have been lost or 'perhaps intercepted by my Spanish friends'. He thanked Mordechai for continuing to host his sisters, and for caring for him when he was mired in misfortune. He signed off 'QBSM' – *que besa su mano*: 'the one who kisses your hands'.

One hundred and twenty years later, the Dutch essayist and historian of South American independence, John de Pool, resurrected and elevated Mordechai's memory. De Pool wrote a 'historical novella', *El Primer Chispazo de Genio* ('The First Spark of Genius'),[119] about Bolívar's few months on Curaçao. The fiction gave way, at the end, for an appeal for due recognition. 'The austere and noble figure of Mordechai Ricardo (is) today unknown and forgotten.' But it was on Curaçao that the cause of South American liberation 'found its first true protector' in Mordechai. He deserved his place among the heroes honoured in the National Pantheon in Caracas.

A formal tribute did come, in 1988. The Venezuelan Post Office issued a sheet of stamps, commemorating 'El Libertador Y Curazao'.[120] They feature a miniature of a white-haired Mordechai from the 1830s, and John de Pool's own imagining of Mordechai Ricardo and Simón Bolívar strolling along the beach, behind them; in the background lies the compact, octagonal house where Mordechai long hosted Bolívar's sisters.

General Juan de Sola

The mathematician John Witney spent years theorising about a 'thing' – that was, it seems, his name for it – which existed in 196,883 dimensions.[121] If that fails to fry your brain, or indeed if you have wrapped your mind around the concept, then consider Juan (né Isaac) de Sola. He was the maternal-first-cousin-of-the-wife-of-my-third-cousin-seven-times-removed. But what a maternal-first-cousin-etc.

The third cousin seven generations back was the Mordechai Ricardo we have just met. His wife's mother, Rachel and Isaac's father, Judah, were siblings. There is haze around where (Curaçao? St Thomas?) Isaac was born, and when (1786? 1795? 1800?).[122] The year matters because it was either at the age of 26, 22, or as an astonishingly enterprising 17 year-old, that he travelled deep into Venezuela, along the Orinoco River, to the city of Angostura. Decades before it had been a splendid Spanish outpost, a jewel set in a valley of natural abundance. In the anti-royalist siege and occupation Angostura had been stripped, vandalised, wasted. But for Simón Bolívar it was to be the capital of his new republic. And a government needed a voice. He founded a newspaper: *El Correo del Orinoco*. Young Isaac joined the staff of writers.

He made something of a name as a journalist. He was restless though, and joined the patriot forces, where he won a new reputation as a brave and able soldier.[123] Isaac was attached to perhaps the toughest army of the lot – and in the war of South American liberation that is some epithet: the Army of the Apure under the hard-bitten, hard-living warlord of the plains, General José Antonio Páez.

As an officer in the *Apure Braves*, Isaac took part in the 1821 Battle of Carabobo. It was the huge, spectacular fight against the Spanish which led, decisively, to independence for Venezuela. It is still celebrated, each 24th June, as the country's Army Day.

Bolívar had painstakingly assembled, from huge distances, across harsh terrain, an array of skilled and battle-tempered fighters. His attack plan depended on the cavalry in which Isaac rode. The events deserve the account of a proper historian:[124]

> 'Páez's cavalry was despatched to the west with instructions to attack the enemy's left flank. Undertaking a forced march for two and a half hours, they rode up and down steep terrain, hacking past tropical undergrowth, fording streams, until they were two miles from the valley where (the commander of the Spanish forces) La Torre had taken position. By the time they reached Carabobo, they were labouring under a broiling sun.
>
> The Spanish general had been confident that no cavalry could possibly negotiate the precipitous landscape to the west, and so he expected the republicans to flood into the valley from the south, where a gap in the hills beckoned. But Bolívar's vanguard did not take the bait. Instead, they moved stealthily along a narrow ravine on the western side. Hacking their way up a tangle of green, they scaled the heights and there, past trees and uneven ground, were able to spy the royalists in the valley, preparing for a frontal attack. The patriots spilled over the ridge, assaulting the Spaniards where they least expected it.'

By 1823, Isaac's name had changed. The spur was, it seems, marriage. The priest who recorded his conversion wrote: 'I proceeded to the instruction of Mr. Juan de Sola, Captain of the Battalion Apure, of the Hebrew nation... I baptised him solemnly according to the Roman ritual and I imposed upon him the name of Juan Bartolomé de la Concepcion.'[125]

By the year-end, Juan had also changed appearance. The Spanish had been holed up in their final bastion, Puerto Cabello – the fortress town from which Simón Bolívar had fled in 1812, before seeking refuge on Curaçao. Paéz, Juan and their band of ferocious horsemen finally dislodged the remaining royalists, driving them to the sea. In the battle, Juan took a swipe of a sabre across the face. He carried the scar for life.

There will be another fight, another knife-marked cheek, to come. It will lead us, towards the end of this story, to the very vault of heaven.

FOUR

On Facts; The Victorians

You can believe that a Jewish and democratic state was always destined to be a contradiction. You can believe that Palestinian nationhood is a chimera, Palestinian leaders incapable of peace. Both statements may be finger-pointingly contestable, but we can have that discussion.

Or you can believe that your small Central American country is being undermined by the US. That foreign-funded NGOs are trying to engineer a 'soft coup d'état'. Again: let's talk.

What you cannot do is just say stuff and hope it works. We learn that from an early age. Be it laziness or malice, lying is wrong. It is also risky at best, self-defeating at worst, because if exposed, it can undermine faith in the rest of your argument.

You will tell me, reasonably enough, that I'm a wishful idiot: that recent experience has shown the power of the flimsy assertion, the alternative fact, the outright lie. But it cannot be – and by whatever historic accident, the BBC's strong global audiences suggest it is so – that the perplexed or pointed question does not still have its place. The claque has its allure. But not everyone wants to check in their faculties at the entrance to the club.

That is the sunny view. There is another, reading backwards, which is darker and more fearful. It is that without an attempt to establish observable, verifiable fact, we have no defence against the totalitarians. This is not hyperbole. George Orwell – in essays and novels – anatomised that danger: from loose assertion to the bastardising of language to the re-writing of history to the control of thought. Hannah Arendt warned that once the totalitarian was in full choke, it was too late: normal rules would no longer apply; it was a fallacy to assume that the weight of lies or the burden of hypocrisy would be too much for the regime to bear. 'The totalitarian system, unfortunately, is foolproof against such normal consequences; its ingeniousness rests precisely on the elimination of that reality which either unmasks the liar or forces him to live up to his pretense.'[1]

Our plodding attachment to the idea of facts may seem boringly axiomatic. It comes from a very deep urge.

~~~~

May 2018. It is two months after that trip to Lisbon where I stumbled over nothingness, and began this journey into family. In Nicaragua, it is now two weeks after protests began to roil the country. It is these demonstrations which the authorities are calling a foreign plot to bring down the government.

Outside Álvaro Conrado's house in Managua, the traffic still bellows and judders, apparently undisturbed by the chasm of despair abutting this stretch of road. But which Álvaro is being spoken of? Álvaro Senior who sits in the near-dark, the air thick with grief? Or his son, Álvaro, bespectacled, serious, curious, now forever 15 years-old? It is he who had asked his father what the protests were about, then asked his friends whether they wanted to go with him to see them. One did. Together they headed to the university. There, as Álvaro was bringing bottled water to the demonstrators, he was shot dead. Actually – more accurately, and more pertinently – there, Álvaro was shot.

Because, although maybe he would have in any case died, what is clear is that the people who took him to hospital were turned away. They were forced to hunt for another. Nor was this one, terrible aberration. We spoke in three separate conversations to doctors – only one of whom was willing to go on the record – who said that emergency rooms at public hospitals had been instructed not to admit protestors with gunshot wounds.

As for the senior figure in government: well, you can always claim that a single incident is a tragedy, and that yes there will be a full investigation. But that avowal comes late in the same interview where you've already insisted that far fewer people died in the protests than is demonstrably the case. And more bizarrely, you've also claimed that the fact that many of the demonstrators who died did so from single shots from snipers' rifles proves that this must have been the work of the opposition – because the security forces 'don't have snipers' rifles'. (Sic), as we never say on air.

In a later interview with one of President Ortega's closest advisors, I ask him about the state of democracy in Nicaragua. We go back and forth a few times. I offer one small illustration: that as we are talking it has been more than a decade since the president held a news conference, where he might have been willing to answer questions. 'Nicaragua,' responds President Ortega's confidant, 'is the country with the most press freedom in the world.' I listen now, teeth on edge, to my forensic on-air follow-up: 'Sorry, you're having a laugh.'

And then there is the Middle East. It was the middle of 2021 when I was rootling through the back-story of a former British Prime Minister. I was concerned about what I was finding. About what I *thought* I was finding. About what I am about, in this chapter, to put on display.

At the time, we had just had the announcement of the latest ceasefire between Hamas in Gaza and Israel. And the programme I'd just presented had two people saying two things, on air, that were simply not true.

A senior Hamas official said, twice, that Netanyahu had 'started this war with the heavy bombardment of Gaza'. No: we can explore, should you wish, whether it is appropriate for Gazan militants to fire a barrage of rockets deep into Israel after high tension in Jerusalem – the heavy-handed policing of al-Aqsa mosque, the threatened eviction of Palestinian families from East Jerusalem. But the sequence is germane. The Israeli air-strikes on Gaza which followed, and caused far more damage and loss of life, *followed* the missile fire into Israel. And predictably so.

And the high-ranking Israeli diplomat, when asked how concerned he was about the unusual inter-communal Palestinian–Jewish violence within internationally recognised Israel that had accompanied the 11 days of conflict with Gaza. Him: 'More concerned than what we saw with Hamas…to see the riots and incitement mainly from the Arabs against the Jews.' Me: that's not entirely correct; there was a lot of violence from Jewish ultra-nationalists. Him: 'That's absolutely a lie what you just said. There were hundreds of attacks of Arabs against Jews; there was one incident (of Jewish violence) in Bat Yam.'

So if I am going to be that punctilious on air, with what care should I make claims about my genealogy? Next to lying, hypocrisy smells almost as bad. It can't be right for me to ask that others stick, in public, to what they know – or are genuinely convinced – is true, and then to begin this chapter with a threadbare theory.

For any other cousin, there would be no need to tiptoe and to hedge: all the circumstantial evidence does point in one obvious direction. But this cousin* is the Jew who wasn't a Jew but was always seen as The Jew: Benjamin Disraeli, for short. When Rishi Sunak became PM, some opined that Disraeli's the reason we shouldn't refer to Sunak as Britain's first non-Christian Prime Minister. It is, after all, there on www.gov.uk, where along with MOT certificates and tax returns, you'll find the official list of past Prime Ministers. Under *Dates in Office* (1868–68; 1874–80) lies the prim heading *Interesting Facts*. Disraeli is allowed just one: 'He was the first and only Jewish Prime Minister to date.' Except: define Jewish. You might argue that Dizzy could barely have done more, as a baptised child or as a committed, practising

---

*Albeit, a third cousin five times removed.

Anglican adult, to prove his Christian credentials. Still, once a Jew and all that.

There's more: in the *Biography* section, in the same sans serif used elsewhere for information on Universal Credit and Passport Applications, we are told that Disraeli 'was the son of Isaac, a Jewish Italian writer'. Come again? Isaac was born in Britain and had just one parent – his father – who was an immigrant from Italy. Even if Isaac's mother had had Italian ancestry, as History – capital H – currently has it (and which I'm recklessly going to suggest is wrong) what does that make my father, born and raised in Manchester to parents who definitely were immigrants? They had come to Britain from 'Russian Poland', the place we now call Lithuania. By HMG's calculations, that must have made Dad a 'Jewish Lithuanian'. I should have let him know.

Re-drawing Dizzy's lineage goes beyond me grafting a crooked new bough on to our family tree. The lineage, which he forever misrepresented, and then others misunderstood, plays its part in that most neuralgic debate: what *is* the place of Jews? More specifically: what does it mean to be a British Jew? Or should that be – a Jewish Brit?

These are questions on which will turn the arrival in 1860s Britain (and at the end of this chapter) of my great-great-grandfather Shimshon Roco. His immigration sparked a mass brawl among Victorian Jews which, in its way, echoed the 'double consciousness' of which W. E. B. Du Bois would write so perceptively and movingly. These Jews' identity was so clearly formed in part by their concerns about how non-Jews viewed them, and what then they should do to mould their identities and shape those views. And please: the key word here is echo. I am not suggesting it was the same. What I am saying is that some passages in *The Souls of Black Folk* may help us understand and – importantly for where we end up – convey the daring subtext that we are allowed to learn from others.

I'll stand my ground on that one. But I'll cut less of a dash to begin. Because given that I'm approaching that argument over

Jewish identity by confounding decades of conventional wisdom about a part of Disraeli's lineage, you'll understand why my step is hesitant.

~~~

THE VICTORIANS (APPOINTED 1868 & 1869)

'She'd thought of herself as a Jewish German, not a German Jew. When the Nazis came to power, and friends, colleagues, neighbours scrambled to forget they'd ever known her, the transformation of her identity stunned her and the question of how it had come about became an obsession.'

VIVIAN GORNICK, OF HANNAH ARENDT[2]

'Where, in recent history, are we to draw the line between the history of the Jews as such and the history of the larger societies of which they happen to be members?'

ISAIAH BERLIN[3]

The Jews are progressing. But to reach the Victorians and the era of Jewish emancipation, we must first lurch backward. Back even before the ship bearing Ester Orobio Furtado – my *marrano* ancestor of Chapter One – beat ashore in Amsterdam in the early 1700s. It was at the end of the previous century that her father-in-law-to-be had reached the same harbour. Ester had swung north-east from Lisbon. Great-great-great-great-great-great-great-grandfather Rabbi Abraham Siprut de Gabay had hauled north-west, over land, over the 1,700 miles from Constantinople.

The Ottoman capital had been home to one of the earliest exiled Sephardi communities, coalescing after the expulsion from Spain in 1492, and five years later, the mass forced conversion in Portugal.[4] It is possible – 'probable', according to the historian Lucien Wolf, because of the rarity of the surname[5] – that the Sipruts descended from the Ibn Xaprut or Shaprut family of

Spain, whose most illustrious member was the 'physician, diplomat, finance minister, and factotum at the Court of the Caliph of Cordoba during the Muslim Golden Age',[6] Hasdai ibn Shaprut (910–979). Hasdai was not just the first of a long series of prominent Jewish statesmen to serve Spanish royalty, but possibly 'also the greatest; in any case he occupies a central place in his people's destiny and pioneered the way for new ages... One might say that when Israel's culture withered in the East, he dug up the roots and planted them on Spanish soil.'[7]

When the Inquisitors did all they could, half a millennium later, to rip out those roots, Constantinople was one of the first to offer a new home. But two centuries later the Ottoman capital had become a harsher home. It was visited, repeatedly, by the plague.[8] In 1660, fire had destroyed much of the city. War with the Holy League had drained imperial finances. A hardline, purist religious faction ascended in court. Jews with palace positions, such as physician, were told to convert to Islam or lose their jobs. They were forbidden to re-build their own razed dwellings, or simply evicted from entire districts.[9]

So Abraham, his wife Reina, their infant son Jeuda, and possibly their baby Joseph, left. Amsterdam – the 'Dutch Jerusalem' – was an immense distance, but an obvious harbour. It already had a reputation as a centre of great learning, with a magnificent house of prayer – the Esnoga, the Portuguese Synagogue, which had opened in 1675.

Rabbi Abraham would become known for his teaching. But his first entry in the community register has him noted for his needs.

If you can't quite make out the point I'm making, here's a close-up from that Amsterdam Portuguese Jewish Community welfare ledger of November 1696:

Four lines down 'Abraham xiprud de gabay' has been donated a blanket. The entry also shows that he's listed under '*Belogrados*'. That was the catch-all for Balkan Sephardim, although in Abraham's case he does indeed appear to have stayed, at least briefly, in Belgrade.* Most of these refugees arrived 'impoverished, in bad condition and in need of support',[12] and then found themselves at the bottom of the hierarchy of deserving poor – to the extent that their welfare payments, raised by the community, were but a fraction of those doled out to immigrants from western countries. Although many had been craftsmen in the Balkans, Jews, en masse, could not routinely gain access to Dutch guilds until the nineteenth century. And so the *belogrados* took on the jobs the other Amsterdam Sephardim would rather not: manual labour and work as a carer. In 1707, Abraham co-founded a charitable society for the sick.[13]

Even then, it was still often not enough. The city, prosperous for some, was expensive for all. The newcomers from the East, many trailing the trauma of persecution, did not always feel welcome. One of their own wrote, in 1691, of his 'face not fitting'.[14] Indeed, the existing Sephardi community often gave them money on condition that they leave town, and return to central and south-eastern Europe, or strike out to Italy, to Germany, to London, to North Africa, to the West Indies: good luck, please don't come back. Between 1699 and 1701, the number of *belogrados* was cut by almost a half.[15] Even in the 1740s, settled and celebrated members of the next generation had siblings and sons to whom the community gave welfare payments on the condition that they move away from Amsterdam for four, five, fifteen years.†

It was not a given, then, that Abraham would stay. One resource he could draw on, as several of the *belogrados*, was a deep well of Jewish knowledge. Abraham was a rabbi, and the son of a rabbi. He would teach *kabbalah* to the eighteenth century's most celebrated Dutch Sephardi man of letters, the poet, playwright, lexicographer,

---

*'בילוגראייד מתושבי מטה חותמי אנחנו' 'We – the signatories below, residents of Belgrade' begins a declaration signed by, among others Abraham, son of R. Jehudah Shiprut di Gabay.[11]

†'A third of the poor' were sent away, writes Levie Bernfeld (p.348). Is this what happened to Abraham Mendez Chumazero (see Chapter Two) in the early eighteenth century, and the reason he came to London?

halakhic scholar, belletrist, astrologer, historian – and protégé and friend of his son Joseph – David Franco Mendes. The young Franco Mendes wrote, giddily, that Rabbi Abraham Siprut de Gabay had initiated him into the 'secret, holy code'.[16]

Even as his reputation grew, Abraham's last years* could not have been easy. The late 1720s was a terrible time for Amsterdammers, and indeed across Europe. David Franco Mendes reported it in his history: a *furiosa Epidemia*[17] swept the city in 1727. It was so bad that the father of American epidemiology, Noah Webster, took note: 'this was a sickly year, see the bills of mortality in...Amsterdam'.[18] His observation is backed by more recent research: the city's death rate surged by a third.[19]

The community did what it could. Those who were well enough gathered within the great whitewashed walls of the Esnoga. Special prayers were intoned 'fervently'. Rabbi Abraham's youngest son, 24-year-old Isaac, was called to sound the gamut of shofar notes.[20] Outside the High Holy Days, it was an exceptional sound of alarm.

Isaac was newly married: his bride, of 1725, the 19-year-old Ester Hamiz.[21] He was an artisan, a diamond worker – one of the few trades open to Jews.† She had brought a modest cash dowry of 800 guilders. They were trying to build a life amid harsh, diseased times. Yet their younger daughter would be the grandmother of a British Prime Minister. How could that have happened?

Until now, History has been no help in answering that question. Because until now, while History has recorded that grandmother – Benjamin Disraeli's grandmother, Sarah Siprut de Gabay – as the daughter of an 'Isaac and Ester', it did not record her as the daughter of *this* Isaac and Ester.

~~~~

You can still see Sarah these days, at her grandson's country retreat in Buckinghamshire, although not immediately. The last time I stepped

---

*He died in 1733, at the age of 67.
†In November 1732, he was paid 75 guilders for teaching his trade to orphans at the religious-vocational Aby Yetomim.[22]

into Hughenden's handsome drawing room, my eye was first drawn to the fireplace, over which presided the high neck and bare alabaster shoulders of Mary Anne, Disraeli's wife; then to the canary yellow upholstery, the magenta carpet, the gilt, the ormolu, the view of the garden. Sarah was off to one side, muted against the damask. It appeared to be her new resting place; either side of her frame you could still see two small, scruffy holes punched through the wall.

23

Her frizzy auburn hair aside, she seems the English gentlewoman, clad in empire dress. The National Trust name her as Sarah Syprut de Gabay Villa Real, a woman of altogether nobler lineage than Isaac or Ester could claim. It appears to be wrong. And more than a detail.

The name would work for her grandson Benjamin Disraeli. He considered the Villa Real family to be the acme of Sephardi aristocracy, and so – not coincidentally – his kin. In 1844, in a letter to his friend, the poet and fellow Conservative MP Richard Monckton Milnes, who was staying in Berlin, Disraeli sent thanks for news that his novel, *Coningsby*, was well-received; he also offered a travel advisory: 'The Germans are now the most intelligent of tribes; but they don't rank high in blood. They are not *Sephardim*, like the Hebrews of Spain and Portugal, our friends the Sidonias and the Villareals.'[24] (Sidonia was the fictional fulcrum of his novel: the zenith of mysterious power and influence.) Four years later, in an introduction to an anthology of his father Isaac's writings he referred to 'the Villa Reals, who brought wealth to these shores almost as great as their name'.[25]

Disraeli was about as reliable with facts as he was adept, in his youth, or indeed for much of his life, with money. But his 'false, unproven, confused or seriously misleading'[26] mythologising of his ancestry has not to this day shaken loose the Villa Real suffix.

Gather your petticoats, because we are about to enter a brambled forest of names and clumped families. But if we are going to make it from Uncle Iz to Cousin Diz, we need to pick through the entanglements.

The titans of early Anglo-Jewish historiography, Lucien Wolf and Cecil Roth[27] both seemed keen to accept Disraeli's claims to the Villa Real name, but both conceded it was conjecture. Wolf ran a line via Sarah's father through Portugal, and by way of the eyeball-straining relation of her mother's sister's husband's brother in Venice. There appears to be no evidence for the first, and he's got the name wrong for the second.* Roth also saw an Italian connection: after all the Benjamin D'Israeli† whom Sarah had married in London had come from the small northern Italian town of Cento. But this doesn't lead us to a Villa Real.

Nor does Roth's other suggested route – the 'Gabay Villareal' family of Livorno. There *was* an Isaac Gabay Villareal from Livorno who had a daughter called Sara. But his handwriting was conspicuously different,[29] and even more conspicuously he had died in Amsterdam in 1739,[30] four years before Sarah Siprut de Gabay was born. And the only record of this Sara marrying was to a Joseph Saruco, from Hamburg.[31] Her father Isaac was not our Isaac.

---

*Wolf guessed that the mother of Isaac 'Syprut' – i.e. Sarah's paternal grandmother – had been a Villa Real. But Isaac's mother was the solidly *belogrado* Reina Aubi, who married a rabbi – not a rich profession – from Constantinople. And the Venetian he had in mind was the poet-rabbi, Simha Calimani. But the Jacob Calimani who married Isaac's wife's younger sister, Simha, does not appear to be his brother.

†It was as a teenager that grandson Benjamin 'now signed himself Disraeli, dropping the foreign-looking apostrophe'.[28]

The Villa Real link seems unproven, then, and Sarah's links to Italy squintingly thin.* But the lure of an Italian connection for Disraeli – even if it came just from his hat-maker grandfather – proved irresistible for the Prime Minister's biographers, keen to foreground his rich tale. Where did Disraeli come from, metaphorically as well as genealogically? They knew their subject was utterly unreliable as a source. That very flaw still enticed some to hurtle on to wild terrain. In the 1960s, one of the most admired – Lord Blake – tried to resist the tug before giving in and galloping off: 'If national or racial stereotypes are to be introduced at all – and they are perilous guides – it is not so much the Jewish as the Italian streak in Disraeli that predominated… Disraeli was proud, vain, flamboyant, quick-witted, generous, emotional, quarrelsome, extravagant, theatrical, addicted to conspiracy, fond of backstairs intrigue. He was also – and this is certainly un-Jewish – financially incompetent to a high degree… Disraeli, unlike his family, was a most untypical English Jew. Throughout his life people remarked upon the indefinable but indubitable impression that he gave of being a foreigner, whether it was the pride of a Spanish grandee, the ingenuity of the Italian juggler, or the plausibility of a Levantine on the make.'[32]

Blake may have careened off-piste. But Disraeli's was indeed a fantastical story: Ken Clarke called him the Conservative Party's unlikeliest leader in its 200 years; even more so than the grocer's daughter, a century later.[33] Born a Jew, Disraeli became the leader of the party of the English landed gentry. He would endure foaming, full-frontal Jew-phobic attacks throughout his life.[34] He never attempted to deny his Jewish lineage; it would have had little effect. Rather, Disraeli tried to co-opt snobbery, building 'edifices of ancestry'.[35] His was no ordinary Jewish stock; it was, to clarify, *consommé juif.*

Which leaves us still needing to make the leap. Isaac's father, Rabbi Abraham, had arrived as an indigent immigrant from the east. Isaac himself had once been a manual worker, who had earned

---

*Her mother's dowry did come with the promise of cash on the death of an uncle who lived in Amsterdam but had been born in Ferrara.

a bit of cash teaching at a vocational school for Dutch orphans. His wife, Ester, had not brought a big dowry with her, and it would have been odd had she. Few marriages straddled class boundaries. And yet their daughter would be rendered in oils by the Swiss portraitist François Ferrière for whom she sat in her country pile. How had that happened?

The answer is clear, prominent, unsurprising – and apparently ignored. It comes at the end of the twizzling string of signatures that prove there was but one Isaac Siprut de Gabay. They begin with his 1725 pre-nup – a great plume of curlicues issuing from a heavily condensed and italicised *IsaqueSiprutdeGabay*: they are the letters of a young man moving at speed and volume.[36] He either has tuition from his older brother, calligrapher Joseph, or perhaps he has just matured a little, because in 1732, he signs more handsomely, less hectically for the 75 guilders he is receiving to teach the boys at the orphanage.[37] The flourish reaches its confident peak in 1749, with the thickly scrolled signature of 'Isaac Siprut de Gabay merchant living in London', granting power of attorney.[38]

And that is the detail that Disraeli biographers seem to overlook: the locale. Perhaps because it is self-evident, that at various points the people who would constitute this Jewish family, these forebears of Disraeli, would have to have arrived in England, probably London, from – well, somewhere foreign. What they may have glided over is not the foreign bit. But London. London may be the key to the mystery.

A year after Isaac had married, and was still in Amsterdam, he and his brother Joseph had bought a house together – almost certainly having been loaned the 4,500 guilders – a short stroll from the synagogue.[39] They had sold it for a thousand guilders more seven years later, in 1733.[40] This was not big money.[41] The change appeared to materialise in 1736. The uncle who had promised the couple a bequest on his death, died in August. Three months later, Isaac and Ester are recorded having sold two houses on Weesperstraat for 12,500 guilders.[42]

Maybe that was the spur to try their luck in London. The couple would not have been heading out of Amsterdam as distressed *belogrados*, palmed a few coins from the communal welfare fund.[43] When, exactly, Isaac and Ester did emigrate is not clear. But that notarial record, registering Isaac as a London-based merchant, means the couple were definitely in situ by 1749. It was fecund soil for the nascent middle class. 'Those who uprooted themselves to migrate to England (in the eighteenth century) were coming to an under-developed Jewish community in a country that gave its inhabitants an extraordinary degree of personal freedom,' writes the historian Todd Endelman. 'In comparison with the rest of the European diaspora, London was a frontier boom town, with all the freedom from authority that this term implies.'[44]

Either to buy the Disraelian fantasy of descent from the *crema* of Sephardi aristocracy, or even just to leave the un-spooling at 'Isaac Siprut, a wealthy merchant', short-changes the story.

Why does it matter? Because beyond me throwing a cousinly arm around Benny, it downplays the role of London, and of England. This may have been the nation – may still be the nation – of the Eton-Oxbridge-Downing Street conveyor belt. But it was also a nation of fluidity and possibility. I sometimes, self-regardingly, wondered what my paternal grandparents, teenaged immigrants from the Russian Empire, would have made of their grandson being posted by the BBC to the heat of the Levant. This is not to compare the scale of Disraeli's ascent: but the familial tiers, the distance travelled, they are comparable. And England is where both happened. London provided Isaac, and in time, his great-grandson, astonishing opportunity – notwithstanding Disraeli's baptism and the anti-Semitism in which he was still soused. To repeat and embroider Disraeli's own account of a noble family line is to diminish the extraordinary nature of his unremarkable background. It is to fail to give due consideration of the second part of Isaiah Berlin's question at the top of this chapter – about the moving parts that make the diaspora Jew.

~~~~

Sarah D'Israeli – née Siprut de Gabay – felt she had an answer; but the people she so desperately wanted to tell were unwilling to listen. That portrait of her hanging in Hughenden betrays nothing, at least on first glance. If anything, the middle-aged woman before us looks tentative, cautious: shoulders rounded, a half-smile beginning to hitch the left cheek. But maybe she was adept at composing herself; maybe the painter was on commission and working from a brief sketch. Her grandson, in contrast, knew her for 20 years. In Disraeli's account, 'my grandmother...had imbibed that dislike for her race which the vain are too apt to adopt when they find they are born to public contempt.'*[45] Her husband, Benjamin d'Israeli, investing her dowry, had transformed his business from hat-making to coral-trading. Sarah only grew more restless. She disdained the company of Jewish London, but found herself unable to penetrate the circles she craved. In 1780, she cajoled her husband into moving to the country. They settled in the village of Enfield, in a fine three-storey house, constructed in 1672 from soft, light red bricks[46] and 'decorated with pedimented gables and a pillared facade "wrought by means of moulds into rich designs of flowers and pomegranates, with heads of cherubim over two niches in the centre of the building"'.[47] There, Benjamin 'formed an Italian garden, entertained his friends...ate macaroni which was dressed by the Venetian Consul, sang canzonettas.'[48]

His life appears girdled in delight; his wife's curdled in fury. She 'never pardoned him for his name', recalled her grandson. Indeed, although 'not incapable of deep affections' she was 'so mortified by her social position that she lived until 80 without indulging in a tender expression'. In private conversation – at least, according to Roth – Disraeli further acidulated the canvas. Grandmother was 'a demon only equalled by Sarah Duchess of Marlborough, Frances Anne (Marchioness of Londonderry) and perhaps Catherine of Russia.'[49]

Her distaste for and disavowal of Jews and Jewishness prompted her mother, Isaac's widow Ester, to all but excise her from her will.†

---

*I'm more inclined to believe Disraeli's account here, simply because he has less to gain from it.
†Her will of April 1784, held in the National Archives PROB 11/1203/20. Ester wasn't hugely impressed with her other daughter, Reina and her husband Abraham de Crasto, 'neither of whom conducted themselves through life towards me with that filial duty and regard they ought to have'.[50] Ester left them one shilling. At least Sarah got the towels, gold watch, rings, earrings and linen.

Ester bequeathed her estate to Sarah and Benjamin's only child, Isaac. She was not to know that her grandson would complete the apostasy, resigning from the synagogue, baptising his children. This was unorthodox but not unusual. London was a land of possibility for Jews, but only up to a point. There would be no Jewish member of parliament admitted until 1858, more than 20 years after her great-grandson had entered the Commons. Isaac was, by all accounts, mild-mannered and bookish. He did not appear to seek repudiation of his religion. Rather, as he argued in *The Genius of Judaism*, written in his late sixties, Jews should be fully emancipated. These sturdy patriots should suffer no civil impediments. But the book also makes clear that Isaac, a devotee of the European Enlightenment, had no time for Talmudic fiddling and finagling, and the great barnacled chains of Oral Law. By then he had long since given up membership of his synagogue, Bevis Marks, exasperated by the rigidity of their petty rules, which saw him fined for not taking up an honorary office he neither sought nor wanted.* At that point he was persuaded by a friend[51] to improve his children's chances by having them brought into the Church of England. Benjamin was 12 when he was baptised.

Disraeli — as Roth told us — set his grandmother alongside her contemporary despot, Catherine the Great. An even more distinctive comparison comes with Sarah's brief appearance in Isaiah Berlin's lecture — *Benjamin Disraeli, Karl Marx, and the Search for Identity*. Berlin takes Disraeli's line about his grandmother's vanity leading her to hate the 'race' into which she was born because of the contempt with which society treats them. 'This,' writes Berlin, 'does something to explain the attitude to his former brethren of the otherwise rational and realistic Karl Marx.'[52]

---

*Isaac was elected warden of Bevis Marks in 1813. He wrote to decline the office. His letter was either mislaid or ignored, and so — in accordance with synagogue rules — he was fined £40. He appealed, to no end. James Picciotto, in his 1875 *Sketches of Anglo-Jewish History* said the rupture could have been avoided 'had the authorities of the Sephardi Congregation displayed more judgment and tact'; he bemoaned Isaac's secession as 'unquestionably...the greatest loss to Judaism, at least from an intellectual point of view' (pp.300 & 295).

Marx's almost unprintably rabid disgust with Jews* interests Berlin less than Disraeli's relationship with Jewry and Judaism. His portrait does not just give us Disraeli in refulgent relief, but the times. That it took the singularity of Disraeli to overcome his otherness helps to set the scene for what follows in our two subsequent journeys through Victorian England: the place of Jews within English culture; the practice of Englishness within the Jewish community.

Disraeli's baptism had done nothing to stop him being thought of, always and often foremost, as The Jew. Disraeli not just saw it, but foresaw that it would never cease. So he created several extended fictions, lapping one atop the other.

'He played the game of politics like an actor in a theatrical performance, except that he played his part so well that he was convinced by his own make-believe,' writes Arendt.[54] And then, says Berlin, this 'fantastic figure', this 'epitome of dandyism and artificiality' convinced others: 'rings on his gloved fingers, elaborate ringlets of hair falling about his pale, exotic features, with his fancy waistcoats, his rococo eloquence, his epigrams, his malice, his flattery, and his dazzling social and political gifts, admired but distrusted and by some feared and loathed, a Pied Piper leading a bemused collection of dukes, earls, solid country gentlemen, and burly farmers'.[55]

Key to Disraeli's intricately constructed milieu was a sumptuous back-story of a caste, a people, a race. Enter the Villa Reals. Arendt is merciless. 'Jewishness, from the beginning, was a fact of origin which he was at liberty to embellish, unhindered by actual knowledge.'[56] This practising, knowledgeable and committed Christian had invented a legend of Jewish ancestral gentry, and then banged

---

*Hannah Arendt is much more forgiving. She says Marx is anti-Jewish (at least in his youthful writings) but not anti-Semitic.[53] In other words, she sets him in the context of those mid-nineteenth century Prussian radicals who were calling for Jewish emancipation and political equality. Marx's *On the Jewish Question* portrays the economic role of the Jew as the pinnacle of the capitalist perversion, and also the defining characteristic of the Jew. So yes: it's not the red-eyed racialism of the Nazis – the Jew as a WMD. But do you mind if I don't contort and contextualise too much? This may be an unusual mode of investigation – but as an exercise, try reading aloud the second part of Marx's essay, particularly the call and response beginning 'What is the secular basis of Judaism?' It's like drinking over-stewed black tea. Before long, your tongue shrivels.

on about it *ad tedium*. As an earlier essayist, Horace Samuel, wrote: 'He…plumed himself to the last on what he may well have called the "Oriental ichor in his veins." If his enemies dubbed him a parvenu he would fling the wretched taunt back in their faces, bidding them realise that they came from a parvenu and hybrid race, while he himself was sprung from the purest blood in Europe.'[57]

It was, in its way, an act of defiance. But it was also a volatile brew, in which everyone might get soaked. Before Berlin, before Arendt, before Samuel, there was Ewald. The first of his five volumes of biography was published in 1881, the year Disraeli died. 'Unlike many men *of his own nationality* (my emphasis), who, when they have attained to fame, carefully shun all allusions to their origin, Benjamin Disraeli gave every prominence to the fact.' And here's the spray: 'With the intense egotism and self-reliance of the Hebrew, he believed in himself and in the superiority of the race from which he sprung.'[58]

Dizzy, then, is a synecdoche for the Jews. And that matters more when he leads us from volatile to toxic. Arendt writes that Disraeli had the insight to become the Victorians' greatest id-tickler. 'Bourgeois society, in its search for entertainment and its passionate interest in the individual, insofar as he differed from the norm that is man, discovered the attraction of everything that could be supposed to be mysteriously wicked or secretly vicious… (He) could, and did, help transform chimeras into public fears and to entertain a bored society with highly dangerous fairy tales.'[59]

Disraeli was obsessed with his belief in the outsized influence of the Jewish people. 'All is race – there is no other truth,'[60] says his most famous – most notorious – Jewish character, Sidonia, the rich, murky, omnipotent puppet-master. This was Disraeli's voice; of that all his biographers appear united. It may be considered not the done thing, these days, to read the author into the words, but Disraeli scholars insist that with this novelist, you do get his voice, distilled. And so for Sidonia's world-view, read Disraeli's. It becomes explicit in his tribute to fellow Conservative MP (and the man who had loaned him the money to buy Hughenden) Lord George Bentinck, where the encomium is interrupted by a long excursion on the power – and danger – of the Jewish race, a thesis that is a nearly exact copy of Sidonia's, in the earlier *Coningsby*. Having denounced 'that pernicious doctrine of modern times – the natural equality of man', the 'cosmopolitan fraternity' that would, if enacted, 'deteriorate the great races and destroy all the genius of the world', Disraeli lauds, in contrast, the Jewish 'bias' to 'religion, property and natural aristocracy'. But be warned, if persecuted by 'ungrateful Christendom', then 'equality of man and the abrogation of property are proclaimed by secret societies who form provisional governments, and men of Jewish race are found at the head of every one of them...the peculiar and chosen race touch the hand of all the scum and low castes of Europe!' This is no theory: it was borne out in the revolutions of 1848.[61] The argument in favour, then, of Jewish emancipation, of allowing them to enter parliament (which Disraeli had initially voted *against*, and 'with the utmost sangfroid'[62]) was not liberal tolerance. Rather, as Sidonia explains to the young Tory, Coningsby, it was that without open admission to the oak-panelled rooms of power, this increasingly influential property-owning class of Jews would challenge rather than work with the establishment, and cost the Conservatives victory in election.[63]

I have rather demonised Cousin Diz. And his fantasies about his antecedents and about the string-pulling mystique of top-drawer Jews are not sufficient to explain his achievements as a politician, nor his legacy to Conservatism. But maybe they were necessary for the man – 'a man,' in Isaiah Berlin's words, 'out of his proper element', in desperate search for a set of operative ideas and an identity. 'If the answer could not be found, it would have to be invented. Disraeli's conceptions of England, Europe, Jews, himself were bold romantic fantasies. "When I want to read a book", he once declared, "I write one". His entire life was a sustained attempt to live a fiction, and to cast its spell over the minds of others.'

~~~~

Disraeli's ludicrously self-centred aphorism about books was supposedly in response to being asked whether he had read *Daniel*

Deronda. George Eliot's sumptuous final novel had been published during Disraeli's second span as Prime Minister. In a sense, his lordship was true to his epigram. Even as PM, he managed to bash out a good chunk of *Endymion*. But if, out of self-regard and lack of time, he did fail to read *Deronda* before his death in 1881, it would have been his lordship's loss. Although, as we will see, one of its most impressive strengths – the ability of this non-Jewish Victorian novelist to visualise and vocalise an array of Jewish characters and themes – was long seen as its fundamental weakness: it was either inelegant and unnecessary, or – for a later camp of critics – pernicious. But even if you belong to one of those camps, the novel is still useful for us. It will help map the terrain for the eructations accompanying the entrance of another ancestor, great-great-grandfather Shimshon. His imminent arrival in London will send the community into a paroxysm, as they use him to thrash out the place of Jews in England.

The other, rather more tenuous excuse for engaging with *Deronda* is a possible family link to the story itself. It comes from the piercing impenitence of Daniel's mother over her decision to sever him from his family and his faith: 'I rid myself of the Jewish tatters and gibberish that make people nudge each other at sight of us, as if we were tattooed under our clothes, though our faces are as whole as theirs. I delivered you from the pelting contempt that pursues Jewish separateness. I am not ashamed that I did it. It was the better for you.'[64] So the Princess Leonora Halm-Eberstein explains herself, at last, to Daniel, towards the end of the story.

Compare Disraeli's account of his grandmother. Sarah D'Israeli's outlook was – as we have already seen – occluded by the shadow of Jewishness, by the indelible reminder of her married name. It would be, she feared, a congenital blight. 'She foresaw for her child (Isaac, Disraeli's father) only a future of degradation.'[65]

How degraded was clear, even at the end of Isaac's life. The year he died, 1848, the young Mary Ann Evans – as Eliot still was, then – wrote to a friend about Isaac D'Israeli's son, the novelist and coming man in politics. 'D'Israeli (*sic**) is unquestionably an

---

*Disraeli had dropped the apostrophe back in 1822.

able man.' Mary Ann did not, though, think much of 'his theory of races'. To her, 'all the other races (including "Hebrew Caucasians") seem plainly destined for extermination'. 'My gentile nature...is almost ready to echo Voltaire's vituperation... Everything specifically Jewish is of a low grade.'[66]

By the early 1870s, she is a different woman – she is England's foremost novelist. She may have changed; her characters – such as those in her greatest novel, *Middlemarch* – still gain credibility by using 'Jew' as a mundane and unflattering reference point.

So was that loud echo between Sarah D'Israeli and the Princess's fears for their sons, just a lucky consonance? Stanley Weintraub suggests not: Eliot may 'possibly' have used 'the springboard' of Disraeli's memoir to create the character of the princess.[67] Eighty years before, Isadore Mudge and Minnie Sears had lowered the odds: the future PM's portrait of his grandmother 'so resembles' Deronda's mother 'that it seems probable' that Eliot at least owed something to Disraeli.[68]

Professor Gordon Haight disagrees. He made his imperious reputation as *the* authority on Eliot, and in his biography, he offers us a regally disdainful view of the sport. Having waved away numerous fanciful claims as the 'so-called "originals"' for Deronda and other leading characters, he cites Mudge and Sears' view on Disraeli's grandmother, whom he incorrectly names: 'of Daniel's mother, who hated Judaism...no better candidate has been proposed than Mrs Isaac D'Israeli! (sic)'.[69] The exclamation mark may imply scorn. But it also perhaps slightly misses the point.

George Eliot's supreme talent and scholarly seriousness did not indeed need a simulacrum to create a character. Gertrude Himmelfarb refers to a 'simmering' – more than a year long – which preceded the writing of *Deronda*: 'a massive work of research into Jewish learning and lore'.[70]

Nor is there anything in the author's notebooks[71] that refers to Disraeli's memoir. But it might be slightly odd had there been: after all, he had published the introduction to his father's anthology more than 20 years before Eliot had begun her slow stew. It remains perfectly conceivable – at least to me – that either Eliot, or her equally bibliophilic partner George Lewes, could have read the brief remarks of Disraeli who was, after all, a prominent member of parliament, a well-known novelist, and the son of a successful littérateur[72] – and the germ of a character or an idea may have begun to fructify.

Eliot did write directly of Disraeli in her final book of sketches, *Impressions of Theophrastus Such*, as her fictional narrator confronts so much that is here: the torsions of the hypocritical English, offering emancipation of the Jews and distaste for the Jews. It is an astringent essay, at times grating. It elevates the idea of nationhood and national characteristics, and the qualities of Englishness; it deplores their degeneration through the 'premature fusion with immigrants of alien blood';[73] it lists the allegedly unpleasant characteristics of the 'negro' and Jew. Yet it also asks: what are we afraid of? How can we can call ourselves confident, advanced, liberal? We should acknowledge our debts and influences and salute the determination of minorities to hold fast. And so for *Deronda* – a novel written just a few years before, dealing partly with the place of Jews in Victorian England – to include a woman who rejected Judaism in an attempt to improve her son's prospects: such a character would not have been a particularly gymnastic stretch of imagination. Certainly not in an author who had a genius for voice and empathy.

What does bind Sarah so closely to this novel is the dread that vibrated from her core. That her ineradicable parentage, her embarrassing married name would forever disqualify her from fitting in. And this animating fear would be borne out, not through the depiction of a character, but in the reception for the book itself. The Jewyness was awkward, unwelcome, and just not needed. Why spoil a perfectly good novel?

That 'pelting contempt' feared by the Princess for her son, prompted Eliot's publisher William Blackwood to follow the novel, a year later, with *George Eliot and Judaism: An Attempt to Appreciate 'Daniel Deronda'*. The author, Professor David Kaufmann, was a brave choice: a 25-year-old from Moravia, teaching in Budapest, writing in German, translated by a Scot for an English audience. Kaufmann acknowledges the scale of his task: 'Loud has been the weeping and terrible the gnashing of teeth in the camp of the critics. Of what has the revered and idolised Queen of novelists been thinking that she should descend to the Jews?... The majority of readers regard the world to which they are introduced in "Daniel Deronda" as one foreign, strange and repulsive.'[74] And yet England remains the country unparalleled in its welcome for Jews, where 'men can give all allegiance to a foreign State without ceasing to belong to their own people.'[75] And so, given Eliot's 'unexampled grandeur' in treating her subject, her lack of didacticism, the vivacity of her characters, 'indignation and perplexity will doubtless some day vanish, however, and give place to joy.'[76]

Kaufmann died young – his belief, as we'll see, only partially realised. Eliot herself had known from the start what was coming. Within weeks of the publication, she had written to Harriet Beecher Stowe that she had always expected 'resistance' and 'repulsion' for writing about Jews. 'But precisely because I felt that the usual attitude of Christians towards Jews is – I hardly know whether to say more impious or more stupid when viewed in the light of their professed principles, I therefore felt urged to treat Jews with such sympathy and understanding as my nature and knowledge could attain to.'[77]

Almost a century later, her biographer Gordon Haight showed that he was not just willing to dispatch lesser academic pretenders, but was even prepared to frown from on high at the subject of his life's work. Of that letter, he writes: 'This frank avowal of didacticism contradicts George Eliot's basic tenet that fiction should represent real life, "never lapse from the picture to the diagram". This is fiction with a purpose. It was not just prejudice that turned readers against it, but her failure to achieve creative realization. As William Cory* said, "It does not go into my blood".'[78]

'Fiction with a purpose'. Yes, now you mention it. Ketchup on your cornflakes. Salt on your strawberries. Fiction with a purpose. Bad taste. Not done.

But even if it were – and absolutely, we paid for a novel, not for agit-prop – then the Jewish characters still simply do not seem

---

*Poet and pedagogue, and contemporary of Eliot.

plausible. And who better to tell us than a succession of eminent non-Jews?

Henry James was the first to enlighten us in December of publication year, in the pages of *The Atlantic Monthly*. His review of the novel was arranged in a conversation between three characters: a wildly critical woman, a pantingly enthused woman, and a deeply reasonable man. 'Constantius' duly 'splains to the ladies that 'there is no-one who admires Eliot more', and he allows that *Deronda* has 'intellectual brilliancy'. And yet, 'it is the weakest of her books'. The earlier parts of the novel – dealing with the English heroine and her English antiheroic suitor – 'are admirable'. But 'all the Jewish burden of the story tended to weary me... Deronda, Mordechai, and Mirah are hardly more than shadows... I think Deronda's mother is one of the most unvivified characters; she belongs to the cold half of the book.' And as for all this blather about a 'Jewish revival'. Not even the Jews take themselves that seriously. 'They have other fish to fry!'[79]

Others followed: Eliot was doctrinaire; the characters mythical; Jews in real life are more diverse and less invariably noble. (It is a weird reading that has the book's Jewish figures as paragons en bloc.)

F. R. Leavis was the mid-century champion of Eliot, when she had rather fallen out of fashion. He helped ensure her place in The Canon, which he did much to order and polish and buff. But *Deronda*, oh dear. There was a 'good half' and a 'bad half'. Eliot was welcome to her views on the Jews. Those ideas were not off *per se*. But they did befoul the book. Without them, it could have been Eliot's masterpiece. Leavis even – please feel free to sit down and grip something firm – twice, and in detail, advocated amputating the Jew-y bit and republishing the book as '*Gwendolen Harleth* – George Eliot's superb last novel liberated from *Daniel Deronda*'.*

---

*The first time was in 1948, in *The Great Tradition*. He pulled the cord on the buzzsaw again in the 1970s, in his essay *Gwendolen Harleth* (published posthumously in the *London Review of Books* in 1982): 'There can be few who have read *Daniel Deronda* to whom the idea has not occurred of freeing by simple surgery the living part of the immense Victorian novel from the deadweight of utterly different matter that George Eliot thought fit to make it carry.'

The big men of literary criticism were agreed. Eliot's last novel: coulda been a late Beethoven quartet, but instead she had made the last two movements into a quintet for two violins, viola, cello – and triangle. All that dreary stuff that the Jews discuss – about peoplehood and philosophy and nation. Not just discordant – self-indulgent, boring.* And the Jewish characters do not ring true. We should know. We, the guardians of English literature. Jews may say that Eliot has displayed astonishing insight and mastery of voice. But that is because they are blinded by the author's generosity. (It is a useful point of principle in discussions: the Jews cannot comment on any Jewish matters that might intersect with the non-Jewish world, as they are irredeemably *parti pris*.)

There is the criticism that the Jews in *Daniel Deronda* are unbelievable, alien and/or pedestrian. More recently, the tendency has tipped the other way, to ascribe the book breath-stopping power.

Paul Johnson, cantering through his *History of the Jews*, waves his arm towards 'this book…little read now and…accounted an artistic failure even at the time'. He then pulls up, and sounds the bugle. 'But in terms of its practical effects it was probably the most influential novel of the nineteenth century.'[80]

Johnson the Zionist is an exception in the bigger-bang school of criticism. Most members see *Deronda*'s landscape-changing power tainted with radioactive fallout.

'If one were asked to vote for the work of literature that has had the greatest effect on the world,' writes the academic K. M. Newton, 'assuming that the Bible or the Koran and other religious texts were excluded from the category of literature – then *Daniel Deronda* ought to be a strong contender. A case can be made that without it the state of Israel might not exist.'[81]

In the post-colonialist school of criticism, Eliot has much to answer for. Edward Said blazed the trail in 1979, in *Zionism from*

---

*Even in her 1999 introduction to the Knopf edition of *Deronda*, A.S. Byatt says of Leavis's hackwork: 'He made the suggestion that the "English" part could perhaps be published without the Jewish part, and no truthful (*sic*) critic could fail to understand the responses behind those desires.' In 2014, the writer Diana Souhami tried to fulfil those desires in her novel, *Gwendolen*: 'breathtaking chutzpah' (*Guardian*); 'convincingly updated' (*The Irish Times*).

the Standpoint of its Victims. A consensus arose: the Jews in Deronda are propagandising a world-view and ideology whose destructive power we can now all see. There are Mordechai's mystic ravings: 'to redeem the soil from debauched and paupered conquerors...a community in the van of the East which carries the culture and the sympathies of every great nation in its bosom: there will be a land set for a halting-place of enmities, a neutral ground for the East as Belgium is for the West.'[82] By the end of the book, Daniel has been converted from gentleman to zealot: 'The idea that I am possessed with is that of restoring a political existence to my people, making them a nation again, giving them a national centre, such as the English have, though they too are scattered over the face of the globe. That is a task which presents itself to me as a duty; I am resolved to begin it, however feebly. I am resolved to devote my life to it. At the least, I may awaken a movement in other minds, such as has been awakened in my own.'[83]

And doesn't he, just? Within the pages of the book, he may appear a restless youth, seeking an 'external event' to 'compress his wandering energy'.[84] Indeed, we don't see him embarking on his voyage to the Mystical Orient, let alone arriving, engaging, responding, maybe even changing. Still, as Professor Newton argues: 'Whatever Eliot's intention, readers now cannot help but read the novel in the context of the situation in the Middle East and almost inevitably wonder whether she would have regretted the proto-Zionist theme if she could have had second sight and seen the consequences of a Jewish state coming into being in Palestine.'[85]

Or maybe not. Eliot is purblind to the sins of colonialism, revealing her 'belief, at a deep level, in the inherent validity of imperialist domination of darker races...(and a) lack of concern both with the situation of the indigenous population of Palestine and with the inevitable conflict between them and the Jews that the proto-Zionist project would create'.[86] It is true, as we've seen, back in 1848 in her unpublished twenties, that she wrote a letter giving vent to such noxious vapours. But much closer in time to Deronda is her final published work, Impressions of Theophrastus Such. She has been far more readily, if imperfectly, associated with the fictional memoirist of the title, who argues 'we are a colonising people, and it is we who have punished others.'[87]*

Still, onwards, as Daniel's Zionist mission spreads oppression westwards as well as east, given that it, 'excludes and marginalizes (the English heroine) Harleth'.[89] I read that line, and find my mouth in the same shape as when I realise the Blue Stilton *is* off. Poor Gwendolen – as Eliot calls her – does indeed have her 'small world' suddenly and disorientingly 'getting larger', as she learns of Daniel's plans for a new life, abroad. But the dislocation – 'for the first time being dislodged from her supremacy' – is hardly unique to her and her previous sense of entitlement among Eliot's characters. So much of her literature involves the puncturing, on a spectrum of gentle to harsh, of English provincial self-regard.

No matter: there's more. All this is even bad news for the Jews. In constructing Jewish characters with 'little freedom in their actions as their identities are determined in advance', Eliot 'perpetuate(s) the Jews' worldlessness and lack of political reality, *indirectly helping to advance political anti-Semitism* (my emphasis)'.[90]

More than 60 years before that observation was made, Hannah Arendt had criticised Jews for their lack of political engagement. But she was having a go at a class of actual, real-life, *parvenu* Jews, at a particular point in history. It seems a bit of a stretch to visit that upon Eliot, for her fictional constructs. A stretch and a wrinkle: Eliot is criticised for determinism in her novels – but those same critics allow Daniel no freedom of movement. Perhaps this romantic youth will have his itch scratched, and return from the east. Perhaps he'll be disillusioned and return. Perhaps he'll stay and envisage a multiplicity of futures for the settling (to some, re-settling) Jews.† George Eliot, who's not averse to telling us what happens to her characters in an epilogue, does not in *Deronda*. Not

---

*Impressions – like *Deronda* – also drew bewilderment and exasperation for having a final chapter about Jews – indeed, apparently, about 'why the Jews are not more popular than they are'. Why should we be expected to care, asks the critic in *The Saturday Review* of 1879: 'we are not prepared to answer these questions at the fag-end of a book avowedly devoted to other things'.[88]

†Claudia Johnson points out that 'neither he (Daniel) nor Eliot ever suggests that Palestine is an empty place awaiting his advent.'[91]

only do the critics remove Daniel's room for manoeuvre, they remove it for the generations to come.

To all of which Sarah D'Israeli — if not the seed, then at least a presentiment of Deronda's mother — might well have changed her posture in the portrait at Hughenden to arms folded, jaw set in grim vindication: why the surprise? I could have told that scandalous Eliot woman she'd be on to a loser banging on about Jewry.

And there were other Jews, closer to Eliot's time, who were, unlike Sarah, still proudly, professedly observant. But they, too, were unsure what was expected of them, and on what terms England accepted them.

On that debate did a great-great-grandfather's arrival in Victorian London turn.

~~~~

The news is brief. A death, written twice. Formal, then prattling.

The Jewish Record: 'SAD DEATH. — *We regret to learn that the wife of Mr. S.J. Roco, newly-elected Hazan of the Spanish and Portuguese Synagogue, died in giving birth to her first child** on Monday. Much sympathy has been expressed towards Mr. Roco, consequent on the sad and untimely loss he has sustained.*'[92]

The Jewish Chronicle: '*It is reported her decease was accelerated by excitement consequent to the election of her husband.*'[93]

It was 1869. Judith Roco (née Judels) was a strikingly old first-time mother for her time. She is recorded, two years before, as *achtendertig* — 38† — on the day of her wedding in 1867 to the 23-year-old cigar-maker, 'Simson' Roco.‡

---

*For whom I can find no record. The baby, it seems, did not survive.
†Her burial registration card from the Portuguese Jewish cemetery in Amsterdam, filled out some time after her death, says she was born in 1849. But along with the entry in the marriage register (Noord-Hollands Archief, Reg.11 fol.96v) is the fact that her parents married in 1821, when her mother was already 35 (Noord-Hollands Archief, Reg.3 fol.26). Had Judith been born in 1849, her mother would have to have been 63.
‡Shimshon, Simshon and — in his naturalisation certificate of 1911 — 'Samson'. His certificate is signed (or at least signed with a stamp) by the Home Secretary, Winston Leonard Spencer Churchill. The family spelling (and pronunciation) followed the Hebrew.

What does seem more certain is that the election of great-great-grandfather Shimshon as junior cantor (*Hazan*) at Bevis Marks Synagogue *was* a shock. His obituary[94] suggests he was not even committed to the possibility of a career in a cantor until a position came up at Bevis Marks.* His decision to apply would not just upend his life; it would spark outrage and rancour in the community he was about to join.

Auditions for the position of junior cantor had spread over six weeks. The *yehidim*, the members, then had a chance to vote. Four of the candidates received none. In second place was Abraham Haim Nieto – the acting junior cantor, the inside candidate, the favourite: but he only scraped just over half the votes of the winner. Shimshon had just turned 25. He was to spend the rest of his life in London, and more than 50 years as the cantor at Bevis Marks.

Why *had* he been picked?

Perhaps Shimshon was singularly talented: his obituary suggests so. But maybe he was helped, inadvertently, by a bit of previous from the runner-up. Abraham Haim Nieto was – as he liked to remind people – a descendant of the celebrated eighteenth-century Bevis Marks *Haham* (senior or chief Sephardi rabbi), David Nieto.† He had also been attached to Bevis Marks for years, during which time, in maladroit attempts to raise his profile, he'd clashed with the other *Hazanim*. 'The *mahamad* (had) found it necessary to restrain him'.[95]

Come the election campaign, though, any restraints were off. Shimshon faced a very well-organised, if not downright nativist campaign. At a 'meeting to promote the election of Mr Nieto' at Zetland Hall in June 1869, and attended by 'gentlemen of the Portuguese and German sections (i.e. *Sephardi and Ashkenazi* communities)', *The Jewish Record* reports that 'resolutions were unanimously passed pledging the meeting to use its exertions to secure return

---

*This may have been, in part, to having not yet had the time fully to train, because of national service. As the *Jewish Chronicle* put it in a profile to mark his 50 years as cantor: 'Mr. Roco has not only served in the army of the Lord of Hosts, for at the age of 19 he succumbed to the fortune of the Ballot, and shouldered a musket in the ranks of the Dutch Army' (JC 19-06-19).

†We met *Haham* Nieto in Chapter Two, at the start of the eighteenth century.

of one of the English candidates.'⁹⁶ Abraham didn't stop there. In the same edition of The Jewish Record, the last before the election six days later, the best part of two broadsheet columns was given to testimonials for him from high-ups, and a letter which hinted at the very Victorian volcano that was about to blow.

It is often regretted, wrote the correspondent, that 'native talent for the ministry is in England so rarely to be found, and that we are reduced to the humiliating necessity of...invoking exotic aid for priestly functions, by importing our ministers.' During Abraham's audition, 'his immeasurable superiority...must have amazed his four foreign competitors at the futility of inviting them hither. Let us hope, this gratifying success will for ever dissipate the prescriptive belief in British incapacity.'

It came to naught. The Jewish Record reports 'the young candidate (i.e. Abraham) had a larger share of the popularity and good wishes of crowds of persons who thronged Bevis Marks, and when the name of Mr. Roco was called out at the close of the ballot as having gained the larger number of votes, a howl of indignation greeted the announcement.'*

Abraham, the 'English candidate' unwanted in London, would emigrate, first to Kingston, Jamaica, then to the US.† It is possible that Shimshon's victory was, in part, and probably inadvertently on his part, down to a quiet stop-Nieto campaign.

Shimshon was, the *mahamad* minutes say, to be informed of his election by letter. His Jewish Chronicle obituary reported that it was 'by telegraph' and prompted 'one of the most tragic episodes of his life. His wife Judith, who was in weak health, received the news while he was out, and died of excitement.'

---

*The Jewish Record 25.06.1869 – the same date on which, elsewhere in the paper, 'much sympathy' was being extended to Shimshon over his wife's death.

†From where, 47 years later, he'd write again to Bevis Marks offering his services: the minutes of 4ᵗʰ September 1916 note a letter from the Rev. A. H. Nieto of New York offering his services as Hazan. 'It was decided that he be informed that no steps were being taken for the appointment of an additional Hazan.'

In London, the excitement was of a different sort. The 'howl of indignation' reported by *The Jewish Record* turned into a howl-round, head-splitting and self-feeding.

First to discharge: 'An Englishman', as he signed himself, in his letter of 25th June.[97] 'Sir — The domestic affliction sustained by the newly-elected Hazan so soon after his appointment, prevented me writing on the subject ere now.' Just to be clear, the writer had waited less than a week after Shimshon's bereavement. 'As an Englishman, I cannot help remarking, what a disgrace it is to pass over the worth of native candidates... Let us only suppose a vacancy for a Hazan being declared in Holland, what Englishman, however talented would stand the remotest chance... It is to be hoped that the German* Congregations will learn a lesson from the apathy (if not the vindictiveness) of the Portuguese†, and when any office become vacant which can be properly filled by Englishmen, they will "look at home".'

From a puff of sulphur, to — a week later — a full magmatic eruption. 'The repudiation of...an able and worthy British brother, mortified and broken spirited, from the employment for which he had been specially and successfully trained, displayed a refinement of cruelty, and a scorn of public opinion that every enlightened Englishman must deprecate and deplore.'[98] The writer — he signs himself 'Mirador' — then suggests such treatment of 'English brethren' will only feed anti-Jewish sentiment among 'Christian fellow-subjects'. It will also lead to Jews deserting en masse: 'Really the Conversion Society should offer us some substantial acknowledgment for the recruits we have sent them.'

At which point, the pointedly nom-de-plumed 'John Bull' skid-stops his penny farthing, and takes aim at both the letter-writers to date, as well as the newspaper editor for allowing such 'severe censure' to spew. 'John Bull' says that there has always been 'a desire to give a preference to English born'.[99] Indeed, the job *had* been offered to two English candidates previously, but both had declined. At that point, the governing body opened up the

---

*i.e. Ashkenazi
†Sephardi

application process. Three Dutch, one French, two English candidates had put themselves forward. 'After a fair contest on the part of the adherents of Mr. Roco, that gentleman was duly elected by a large majority.' The members 'were liberal enough to think that a Jew is a brother, whether born in Great Britain or the Netherlands'.

On, into August, the lava pours across the letters pages. Nieto – 'one of (our) own' – was 'far superior in every point to *any* of the other competitors'. So says 'Justice'.[100]

'E.C.' in Manchester may not have quite such a DC Comics name as 'Justice', but he does ask: 'which is the greatest honour, that of electing the competent man of whatever country, or allowing a deep, ignorant prejudice to have sway over their better feelings. I think the former; the latter is in one word *un-English*.'[101]

On the argument raged. It spread to other communities. In the end, the editor of the *Record* appealed for the letter-writers to draw breath and change subjects.[102]

The huffing may, now, seem hilariously overblown. But this was – this is, perhaps – the searing dichotomy of the diaspora. Take the US, where, as Dara Horn explains, the 'founding legends' of the local Jewish communities were often total garbage. 'These stories express the Jewish community's two highest hopes and deepest fears. The first hope is that the Jews in this new place will remain part of the chain of the Jewish tradition, and the second hope is that the local population will accept them.'[103]

Some hope, according to the French political scientist – and later member of the Vichy government – André Siegfried. 'The Jew gives the impression at first of being very quickly Americanized, for no other foreigner has his easy adaptability...(but) the fact remains that notwithstanding its material adaptation, the original traits of the race persist and leave their indelible mark on every thought and action... The knowledge that the Americans have encountered something which they cannot assimilate has long stirred up an anti-Semitic feeling.'[104]

That viral hit – the American translation of Siegfried's analysis came out in 1927 and was into its *thirteenth* printing by the end of 1928 – sets the backdrop for Hannah Arendt's white-hot ironywork in 1943. Just arrived in the US, she hammers out the essay, *We Refugees*. 'If patriotism were a matter of routine or practice,' she writes of Jews, 'we should be the most patriotic people in the world... But since patriotism is not yet believed to be a matter of practice, it is hard to convince people of the sincerity of our repeated transformations... The natives confronted with such strange beings as we are, become suspicious; from their point of view, as a rule, only a loyalty to our old countries is understandable.'[105]

So the Victorian neuroses sat in a long tradition — all of which must have proved hard pounding for the 23-year-old Shimshon. Subsequent synagogue records suggest he emerged more toughened than tenderised.

What is clear is that he didn't maunder. Just seven months after Judith died, he re-married. Simcha Chumaceiro was the daughter of the long-serving *Hazan* at the Esnoga in Amsterdam;* she was the sister of one of the candidates whom Shimshon had beaten to the post of *Hazan* at Bevis Marks.† And she is — you'll have picked up on this — a *Chumaceiro*. In fact, for me, she was the original Chumaceiro, the first ancestor I encountered who bore the name: the vaguely-recalled great-great-grandmother whose span of separation from me mirrored her own generational distance from the Portuguese Ester Orobio Furtado. There is a further symmetry: Ester had sailed from Lisbon to Amsterdam where she married; Simcha married in Amsterdam and then sailed for London.

Pictures of Shimshon — at least from later in life — show him looking the part: dapper, precise. A broad rectangular face, emphatic eyebrows, trimmed hair, and a neat isosceles beard.

---

*Jozef Chumaceiro (1818–87) — referred to as 'Hazan Joost Chumaceiro' on p.48.
†Jacob Chumaceiro (1843–1912), who would become the *Hazan* at a new small Sephardi synagogue on the Essex Road, in Islington, north London.

This might, reasonably, strike you as the thin scrabblings of unmerited extrapolation. But it is certain that Shimshon's appearance, whether in family photos or synagogue publications, fit with the exacting demands of this frock-coated pillar of the Anglo-Jewish establishment.

For the clergy, standards had long been set high. Since 1862, Bevis Marks had expected that not just its rabbis but its *Hazanim* 'preach...in English at regular intervals'. So Shimshon would have needed to learn, fast.

Sermonising was the least of it. The *Hazan*'s job was to lead the congregation in prayer. That would partly be through song. Bevis Marks, though proudly *Sephardi* had, along with its older sister synagogue in Amsterdam, largely sanded down the complex cadences,

---

*This is a cropped picture. From left to right Samson Van Ryn (Esther's son, about six years old. My mum spoke very warmly about her childhood encounters with this beguilingly rough-edged uncle, rather frowned upon by the more proper members of the family). Isaac Duque (husband of) second daughter Julia Roco, Shimshon Roco, Hinderina Van Ryn (Esther's daughter, my grandmother, about seven), first daughter Esther Van Ryn (née Roco), Simcha Roco (née Chumaceiro), (husband of Esther) Henry Van Ryn — who we'll meet in the next chapter, third daughter Dolly Roco. In the background, just visible, chicken wire. Who knew, in 1912?

modes, rhythms and quarter-tones of Oriental or North African or Iberian melodies.*

Dissonance remained. 'The (Bevis Marks synagogue) choir or choirs were always a source of trouble, and in the minutes of the Congregation over a long period (from the 1870s) there are frequent records of complaint about them.'[106] In the twentieth century, there was even greater resistance: the *Haham*, Solomon Gaon, opined that the choir had no historic place in Sephardi ritual, that it should not become too 'polished or musically precise', they should follow rather than lead the congregation, and so 'directed that the choir no longer sing in harmony, but in unison'.[107]

The *Hazan* also had to *leyn* – to chant long passages from the *Torah* scroll, hand-written without vowels, punctuation or musical notation. Bevis Marks had had stringent expectations from the start. From the early eighteenth century, there are accounts of *Hazanim* being fined five shillings a pop for any mistakes in reading from the *Sefer Torah*. [108]

Bevis Marks was known, then, to be a stickler for rules and penalties, laid out and rarely updated in its *Ascamot* or constitution. There sometimes appeared to be little room for flexibility or mitigation or even a modicum of empathy: Exhibit A would be the pettifogging treatment of Isaac d'Israeli.† His final very courteous letter of appeal is from someone who finds himself driven both up the wall and round the bend.[110]

Add to this the traditional synagogue politics and rows. The great, leather-bound volumes of the *mahamad* minutes drily – and severally – record the 'official and personal differences' between Shimshon and his fellow *Hazan*, J. Gomes de Mesquita, and the interventions needed with the 'reverend gentlemen'. The long-serving archivist at Bevis Marks, Miriam Rodrigues-Pereira, provides a fingertip link to this history. From 1910 onwards, Shimshon gave her father,

---

*The acculturation rings out between rigid bar-lines of an 1857 compendium of *Sephardi* music. More than a century later, the *Hazan* Abraham Beniso recalled his war-time evacuation from Gibraltar to London, where 'I found the melodies being sung quite "staccatto" (sic) which ran counter to my Latin (or real Sephardi) temperament.'[109]

†See footnote on p.96.

Benjamin, lessons in *chazzanut*. Miriam recalled,[111] presumably from what her father had in turn told her, that Reverend Roco had a reputation for being, on occasion, 'a difficult man'.* He spent his last days, she'd been told, 'in an asylum'.

Perhaps Reverend Roco's bloody-mindedness – let's call it resoluteness – fortified his part in keeping Bevis Marks on its present site, despite advanced plans for relocation.† (The synagogue remains the oldest continually functioning synagogue in Europe.) Towards the end of the nineteenth century, much of the community had moved away from the City of London; Shimshon and Simcha had also left their tiny flat next to the synagogue for a house in Canonbury. That meant – given the Orthodox prohibition on taking transport on *Shabbat* or festivals – a good hour's walk to and from Bevis Marks. The dwindling attendance reached its nadir during the air raids of World War One. Shimshon – in the interview he gave to the *Jewish Chronicle* on the fiftieth anniversary of his appointment – recalled what presumably was the daylight strike of 7th July 1917: 'The synagogue nearly fell a victim to an attack from the air, and I shall never forget the Sabbath morning when shrapnel fell on the *Bimah* during the reading of the Law. The congregation took cover until the danger had passed, when we all recited a united *Hagomel* (prayer of thanksgiving) and I resumed the reading of the *Parashah*.'

A vigorous dash of aplomb. It was, perhaps, a story that had been burnished in the memory. And if so, maybe subconsciously, told and re-told so that the cavillers of 1869 could, now 50 years on, be convinced of the Reverend's patriotic chops.

But maybe also, by now, he was done with all that: he had the proof he needed and would never have wanted. How much more loyally British could you get, than having the Great War rip a hole through your family?

This was no neat anecdote. This was ugly, jagged fact.

---

*Shimshon, for his part, states that it had been 'one of his pleasures to have prepared several young men to officiate in Sephardi congregations' (including Benjamin Rodrigues-Pereira) (50th anniversary interview with the *Jewish Chronicle*, 20-06-1919).

†The plan to demolish Bevis Marks, sell the land, and finance a new synagogue in Maida Vale was approved by the Board of Management in 1885 (Sharman Kadish, *Bevis Marks Synagogue 1701–2001*, [Historic England, 2001]).

FIVE

On War; The Soldier

Wars are terrible. Wars are exciting. They may begin by design or by accident, they may be pursued methodically or chaotically, they may be long or short – but they all tend to force fighters and civilians to extremes. Reporters too. That is why so many of us are so drawn to them.

Why would you *not* find it stimulating? Does that sound callous? If much of journalism is to reveal what is going on, what is going wrong, then why would you not want to cover the worst type of breakdown? The one that leads to mass violence and often the most appalling crimes.

The question then: how to convey the extremity? How, perhaps even before making people understand, do you make people care? We'll get on to that.

There is a potential cost, of course. Believe me, I understand that. I have been terrified in the field, and knotted in the anticipation. Am I being an idiot to want to go there? Worse, a selfish idiot? And this is just me: there are legions of reporters far braver, far more experienced and enterprising – and no less doubting and self-aware.

It was in my twenties, even before I was made a full-time reporter, that impatient and ignorant, but with what might prove a useful disregard for rules, I took a fortnight's holiday and didn't tell work I was heading for Bosnia. It is astonishing that on my return, with a bagful of radio pieces, I was merely bollocked rather than sacked. (The reports were aired, prominently.) But I now had a sense of the landscape. Thanks to the kindness of a friend who was based in the region, I had met the fighters, the warlord (later indicted for war crimes), the corrupt business kingpin, the impotent international peacekeepers, the would-be president, the civilians — displaced, dispossessed, battered, angry, sullen, sunk. The guns had been distant. But the damage and the drunkenness and the disorder, they were everywhere.

It was an artless and amateur venture, certainly of far more value to me than to journalism. A decade later, I went from the freelance jaunt to the tightly organised deployment. At least that was the idea: being embedded with the British Army for the invasion of Iraq. There remains a good deal of sniffiness about embeds. That they are a sell-out. That you will be constrained, a cipher.

All of which is, of course, possible. You end up seeing only what one of the warring parties allows you; relaying only the information they tell you. But why? Although I had gone to the war from my posting as Europe Correspondent, I was not long out of several years at Westminster, as a political correspondent. The embed was rather like being in the Lobby (albeit with worse food, appalling bogs, and some close calls with targeted mortar and gunfire): you had privileged access to information, to people and to places. It was then your job to hold what you see and what you hear up to the light. Does it withstand scrutiny? Does it mesh with what you are observing elsewhere?[1]

As we made camp in the desert of northern Kuwait, a senior officer took me to one side. Once the invasion begins, how would I feel about going ahead of most ground troops, in a chopper, into the southern Iraqi city of Basra? Just me, a fellow British TV correspondent, an American anchor. The working assumption — I was told — was that the Shi'ites of the second city, so brutally suppressed by Saddam after the war 12 years before, would lay down their arms and strew rose petals at the feet of the liberators. The coverage could destroy morale in Baghdad. To which the obvious answer was, yes. Unsaid was: you get me in, I'll tell the story as I see it. The bargain was not complex. It didn't happen, of course — and the weeks-long battle to take Basra hinted at a tougher fight to come, and perhaps the wishful – worse, casual – thinking that would come to mark the post-invasion planning.

As those days of hard pounding stretched on, we managed to get our own BBC armoured jeep, fiercely resourceful fixer Yusuf, and adept and unflappable security man Jed to lead some unofficial expeditions. There I met that most bracing novelty: Iraqi civilians without a government goon hanging around to check that Saddam's feelings were not hurt. It had not happened for years. The war, let alone the occupation, had barely begun. And yet they expressed what was to come: already, they were exhausted, exasperated, bewildered, distraught.

The lesson to the journalist is unremarkable: keep an open mind. As a concept, it may read as if it belongs on a page-a-day motivational calendar on the wall of your local caff; in practice, it can be demanding.

That is on the grander scale. Covering violence and unrest – at least for broadcast journalism – also demands intricate measurements of taste. I have seen people just after they have been killed: shot, crushed, run over – deliberately. Men, women and children. How far do you convey the trauma? The sounds, the sights, sometimes the smell – although that may come after. That's the wrong question: we show it as far as we can. How do we show it? How do we balance between unduly shocking and unduly sparing the audience?

There is one way we can at least try to tell a story properly. It is to return. We are not the caravan that only sweeps in when we can crouch in our flak jackets.

Do you want to understand what it is like when a tank shell rips through a crowded neighbourhood, and young lives stop in a supersonic burst of metal, glass, concrete, plaster, schoolbook, hairbrush, bone, blood? Dr Izzeldin Abuelaish showed me. It was the second time we had met. The first had been at a hospital in Tel Aviv. The second, a few weeks later, was at what was left of his home in Gaza. Three daughters had been there. We stepped into the rooms together. They were undisturbed, shattered. Many times I have picked through streets and buildings wrecked by ordnance, ripped by shrapnel. I had never done so in the company of a father, stumbling across his dead daughters' homework and trinkets and clothes and drawings and diaries, writing neat, pages torn and stuck with blood. Sometimes we were quiet. Sometimes he spoke, picked up a belonging. The eye roamed, incessantly. Down here: rubble, wire, dust, bracelet. Up there: hair-clumps glued on ceiling.

There was Victor, the man in the ironed shirt, sitting on the flimsy plastic chair under a tree in the South Sudanese capital, Juba. He was a local government official. Had been, before his country had collapsed into the English language's worst contradiction: civil war. Except the fighting was supposed to be over, now, or at least, in abeyance. So why didn't he return to his home city, in the north? 'You don't know about Malakal?' Victor asked me. 'It is ashes.' We – producer Mike and I – managed to hitch a UN food flight into Malakal. Other – less official – flights followed us in: Russian-made planes with no tail markings, there to resupply the SPLA, the government forces who at that point held the city.

First had come the killing. Mothers and brothers shot, their bodies left to rot. Children who had disappeared in the chaos of fleeing. All this we heard in the UN displacement camp, just to the north-east. My notebook filled with a tangle of names and questions. The next morning, we got a rare tour of the city, in a UN military patrol, with an SPLA escort. This was different. Now it was the city speaking.

Malakal was – is – South Sudan's second city. Once, it thrived. Now it was empty; neighbourhoods silent. Rival forces allied to rival tribes had coursed with the tides. Twelve times during this short war, the city had changed hands. Parts had been razed in the familiar rage of warfare. But much had simply been despoiled.

The children's hospital was built as a prize of independence, won in 2010. Now it was a shell: scorched, roofless, slowly strangled by the returning bush. But I could see no bullet holes, no splashes of shrapnel. It, like the Red Cross headquarters, had been pillaged by fighters not battling for a front line, but high on ownership. Inside the Red Cross offices, amid the dust and debris and fug of faeces, I found a discarded notebook. 'Rules for the Red Cross', a neat hand had written. Avoid 'real or perceived breaches of neutrality and impartiality for multiple reasons, including ethnicity'.

I had seen places destroyed by war. But never a city vanish like this.

And there was Lucie, the young Burundian woman, her voice low, her eyes averted. She had her life before her, and it was already in pieces. She had been 14 when she had taken the long walk home from her school back to her village. A soldier – a man who had been caught in Burundi's protracted ethnic war, a rolling rampage which saw hundreds of thousands killed – a man who had returned hollowed and unstable, a man whom people knew to avoid, a shiftless man; he had raped this schoolgirl. Now, in her tiny, dirt shack, sitting on the floor, her legs stiffly in front of her, she spoke in short, murmured sentences. It became clear that she was being punished twice. Being raped meant being ostracised. Her subsistence life must be led alone. Except there were enough women like her, young and old, that a small women's collective in a nearby town was trying to offer some help, some co-operative work. That was how we had come to meet her.

So many stories. And – at the start of the century which would lead, at its end, to the neighbouring disasters of Burundi and Rwanda – so many deaths. The twentieth century had begun, after all, with the war to end all wars. The Great War was extraordinary in its scale, in its redefinition of struggle and futility. It was extraordinary too for the testimony sent from the front lines. But why, when there are still all these conflicts, all these victims, should we hear another story from more than a century ago?

Because this young man's charming voice – particular and universal – still sings. Because he is also caught in the grand schemes of great men and big powers. And because he is a different figure to those we have met, and one who asks us a potentially tricky question.

The last chapter – of Jews in Victorian Britain – was about the ructions over the placing of Jews. How do we set them in the times?

Disraeli gave us the Jew who succeeded, having rejected Judaism and mythologised Jewishness; the establishment appeared both repulsed and fascinated by him. England had in fact offered Disraeli's antecedents – my remote ancestors – more opportunity than he or some of his more prominent biographers gave credit for. But the opportunity was not unfettered. The limits, the conventions – they laid the frosty groundwork for *Daniel Deronda*'s reception, and the fears and self-doubts which accompanied great-great-grandfather Shimshon Roco's appointment to even a junior position in the Anglo-Jewish Establishment.

Now, after those three characters – Disraeli the Eternal Jew, Deronda the Fictional Jew, and Shimshon the Immigrant Jew, David Van Ryn is perhaps a Perfectly Ordinary Jew.

And that presents a problem. Why should he be here? His role, surely, is just to play his part as one of 20 million extras. A micro-organism abraded and rubbed out in the continent-mincing claws of the industrial war machine. He needs to die for the war to be Great. Admittedly, from his remains will sprout a specifically Jewish varietal of anguish. But is that it?

It's a question I will answer – at least give my answer – at the end of David's story. The previous chapter was about the awkwardness of Jews: trying to work out where they fit, if they fit, and if so, how. This chapter is about a young Jew who can do no more to earn his place for his country. But does that disqualify him from our enquiries? Does this Jew belong? Britain and His Majesty the King say yes, of course. You, on the other hand: what do you think? What do we want from our Jews?

~~~~

THE SOLDIER (FOUGHT 1915)

'The Hebrew identifies his interests with those of the country... On several trying occasions, both in England and in Holland, they have laid on the altar of public safety noble sacrifices of their lives and their fortunes. In recent times, faithful to a paternal government, they have marched in the armies of European sovereigns. Prussia has many Jewish officers; France, since her regeneration, has counted numerous Israelites in her École Polytechnique, and the blood of Israel profusely flowed in the fields of Waterloo. The King of Holland has a complete

regiment of gallant Hebrews. All this confirms what I have already asserted, that every native Jew, as a political being, becomes distinct from the Jew of any other nation. If the Jewish military under the King of Holland were to encounter the French Israelites, the combat would be between the Dutch and the French.'

ISAAC D'ISRAELI[2]

'...and grey fathers know nothing to seek for but the corpses of their blooming sons.'

GEORGE ELIOT[3]

The first thing you notice is how damn handsome he is. Alluring, if you can say that about your great-uncle. The photograph is another world from its contemporary — that wedding party of 1912 from the previous chapter. No stiff pose, no group shot. This is fin-de-siècle, start-of-a-new-siècle — a turn-of-the-century image closer to the Vienna Secession than the Alexandra Atelier of Photography. It is sexy. This is David Van Ryn – Dave, as he called himself – hair raked, brow even, eyes smouldering, up to his thighs in water. He looks up, as if he's just been caught in the moment. He is a young man: 20 or younger. He must be. He was dead before he could turn 21.

Perhaps the photo was taken in Canada. That is where his earliest surviving letters and postcards come from, from deep in the interior. A 1913 postcard, addressed 'Dear Kiddies' is postmarked Kamloops, 'a town in the heart of cattle country', in the far west, in British Columbia. Just a few years before Dave arrived, the poet Robert Service had worked there. It was a place which appealed to his sensibilities, 'riding over the rolling ridges, or into spectral gulches that rose to ghostlier mountains. It was like the scenery of Mexico, weirdly desolate and aridly morose. A discouraged land, forbidding in its weariness and resigned to ruin.'[4]

Dave appears to have made his way slowly westwards. Aged 17 or 18, he is writing from South Monaghan, Ontario. 'By the time you receive this jumble, excitement will be at highest tide and the Roco name poorer by one.' He is addressing his Aunt Julia (his stepmother's sister)[5] and soon-to-be uncle Issy — the couple in that wedding photo. The handwriting and language are upright, stilted. That will change soon enough. The tone won't: he is affectionate and unaffected. He asks for a piece of wedding cake to be sent to him, as long as he is allowed to eat it (presumably because of a tradition that cake not consumed on the day of the wedding be saved for eating when the first child is born). If not, 'don't send it as it would be cruelty to animals.'

A year later, Dave has wound up 2,500 miles further west, at the confluence of the North and South Thompsons. He's writing to tell his parents that 'today I secured two jobs, one for the coming week and the other to follow'. The second is with a 'threshing outfit' — some of the most strenuous agricultural work of the time. Whatever his first job is, it will be some way out in the endless cattle lands: he explains he won't be able to send another letter for a week. The writing has taken on a fluent, italicised slope. He signs off, as he will from the Western Front, *Yr Loving Son, Dave.*

~~~~

His horizons stretch. He has his youth, his health, and the unbounded, far Canadian west. What is so normal now was still abnormal then: for a teenager to strike out, to have an adventure far away. And for a member of this family of Jews to head abroad because they were tugged by a desire rather than pushed by a fear.

Viewed through the thickets of the family tree, it is a change, but it is not unprecedented. His stepmother's father, Shimshon Roco, left nineteenth-century Amsterdam for a job offer in London. His father, Henry, made the same journey, but perhaps just on a punt. He, too, was a young man, the middle of seven siblings and half-siblings. His move to England would save his descendants from the terrible odds of surviving Nazi occupation of the Netherlands. It would also lead to a son fighting and dying in Flanders Fields.

The only photos I have of Henry are, like Shimshon, of him later in life. Now he is bald; but perhaps he always had that great, shag sweep of a moustache, echoed in the long and lustrous curve of his brow. His pupils are small, his gaze direct, and he hints at a spry detachment. I may not have pictures of a young Henry, but there is documentary evidence of him getting into scrapes. Having just turned 21, he makes his first – unwelcome – appearance in the Jewish press: a classified announcement placed by S.A. Almosnino, Secretary to the Board for Affairs of Shechita,* in March 1871. That 'Mr. H. Van Ryn of 48 Shirland Road Paddington, having notified his intention of suplying (sic) Jewish inhabitants of West London with Kosher meat, and he had engaged a Solomon Van Nierop as Shochet†; this is to give notice that neither Mr. H. Van Ryn nor Mr. Van Nierop has been licensed by Ecclesiastical Authorities to supply the Jewish community with Kosher meat, and according to Jewish Law, meat so sold is prohibited to be eaten.'

One door is shut. He crosses London, perhaps choosing this moment to change his name from the Dutch Hartog to the English Henry, and alters direction. No meat, in his classified *Jewish Chronicle*

---

*The process of slaughtering of animals so that the meat can be considered kosher.
†Slaughterer certified to comply with the rules of *kashrut*.

ads of April to June 1873; rather, a promise from this 'Family Grocer and importer of Foreign Produce' on Commercial Road, that he 'has on sale all articles of GROCERY of the choicest quality at the lowest possible prices. Good FRYING OIL at 9d per pint; Best ditto, 10d. and 1s. per pint.' He serves all parts of London, but 'special attention devoted to Country orders'.

Maybe business does not thrive. Maybe he wants a more stable job to provide for his first wife, Phoebe and their seven-month-old son, Maurice, but a month after the last of those adverts appeared, in July 1873, Henry crosses London again, back west. He is elected to the post of Superintendent of Willesden Cemetery. It is the new burial ground for London's Jewish community, a 21-acre site granted by the Home Office. Henry's wanderings are over. He remains in the Lodge and as superintendent for 55 years.[6] In his seventies, Henry, now on to his third wife, my great-grandmother Esther (née Roco),[7] is granted yearly extensions to his contract. The United Synagogue Burial Committee pays tribute to 'the standard of excellence' attained at the Cemetery – 'due in a great measure to his unremitting care and attention'.

What drives Henry to work on almost to his death, in 1931, at the age of 81? Perhaps it is what my mother recalled of the Van Ryn energy; they were loud and amused and not altogether approved of by some of the in-laws. (For his breakfast, family lore has it, Henry took meat with a fried egg and a glass of whisky.) Perhaps it was the money, or lack of it: the Burial Committee may have been lavish in their praise; in their wages not quite so. The residence was free, but at the start of his contract extensions in 1920, his annual salary was £200 – the equivalent, just over a century later, of £7,500. (Which sadly might appear to undermine the breakfast story.)

Perhaps, also, part of him wanted to keep himself busy: overseeing what he was never able to provide his second son: a decent burial. Indeed, a burial at all.

~~~~

Britain declared war in August 1914. Weeks later, Dave sailed from New York. Why? Perhaps his then nine-year-old half-sister, my grandmother Hinderina, would later ask herself the same question. In her 1934 edition of Vera Brittain's *Testament of Youth*, a few passages about the build-up to the war and then its ghastly course are highlighted. On the night that the British ultimatum to Germany expired, 'uneasily I recalled a passage from *Daniel Deronda* that I had read in comfortable detachment the year before.' Those words are Vera Brittain's, but it is Hinderina who scores two thick lines down the margin of the ensuing quotation. 'There comes a terrible moment to many souls when the great movements of the world, the larger destinies of mankind, which have lain aloof in newspapers and other neglected reading, enter like an earthquake into their own lives... Then it is that the submission of the soul to the Highest is tested and...life looks out from the scene of human struggle with the awful face of duty.'

That duty had already been scored into generations of Van Ryns. Unlike England, the Netherlands had long had military conscription. At the start of the 1800s, Louis Bonaparte, the King, had allowed Jews to join up. David's father and grandfather appear in Amsterdam's military ledgers.[8]

In any case – with apologies to George Eliot and Vera Brittain – duty's mien appears, in those early months of the war, upbeat more than 'awful'.

It is 22nd January 1915. David is 20.

'*This will be my last letter from England for the War. We embark for France at 2pm today. Further address: Queen Victoria Rifles, Expeditionary Force, France. Had a jolly time here, went to Hippo'me last night... No time for longer letter. Will write when possible. Love to all, Au Revoir, Dave*'

The message is written on a postcard; its facing side shows a company of trench-diggers. I'm not sure why, but I think – perhaps I've been told, or perhaps once assumed – that Dave is second from the right.[9] His face is certainly close to the formal portrait which is printed in the *Jewish Chronicle* 'War Number' of November 1915, among the gallery of 'Killed In Action'.

A month later, Dave writes from France. As with all the letters that now arrive from the field, they are on thin paper of varying size, lined and un-lined, but all covered neatly in soft grey or mauve pencil. The cursive is gentle and the writing remarkably fluent: there are few, if any, crossings-out.

A century ago, they were sent out of the noise, the violence, the smells, the tumult. Now, I draw a blind against the winter sun to shield the tracks of purple pencil; I clear a desk and turn my hands to check they're clean; sound and movement are damped to a new scale. What I hear is the faint, treble shush as the sheets are unfolded from the shape they've held for decades. Even with the light low, I can see the outline of my fingers through the thin page. There's the merest waft of must.

Dave's been made a machine-gunner, which means leaving his friends in 15 Platoon. He's trying to return to them – although he doubts whether he will be able to. (He won't.) Dave has learned one of the basic tenets of a soldier's life: hurry up and wait. And if you're told you're about to have a week or more's rest, don't believe it: you'll be woken at midnight; instructed to move at a moment's notice; march four miles; wait several hours; march another nine miles; be instructed you're not needed; march three miles to a farm; wait for two days; march 11 miles back to HQ. Prepare to repeat.

Still, that flow of adrenaline and ebb of monotony had been broken two days before, when 'I received your letter and parcel for which I thank you very much. The handkerchiefs and tinder lighter were most useful, and the chocolate most delightful.'

Dave is sorry that he missed his father's birthday on 17th February, 'but under the existing circumstances, I am well contented not to have been present.' The weather's been filthy and he has a bad cold. 'I hope to shake it off soon. Otherwise all is Merry and Bright.' Later that winter, 'the intense cold has caused much frostbite, in fact I have a touch of it, but it does not bother me much. Otherwise I am feeling in splendid shape. I hope to hear that all are well at home. Love to all, Yr loving son, Dave.'

The worst of the winter passes: those freezing, grey and sodden months in trenches hacked out with little care for drainage, with the German lines sometimes just 75 yards away. Now it is 1st April. It is also the third day of Pesach — because Dave is thanking his parents for the 'passover cakes and *grimaselish*' (Dutch matzo pancakes). 'I am sorry I could not be with you, but must hope to be at home next year.' He asks after the family, and marvels at the news that the Canadian post office has sent on a waterlogged old postcard from Calgary. There is some news about his rotations 'in the firing line', which last four days or longer. There is more news, but it is lost, along with the rest of the letter.

Soon thereafter, though, there are a full seven pages of Large Post Octavo — eight inches by five. Dave has less than two weeks to live. He deserves to be heard in full.

Machine Gun Section
British Expeditionary Force
11 April 1915

Dear Father + Mother,

We came out of the trenches last night and arrived at our billets at 3.30 this morning. We were not so tired as usual considering we had done five days in firing line. For the first two days it rained hard and there was from six inches to nearly a foot of water in the trench where we were. To appease our anger we did an extra amount of firing, with such good effect that we silenced the German fire. The result was we did not get a quarter of the casualties that the other half of battn did during their five days in firing line. Seen thru' the glasses their trenches were ripped to pieces. You understand the trenches are largely made of sandbags. When torn like theirs were they are not safe as bullets penetrate them. Of course repairing is only possible at night + it must have cost them some casualties. Once or twice they tried to silence us with rapid fire, but found we were the more rapid of the two.

The last days the weather turned very fine + we bailed out the water + everything was lovely. We had lots to eat + drink. Being Easter time we thought we would have some Bank Holiday sport so we put up dummies + started throwing them at the rear of trenches. There were Welsh engineers in with us who were fine singers so we had some concerts. All this with the Germans fifty yards away. You see war is not so awful after all, at least we are determined to have all the fun we can get. Had you been in trenches you might have thought us callous, for its an old French trench + they have a nasty habit of leaving their dead where they fall or throwing them to the rear instead of a decent burial as our own troops have when possible. There were dozens of them laying round + the parapet was largely built up with them. Still its curious how little anyone bothers. Death is so common that is thought nothing of + had no depressing influence on us.

I received your parcel last night + thank you very much for it. By way, our cigarette supply is not very good now so I would like to have a few sent out when you are sending parcels. I have now quite a reserve of handkerchiefs + shall not need any more for a long time.

Have just this minute received your letter of 6 April. Am pleased to hear all are well + enjoyed the holidays but I would like to hear that you were in better spirits. If you could see us out here you would be surprised. There are very few glum faces. Going to or coming from trenches the noise of singing is great. Everybody is happy, especially now we have some lovely fine days.

Well I must finish up now as they are collecting the post.

Hope all keep well. Love to all

Your loving Son

Dave.

Four days later another letter, far briefer – to ask his parents not to send any more parcels for the time being. He is writing from a field ambulance, having 'met with a slight accident'. The other night he slipped while carrying guns out of trenches. He suffered a 'strain', didn't initially think it was anything, but as it continued to bother him, saw the medical officer who has ordered him to go to the hospital for a check-up. Parcels tend to get lost at hospitals, so please don't send anything further. And please don't worry. 'It's nothing serious.'

But history's gravity is pulling. Two days later, the 9th County of London Territorial Regiment, Queen Victoria's Rifles will be pitched into unremitting, close-quartered slaughter. Dave will play his full part.[10]

~~~~

'Hill 60' may have been little more than a hummock, but in the flatness of Flanders it was raised into a strategic crux. In the spring of 1915, the Germans controlled the feature, having wrested it from the French at the end of the previous year. They now held a surprisingly sweeping view of British advances to the front. It was an artificial hill they were atop, 60 metres above sea level (hence the British military's name for it). This was its third iteration. It had begun as a heap of spoil from a railway cutting. Then, 'over several decades trees shot up in the fertile soil, and shrubs and rambling wild flowers made the mound an attractive spot, known locally as La Côte des Amants; it was popular with summer-evening strollers.'[11]

Initially, Dave was dug in with his fellow QVR Machine Gunners about 300 metres from the hill, just to the east of the railway line. But German lines were closer by: in his letter of 11th April, he says a mere '50 yards' away. Was Dave's position one of those to be bombarded in a different way the following night? Into British trenches, the Germans had hurled two notes tied around stones. One, addressed to 'Dear Honoured Comrades', pointed out that this devastating fight had already lasted nine months. 'We are all tired of this savage life, and you must be too.' The other note concurred that it was past time to stop all this, especially as British losses must be three times the Germans'. 'Let us have Peace on Earth before the cherry blossom comes out…or do you want to go on for ever sitting in these damned trenches?'[12]

The answer to that question, whether low-grade psy-ops or genuine, was presaged in that same 11th April letter from Dave. The 'Welsh engineers' whom he mentioned were not just fine singers, they were miners, and they had been working alongside Royal Engineers. They had tunnelled under the hill and two nearby trenches. Five enormous mines had been laid. 'At seven in the evening of Saturday, April 17, the whole was exploded with terrific effect. Before the smoke had cleared away the British infantry had dashed from their trench and the hill was occupied. A handful of dazed Germans were taken prisoners and 150 were buried under the debris.'[13]

So far so good for the British. It had taken just two minutes for the storming party to rush the hill. Fifteen minutes later, the machine-gunners of the QVRs – Dave's section – were also up in support.

But it was about to get much, much more costly. In the dry words of Brigadier General Sir James Edmonds, the army's official historian, 12 years later: 'To retain the hill was another matter.'[14]

Indeed, the official history expressed grave doubt as to the worth of the fight. The British had placed themselves on 'a small but pronounced salient, exposed to attack on both sides'. Its value as an observation post would mean that the enemy would spare no effort attempting its recapture, 'and unfortunately, in the spring of 1915, he was far better equipped for such warfare'.[15] It would have been better, General Edmonds concluded, had the British raided the hill, withdrawn, forced the Germans to garrison it much more heavily, drawing further British fire, and so sapping enemy resources.

This was not the path chosen. Instead, the British forces clung to the prominence of the hill under fierce fire, and on land made all the more difficult to defend not just because it was exposed, but so heavily cratered from those initial mine detonations. After 48 hours, the battle eased in intensity. But it was a temporary, as well as relative, reprieve.

Over the ensuing two days, beginning on the 20th, the fighting reached a new pitch of grim, compressed fury. The Queen Victoria Rifles were in the thick of it. A QVR Lieutenant – G. Harold Woolley – won the first Territorial Victoria Cross of the war, as the Germans, close by, poured in shells, mortars, grenades and machine-gun fire. 'Officers of experience,' wrote Arthur Conan Doyle, 'described this concentration of fire as the worst they had ever experienced.'[16] What's more, there was no cover. The trenches had been blasted into nothingness. The army historian takes over from the celebrated novelist to summon the images: 'The surface of Hill 60 was a medley of confluent mine and shell craters, strewn with broken timber and wire: and in this rubbish heap it was impossible to dig without disturbing the body of some British or German soldier.'[17]

In the afternoon of the 21st, the explosions and gunfire lessened at last. More than '3000 of our men were stretched upon that little space',[18] which even Conan Doyle, writing well before the end of the war, and in unflaggingly patriotic, chin-up bent, had to concede was 'an excessive loss of life' which 'the little mound...could not justify'. He then went on to attempt to do just that: justify it. What was being fought for was the 'ascendancy of the British or the Prussian soldier', that 'subtle thing which would tinge every battle' to come. 'Who would cry "Enough!" first? Who would stick it to the bitter end?' That, he decided, was 'worth our 3,000 slain or maimed to have the God of battles to strengthen us hereafter'.

A fortnight later, Hill 60 would be back in German hands.[19] And Dave would be dead.

~~~~

In 1899, the 'Plenipotentiaries of the Powers represented at the International Peace Conference' in the Hague agreed, among other rules to govern the conduct of war, 'to abstain from the use of projectiles the sole object of which is the diffusion of asphyxiating or deleterious gases.'[20] Germany ratified the declaration the following year. The UK waited until 1907. It would be an early example of how thin an armour international law can provide, how little it can constrain.

It was 22nd April 1915, 'a glorious spring day'.[21] After five of those spring days, the butchery on and around Hill 60 had paused. The Germans adjusted their sights from the hillock to the main prize a few miles north: Ypres. They also deployed a new weapon. 'A great yellow, greenish-yellow cloud,' 5,830 cylinders of the 'damn stuff',[22] was loosed across a wide front held by troops from France and its north African colonies. 'Colonel Mordacq on 90

Brigade thought that his regimental commanders were deranged when he first heard their telephone calls, but soon he saw the fleeing soldiers: "haggard, their overcoats thrown off or opened wide, their scarves pulled off, running like madmen, directionless, shouting for water, spitting blood, some even rolling on the ground making desperate efforts to breathe."'[23]

Conan Doyle gives full vent in his near-contemporary record: 'So long as military history is written, the poisoning of Langemarck (a village north of Ypres) will be recorded as a loathsome incident by which warfare was degraded to a depth unknown among savages, and a great army, which had long been and honoured as the finest fighting force in the world, became in a single day an object of horror and contempt'.[24] Five months later, at the Battle of Loos, it was the British who, for the first time, deployed chlorine. This time, Conan Doyle's account is rather more spare: 'At 5.40 A.M. the gas-cylinders were turned on. At 6.30 A.M. the guns ceased fire.'[25]

Through the shattered northern edge of the salient the German infantry advanced, although perhaps not as decisively as might have been expected from the jagging four-mile-long rip that the poison had torn. The Germans, it seems, had not counted on just how effective their new munition would be. Canadian soldiers, with British support, were ordered to counter-attack. Even by the standards set along the Western Front, the action was chaotic, frantic, bloody, and – for the Allies – utterly exposed.[26]

The Canadian rear had been out at St Julien, north-east of Ypres. That tiny village now became their front line. On the morning of Saturday 24th April, 'the Germans turned their attention to the exposed apex of the Canadian trenches, releasing gas cylinders well before dawn.'[27] Within a few hours, the fight became an unequal exchange of artillery, the Germans more heavily armed and in better position to smash support roads and destroy signal lines.

And then, for Dave, perhaps the fateful moment: the briefest of orders, at 4.15pm, from the Commander-in-Chief of the British Expeditionary Forces, Sir John French, to Generals Smith-Dorrien and Plumer of the Second Army.

'*Every effort must be made at once to restore and hold line about St. Julien or situation of 28th Division will be jeopardised. Am sending General Staff Officer to explain Chief's views. Acknowledge.*'[28]

To which the response now must be: why? St Julien had no obvious value. It was a hamlet, a clump of cottages which had been pulverised in a single day of fighting. The Germans could and did flood the battlefield with enfilade fire from their superior artillery and machine-gun nests. A day later another brigade would be dispatched to fulfil – to attempt to fulfil – French's order. From their 4,000 men they lost 2,500. Again: why?

But there was another factor at play. It centred on the man who had ultimate command over Dave, albeit at the most elevated remove. In Alan Clark's acidic survey of the quality of military leadership in World War One – the book is called *The Donkeys* – out of the gallery of blithering Victorian old-timers, French is dismissed as a 'weak-willed man of medium height'. It would be fair to say that he divided opinion: along with the vilification, there was praise from some military and civilian leaders, including Churchill. But even his most sympathetic biographer, Richard Holmes, concludes that, while a brave man and one who cared about his profession, 'it may well be argued that French's temperament and experience made him totally unsuited for the BEF (British Expeditionary Force).'[29]

What is unarguable, is that by the spring of 1915, Field Marshal Sir John French was rapidly reaching the end of his tiny tether over the commander of the Second Army, General Sir Horace Smith-Dorrien. Sickness rates in the Second were three times that of the First, which was under Haig's command. The Second Army's lack of 'good work' and susceptibility to 'minor reverses' might have been averted by 'firmer leadership'.[30] In late April, the seething impatience had become an angry boil: French wrote in his diary that Smith-Dorrien was 'unwise…tactless…wordy…unintelligible…his pessimistic attitude has the worst effect on his commander and their troops.'[31]

Smith-Dorrien's briefings up the chain to General Headquarters do appear wordy, even needy: but his appraisal of the situation seems sound. In the words of a later military historian, following the first gas attack and the horrible rupture of Allied lines, there should have been a full tactical retreat, as 'a less defensible salient would be hard to devise'.[32] In fact General Smith-Dorrien insisted he had strongly believed in the value of an Allied counter after the German gas attacks on 22nd and 24th April, but that had depended on co-ordination with the French forces, who 'did not budge'. His own troops were 'exhausted'. The only thing was to withdraw west. 'On ST. JULIEN itself, and to the east of it, I did not think it advisable to ADVANCE to the attack (until ground was gained elsewhere, as) an advance on that front would merely accentuate the salient and entail loss without advantage.'[33]

On the same day that the Commander of the Second Army was vainly pleading to keep his job, and attempting to justify his scepticism about the value of St Julien, a Lance-Corporal in the Second Army was writing to an English family about what happened to him and his men on the road to that same village.

Machine Gun Section
Queen Victoria Rifles
British Expeditionary Force
April 30th 1915

Dear Mr and Mrs Van Ryn,

It is with the deepest regret that I have to inform you of the death of your dear son, no.3447 Rfn D. Van Ryn. During the afternoon of the 24th inst we received orders to advance and reinforce the front line. While crossing a road we came under a terrible shell fire which either killed or wounded all the section, except seven, including our officer (wounded). I trust you will forgive my writing, but during the time Dave was with the gun section he was on my guns, I always found him ever ready to help in every possible way. Not only has the Battalion lost one of its most fearless soldiers, but also we have lost a sincere friend. The remaining boys on the section wish you to accept their deepest sympathy in your sad bereavement.

I remain
Yours truly
L/Cpl H.J. McMorran 1398

~~~~

A decent burial, a good burial was what Henry Van Ryn had been supervising for more than 40 years at the Willesden Jewish Cemetery. Judaism places a great weight on k'vod hamet – on honouring the dead. For traditional Judaism, central to that is interment, returning the body to the earth.

Henry would make repeated efforts to try to find where his son lay. Shortly after Lance Corporal McMorran's dread letter, a brief note arrived at the Cemetery Lodge, dashed off in skittering black ink that denotes a man who has many, many such letters to write. It was from Rev. Michael Adler, 'Jewish Chaplain to H.M. Forces.'

> 'Yesterday (19th May), I met Pte. L. Nathan here at a service I held in the local synagogue (in Rouen). He told me all about your poor boy. He fell near St. Julien + a record of his interment has been kept. I expect an official statement about this soon + will forward it to you.
>
> I showed Nathan your letter + he was very pleased to have been some service to your son, who was a true friend to him.'

The service that Private Nathan had extended to Dave, was to have 'said a small prayer'[34] as he was buried. And indeed, possibly, to have been part of the small company who did bury him, close to where he died. How quickly, and at what risk of German guns, they must have had to hack out enough clods to cover Dave and the dead. A note was made of the location: he had been 'buried at a point 20 yards East of the Wieltje – St. Julien road'.

That line came in a letter from the Territorial Force Record Office in London, in early June, along with an imprecise OS Map reference: 'C. 23c'.

More than four years later, the war over, and Henry was still trying to locate where his son had been buried. The letters – from Reverend Adler[35] and from the staff of the Director-General of Graves Registration and Enquiries at the War Office – all respectfully refer to the 'grave' of Rifleman D. Van Ryn, which had hitherto unsuccessfully been located. Given what carnage moiled that blasted land of Flanders between Dave's death and the end of the war, 'grave' could only have been a fiction borne of courtesy.

No site, then, for the ageing Henry to contemplate travelling to. No place to stop, to stand, to recite *Kaddish*. His daughter Hinderina, Dave's half-sister, had marked that passage in *Testament of Youth*, where Vera Brittain had in turn quoted *Deronda*: that passage about the 'terrible moment' when 'great movements...an invading army...enter like an earthquake'. What Brittain hadn't included was the line that follows. They are plangent words which sing of Henry: '...and grey fathers know nothing to seek for but the corpses of their blooming sons.'

The Menin Gate was unveiled in 1927 by the – now Field Marshal – Lord Plumer. Henry was 77, and still supervising funerals at the cemetery in Willesden. His son was one of the 54,609 names who had no burial site in Belgium. They were instead inscribed in stone. You have to bend your back to find him, high on the panel, VANRYN D.

~~~~

There is another memorial. The letters: his, and others. Harold McMorran wrote again, a month after his first letter, five weeks after Dave was killed. He was Corporal McMorran now, the second chevron perhaps for his experience and bravery and leadership, perhaps just to fill the bloody gaps in the ranks. The letter bore traces of Dave's, the purple pencil across four thin sheets. The writing was a little smaller, the letters flowing a little less easily.

> *May 30th 1915*
> *Machine Gun Section*
> *Queen Victoria's Rifles*

Dear Mr + Mrs Van Ryn,
   I must ask you to forgive me for not writing before. We have again been in action and I have had very little time. I will try and give you an account of the events leading up to the 24th of April. The day on which your dear son was killed. We had been in action at Hill 60 for about five days and were being relieved...

> In the afternoon of the second day we had orders to reinforce the Canadians. While on our way to do this, the Battalion came under heavy gun fire. The machine gun team had almost reached the trenches with the loss of but one man, but while we were on the road near St Jean,[36] the team had three shells dropped in our midst. This killed six men including Dave, and wounded nine. Since then three more have died from wounds. Your son was wounded in the neck and died almost immediately. He just asked for our officer and then he knew no more. He had been on my gun during the greater part of time he was a Machine Gunner and I had ample time to know what a splendid man and soldier he was. However black things seemed, he was ever cheerful.
>
> We buried him near the spot where he fell after a friend who was of the same persuasion said a small prayer.
>
> Again assuring you of the deepest sympathy of all his comrades.
>
> I remain
>
> Yours very sincerely
>
> Corporal H.J. McMorran

~~~~

My initial question remains unanswered. Why, you might ask, is Dave here? What has he to do with a book about Jewishness, and about identities: the forces which create them, and our process of understanding them? Elsewhere – everywhere else – we see the characters engaged in struggle: with themselves, within their families and communities, in the countries where they live, in the countries – soon – where they will be condemned to die. Dave's story may not be of struggle in that sense; but he's here because I demand it. I demand the right of Jews to be unexceptional. It is one of the greatest privileges you can grant a minority.

~~~~

2006.

It is a warm, dry day in early spring. Hill 60 has regained its unremarkableness. It is home again to trees. A beech amiably extends its arms across the beaten path. Its height, its reach, its cracked and weathered bark make it seem old, but only on a human scale: it can't have lived before the Great War. Under its branches, Sarah holds our youngest son. He is named, in part, in tribute to his great-great-uncle.

Ninety-one years before, in Belgium, David Van Ryn died.

Five months before, in Belgium, Aaron David Franks was born.

SIX

On Precision and Concision; The Lost (Part 1)

By precision and concision, I mean:

Civil wars are not 'vicious'. Rape is not 'brutal'. Nor, God forbid, gang rape. If I am wrong, show me the crime or construct the sentence which is otherwise. Nonetheless, you hear these adjectives deliberately, thoughtlessly prefixed to those nouns, just in case you thought any of this might have been even-tempered, caring, solicitous.

Tautology is one unnecessary superfluity (see?). Inflation – of pitch and loudness – another. This can be more difficult to deal with, when it is politicians who are devaluing the language. How far do we repeat their hyperbole? Because not all mass killing is genocide. Not all murderous bigots are Nazis. And no: it doesn't strengthen your case to say that your antagonist has, in recent decades, committed 'dozens of holocausts'. The third weapon of mass desensitisation is cliché: overworking a word or a phrase can dull it for good, in a not-good way. The *mot juste* is not just about delight; it is about exactitude, clarity and wresting us from our torpor.

That question, then, from the start of Chapter Five: how graphic should you be? That line is less easy to scale. I tend to be more conservative, even when it has been my colleague and I who have run against the crowd, towards the mayhem, and witnessed – filmed, close up – the struggle which ended with the killer no longer rampaging, indeed suddenly no longer moving. One point-blank gunshot, two windows of the stolen tractor cab sprayed with half his head. For footage, read also descriptions of violence: the acts and the aftermath. If you have the chance to be among people in acute distress, particularly those in the thick of trauma, what can your painter's eye see? Maybe it is the absence of sound. Maybe, as the rescuers scrabble at the concrete, they are the elderly relatives sitting, into the night, mute, on uneven hard-backed chairs around the edge of the crumpled school, their heads tilted as if listening for an answer.

What am I telling you that you can't already imagine? Earthquake hits small town in southern Italy. Primary school collapses. Twenty-six children and one teacher will die. It is going to be a straightforward story, at least for the first day or so. What is useful? What is pertinent? Where does your reporter's presence stray into intrusiveness?

It was the first mass death I had been at. The day after, I didn't know whether I should go into the sports hall to see what I knew was happening inside. I did, and it was right to do so, and to talk about it. Each wake was a tableau: a child, lying on their back, beautiful, clothes clean, faces and arms incongruously sooty with bruising; around them their families, rocking and writhing in tight waves of grief.

I had limited resources. There was just me and a producer, and neither of us spoke Italian. Nor had the story at that point moved on to its next potential phase, despite a phone call the morning after the first sleepless night from a high-profile programme just out of its editorial meeting. They wanted me to doorstep one bereaved parent who, because of his position in the town, could well have been involved in granting planning permission, and 'isn't it obvious that...?' 'No, it's not obvious.' 'But isn't it ironic that...?' 'No, it isn't ironic.' 'But the editor wants it.' The conversation did not end well. A story that arrant, you have your senses and you have your words. Choose them with care.

And if you are a broadcast journalist, prepare to be brief. That can be word count, alone. Just to remind you: the dappled expanse of a five-minute *From Our Own Correspondent* is covered in a mere 800 words. Even in documentaries, complex ideas and structures rarely survive. You may think it is agony to lose a voice, a location, a thought. All that effort. Can't a corner be turned, a parenthesis curved? Probably not.

I had a different problem in this chapter. A sense of duty. If I knew when they died, how they died, who they even were, I needed to write about them. If it was exhausting, unrelenting, difficult to follow – tough. Genocide is the attempt to obliterate. Our task is to get down on our hands and knees and pick the shards, reassemble the picture.

But in the end I have pruned. Who am I to say that my unbordered topography of terror was anywhere near complete? Rendering it even less readable makes it a service to no one.

~~~~

THE LOST (1941–5)

> 'For all our wealth of historical experience, we do not know how to think about victimhood. Almost everything one might say would be unfair, self-serving, undignified, untrue, self-deluding, contradictory, or dangerous. Perhaps the best intellectual response is simply to write the history of the victims and victimizers as truthfully and accurately as possible.'
>
> JUDITH SHKLAR[1]

> 'One thought foolishly: Everyone, everyone should have his day in court.'
>
> HANNAH ARENDT[2]

The sap-lines of the tree pour upwards. And as they do, so the species changes. The family – for the sake of this story, it is a precise taxonomic group, this family – it remains the same: it is a Family of Jews. But we never sprout and blossom and stunt in settled, predictable shapes. That much we should expect, and – as often as we can – celebrate. In the years that remain, we will change – mutate, if the term is not loaded – in ways beyond my imagination.

But we have also learned that once in an aeon, there is a cataclysm. Those sap-lines are sundered. Our catastrophists, and there are many, say that this, too, is predictable. The Jew is the outsider – hated and hacked at even when, and maybe particularly when, they have come inside the establishment.

I can't say whether the periodic cataclysm is the fate of Jews. But this is the experience of Jews.

And so this is the point where we halt. We will hang our heads. We will ask what if? Some will thank God our parents' parents got out, stayed where they were, made those choices when they did. Some will ask God how could you?

But I will also hang my head because often I can't bring you an elegy to most of the murdered. Not yet, anyway. And, quite possibly, not ever. Many times I can't share a photo, or a description, or a recollection, or any whit of life. In the most direct cases, I am not sure of places and times of terrified or exhausted or sudden or lonely or industrialised death. I am not even sure of their names.

It is a minuscule speck on that continental crime. But for me, it is a source of continuing shame: that not just their lives but their memories have been effaced. They have been disappeared. Some of what follows, then, is an admission of failure.

I realise, at the same time, that my very attempts at cataloguing and form-filling have the most sinister echoes. I am being driven to trace – I can't quite say chase down – the family members. There was, after all, a thoroughness and a meticulousness to the sociopathy. These people must be accounted for. The children have to die; of course they do: otherwise they might grow up. I follow their paths to the gas chambers, grandparents, parents, children. Sobibór, Bergen-Belsen, Auschwitz. Transports no. 63, no. 7, no.13, heading east from Westerbork. Some are split up from the families. Others are deported on the same day; killed on the same day. Did they all know? Did they get to say goodbye? So many children. So few – indeed, almost no – photos of the children.

~~~~

Roco Family Tree

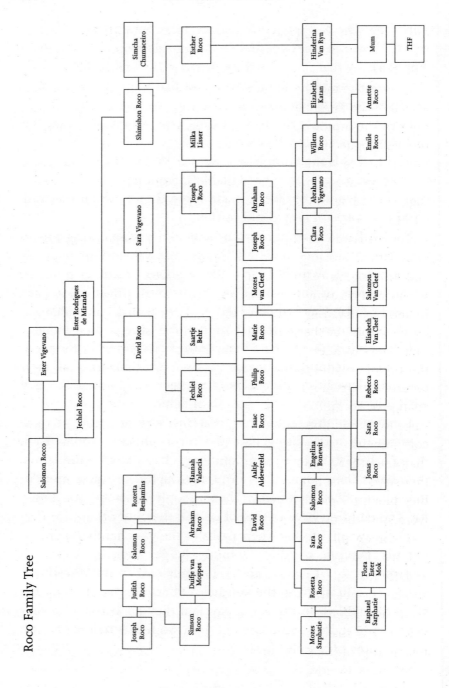

Part One: The Netherlands

The Rocos

Great-great-grandfather Shimshon Roco had done what two generations of the family had not: he had left Amsterdam. The unlikely offer of the junior cantorial post in London had been a punt for the synagogue and for him. But it was a risk which dramatically lengthened the odds for his daughters and their families.

They would live. The descendants of his siblings overwhelmingly would not. Their dates blunted; stopped. −1942. −1944. −1943. −1945.

The patriarch of the Amsterdam Rocos had been Shimshon's grandfather, arriving at the toe-end of the eighteenth century, and twirling an extra Italianate 'c'. His name was *Rocco*, Salomon Rocco, and he came from Ancona.[3] For centuries, Jews had swung in and out of favour in this Adriatic port. After the expulsions and escapes from the Iberian peninsula, the community grew as Jewish merchants were encouraged to build trade with the Levant. From the middle of the sixteenth century, as the city came under the control of the Vatican, the clouds lifted or descended with each change of Pontiff. Salomon Rocco was still a child when Giovanni Angelico Braschi became Pius VI. The new Pope quickly issued his comprehensive *Editto sopra gli Ebrei*, its 44 clauses 'one more degrading than the other'.[4] Jews − on pain of death − were limited in where they stayed, what religious texts they held, items they owned, trades they plied, people they visited, employees they hired, clothes they wore. And 'the distinguishing yellow badge was to be worn by men and women alike, both inside the Ghetto and outside.'

Lives closed down; penury spread. And yet, it seems, in Ancona embers may still have glowed − because ten years later, in 1785, another decree was needed to stamp out the 'heretical depravity'. Tommaso Lorenzo Matteucci, Grand Inquisitor of the city, ordered that 'no Jew shall have the temerity to take Lessons from Christians for any kind of (Musical) Instrument, and much less that of Dancing.'[5]

Salomon, by now, had not long turned 20. Perhaps he had already decided he had had enough, and trekked the 1,000 miles from the

Adriatic to the North Sea. An account from 1793 – the year before his wedding in Amsterdam, and the year of a plot (borne of an allegation of blasphemy against the Jews) to burn the Ghetto to the ground – spoke of the quandary of daily life in Ancona: display the yellow badge and advertise your faith, you may well be beaten up; forswear the badge, and you may well be thrown in jail. Down in Rome, Jewish children were being abducted and converted.

For the ensuing 150 years, after Salomon's immigration to the Netherlands, the Roccos graduated to Rocos[6] and sank their foundations into Dutch soil. You can see it in one repeating riposte to the canard of Jewish disloyalty to their home nation: the family name written across the decades in the ledgers of military service. That tradition of rigorous bureaucracy would, in time, be used for another purpose.

Salomon had made the big move – from Ancona to Amsterdam. His son, Jechiel, made many more, but all within a few minutes' walk. He, his wife Ester Rodrigues de Miranda, and their six children shuffling from one set of rooms to another, across the narrow canals. This was a life far from Disraeli's fantasies about brocaded, bejewelled Sephardim. Jechiel was a cobbler. His children and their children would also be artisans: many of them in the city's diamond workshops, each with their specialism – cleaving, sawing, bruting, blocking, polishing, adjusting.

Jechiel's youngest son was the only one to leave a manual trade – in his case, cigar-making; he was also the only one to leave Amsterdam. You may recall that my great-great-grandfather Shimshon's successful audition in London was so unexpected that, according to newspaper reports, his first, heavily pregnant wife had died from 'over-excitement'. But the posting was also a lifesaver. Seventy years later, survival rates in the Netherlands would be among the worst of the occupied countries: just one in four Dutch Jews survived the Holocaust.[7]

David Roco's family

David was one of two brothers to Shimshon: 11 years older, and, like their grandfather Salomon, he had married a Vigevano – Sara. The couple had ten children across 23 years. Six of the children were still alive come the 1940s. All those children – and all their families – would be pitched into the era of destruction.

Perhaps we should leave the metaphor of the family tree. Maybe a tent. An identity – to be embraced or escaped – affixed by guy-ropes, each wooden peg a person, the thread of more distant relations a little thinner, a little further out. Those are the moorings that were consumed, utterly, in fire. A Holocaust.

David's son Jechiel, and his family

Jechiel was David Roco and Sara Vigevano's first son, and fourth child. He was born in 1868. Like most of Amsterdam's Jews, he was working class.[8] In his fifties, he worked on the boats. In his sixties, he was a gardener. He lasted, somehow, until he was 75. He died* in Auschwitz, at the tail-end of another bitter Polish winter, on 6th March 1944. That meant he outlived his seven children and seven of his eight grandchildren. All of them had already been murdered by the Nazis.

Saartje; Joseph; Marie; Mozes; Elisabeth; Salomon
Amsterdam – Westerbork – Sobibór

Jechiel also outlived his wife of 43 years, Saartje (née Behr). She, along with one of their sons, were the last of his close family to be killed before him. It was to the east of Auschwitz that they had their lives poisoned and suffocated out of them.

As with the great majority of the other Dutch Jews listed for slaughter, Saartje had first been sent to Westerbork. This was the bleak, wind-swept barracks in the north-east of the country, set up by the Dutch government in 1939 for the internment of Jewish refugees who had entered the country illegally. It took on a new purpose after the Nazi invasion and occupation of the Netherlands in 1940. The camp – aided by its location, a pliant Dutch bureaucracy, and an efficient Dutch transport system – became a model for holding and processing and deporting the Jews.

So it was that Saartje became one of the 97,776[9] to make her final journey from Westerbork. Transport No. 63 to eastern Poland.

---

*'Died'. This is where evidence meets euphemism. It is not recorded in Yad Vashem's database how he died. But he was 75, and he had been deported to Auschwitz.

It was 11th May. A Tuesday. It was always a Tuesday, when the cattle-trucks came for their human cargo.

Perhaps Saartje had travelled with her second-youngest son, Joseph. He certainly would have been on the same transport. Their terminus was Sobibór, on the Polish–Ukrainian border, where they were both murdered on 14th May 1943. Joseph was deaf, and a *pantoffelmaker* – he made slippers.

Mother and son would have learned on Monday 10th May that they were to be deported. By then, few – if any – Jews were taken in by the euphemism of 'work camps' to the east. But it seems that few also knew quite how darkly the future loured. How could they?

The barrack leaders at Westerbork had the job of announcing the names on the final list for the Tuesday transport. 'It was always the same. While some threw fits or burst into loud tears, others would pack their bags and quietly obey the orders. Others would again make a last despairing effort to get exemption. But not seldom one was struck by the proud bearing of people whose fortitude put to shame the abject creatures of the Nazis.'[10]

The Dutch journalist Philip Mechanicus kept an unblinking diary of camp life in Westerbork between 28th May 1943 and 28th February 1944.[11] His entry for 1st June 1943 was written three weeks after Saartje and Joseph's journey. It is difficult to imagine theirs would have been any different:

'Men and women, old and young, whole and sick, children, babies and all were bundled into the same truck. Healthy men and women between old people who could not look after themselves, next to people who had lost control of their bodily functions; between the halt, the deaf, the blind, and the insane. All huddled together on the floor, between and on top of the luggage, helplessly entangled. One small bucket in the corner of the truck where they all had to relieve themselves in front of everyone else, just one little bucket for all those people. Next to it stood a sack of sand, from which everyone could scoop up a handful to cover the excrement. In the other corner stood a vat of water with a tap to it, from which you could quench your thirst.'[12]

The journey took three days. Saartje and Joseph were two of 1,446 on board that transport. From those 1,446, one person would survive.[13] Indeed, of the 19 train-loads (one of which carried a mighty 3,000-plus: this was the 'children's transport'[14] of June), Jacob Presser – the great Dutch historian, poet and survivor – reports that only 20 survived. Others put the number lower.

There is extensive testimony of beatings, punishment, humiliation and torture, of hangings and shootings at Sobibór.[15] But the Nazis also had a job to do: the ideologues and the bureaucrats (with a wide intersection of the Venn diagram) knew that there must be an *Endlösung*, a Final Solution.[16] By the middle of 1941, Heinrich Himmler understood that mass shootings were only efficient up to a point; he was also, it seems, concerned about their humaneness: not for the victim but for the perpetrator. It had been reported to him that there could be a 'psychological burden (in) shooting women and children'.[17]

In February 1943, Himmler made his second trip to Sobibór. An exemplary gassing of hundreds of young Jewish women and girls was specially laid on for the *Reichsführer*, before he and his company retired for a slap-up lunch.[18]

The pace could now pick up. The following month, until July, 19 trains took 34,313 Dutch Jews to Sobibór. Among them, Saartje and her son Joseph, and six weeks later Saartje's sister-in-law, Marie – Jechiel and Sara's fifth child. Marie Roco had been a seamstress; her husband Mozes van Cleef had been a greengrocer. On 29th June 1943, they and their two children, 12-year-old Elisabeth and eight-year-old Salomon were packed into the gas chambers at Sobibór, along with 2,394 others.

As with other death camps, although they had a single purpose, there was subterfuge. Having disembarked from the train, Saartje, Joseph, Marie, Mozes, Elisabeth and Salomon would have been addressed by one of the SS guards:[19] you are to be sent on to settle in occupied German territory; first, you must be showered and disinfected. They were told to undress completely, there and then. They deposited their valuables. They then had a 250-metre walk down *Himmelfahrtstrasse* (Heavenly Avenue). They may have been given a little piece of soap. Above the entrance to the gas-chamber was a plaque that read *Seuchen-Bekämpfungsstelle* (Department for Combatting Infectious Diseases).[20] They entered the low-ceilinged room with their hands above their heads: that way you could cram more people in. Unlike Auschwitz, the gassing was by carbon monoxide. It was slower: it took up to 30 minutes for death to be certain.[21] Later, the floor would cantilever, and the corpses tip out.[22]

We started with these cousins because their story is so typical of Dutch Jews, unable to prise themselves from the grip and ravening appetite of the genocidal machine. These six were killed in Sobibór. For many of the other Dutch cousins, as with most of their compatriots, their murder was elsewhere in Poland, in the biggest death factory of all: Auschwitz-Birkenau.

~~~~

Isaac; Abraham; David; Aaltje; Jonas; Sara; Rebecca; Philip
<u>Amsterdam – Westerbork – Auschwitz</u>

As we read a few pages back, Auschwitz was where Jechiel Roco died in March 1944. It was also where his third child, Isaac, was killed on 25th January 1943, at the age of 40. It had been then – January 1943 – that 'Himmler had no illusions that Germany would win the war, but at least he could dispose of the Jews. That was one good deed he could accomplish.'[23]

Isaac had worked in the Central Market, alongside his greengrocer brother-in-law, Mozes Van Cleef.

24

'Had worked'. Long before the filth and the desolation of the internment camp at Westerbork, and before the wholesale deportation of Dutch Jewry which preceded Isaac's murder, the system had closed in on people such as him. From 15th September 1941 Jews were disbarred from 'direct or indirect participation in public markets, public auctions or abattoirs' (along with public parks, cafes, wagon-lits, theatres, sports grounds, art exhibitions, public libraries etc., etc.).[25]

The Jewish Council, the body created by the Nazis to be a conduit between the occupiers and the occupied,[26] protested, to no end: 'Market trading in the Netherlands, both retail and wholesale, is of extremely great economic importance to the country. The expulsion of Jewish traders from markets and streets will have catastrophic repercussions on Dutch economic life as a whole...'[27]

It was a moment, in the gathering maelstrom. Another click on the ratchet.

But maybe I have fallen into the trap. Ratchets turn only one way. Maybe that tired imagery belies two of the most searing questions from the Holocaust: of responses and responsibility.

So let's unlock the ratchet for a moment, and spin further back, and think first about the response of Dutch Jews.

In May 1940, the Germans had swept into the Netherlands. There was fear and dejection among the estimated 140,000 Jews. Escape was difficult: partly because of the geography; partly because of a failure of imagination: especially at the start, no one could guess quite what lay ahead.

In January 1941, all Jews had had to be registered. In February came the first pogrom, and the first report of resistance groups forming. The reaction was rapid: on 22nd February 1941, hundreds of Jews were beaten up, abducted, interned. In April, Jews were issued with ID cards showing a large 'J'. (The yellow star would follow a year later.) Decrees were issued, prohibiting them from swathes of public life.

The maw clamped ever tighter. Raids, often apparently random; the old to the young, dragged from their homes, thrown into the back of a truck. Sometimes, with the help of locals. The Jews confined into ever more cramped quarters in Amsterdam (and remember a third of Jews, pre-war, had lived elsewhere in the country). The line-ups for deportation, with a Nazi leaning against a wall, splitting family members with a wave to the right, a wave to the left.[28] For a time, the choice – and you had hours to make it – between sterilisation and immediate deportation. And on, and on.

There is a reflex, perhaps empathetic, more likely egocentric, when reading the accounts, or talking to survivors – as I have had the privilege, as a journalist, over many long hours – to ask the questions: what would I have done? how would I have coped? would I have survived? (Almost certainly not, was my answer.)

There is, equally, a question which is less empathetic. The cliché is that it is asked by the suntanned Sabras of Israel. And, like many clichés, it contains a truth: they did raise it, and sometimes still do: 'How could you let it be?'

It was a point returned to, repeatedly, in the trial of Adolf Eichmann; in Hannah Arendt's account, the prosecutor thrusts the question in the face of his own witnesses, contrasting 'Israeli heroism and the submissive meekness'[29] of European Jewry. Fifty years later, it was still a puzzle for the founder of Israeli military intelligence. Mordechai Gichon was born in Berlin in 1922, and had moved to Palestine in 1933. In an interview in 2010 with Ronen Bergman for his book *Rise and Kill First: The Secret History of Israel's Targeted Assassinations*,[30] Gichon recalled meeting a Jewish refugee in central Europe in June 1945. 'My brain could not grasp, not then and not today, how it could have been that there were tens of thousands of Jews in a camp with only a few German guards, but they did not rise up, they simply went like lambs to the slaughter... Why didn't they tear (the Germans) to shreds?'

Leaving aside the casualness of the exaggerated odds – in 1943 the network of camps at Auschwitz-Birkenau contained 80,000 prisoners and more than 1,000 guards[31] – I can only offer several other vague answers: that there *was* resistance (beyond the heroic, doomed Warsaw ghetto uprising), albeit sporadic. An insurrection, for example, eventually led to the early closure of Sobibór. That attempts to escape would not just mean almost certain death for you, but particularly sadistic, lethal retribution on many, randomly selected, others. That to those not yet deported, hidden radios had spread the news, broadcast from London, of gassings, of murders, but how much was certain, and was it really everyone? After all, people embarked on trains to Auschwitz still hugging their musical scores. And there were those — among them, the eight in Anne Frank's 'secret annexe' who were hiding, waiting, praying for the Allies to come and free them. But far and away, before even the slate-grey gloom and horror of the camps, I think of the slow suffocation of hope and stamina in the long months before, made even more debilitating by the rushes of fear and adrenaline, by the constant dislocations of normality, of predictability. To those proud, aggressive, resourceful Sabras: think of that prisoner-training you endure to become a member of a security agency. How many of your muscular number break?

The response of European Jewry was not lamb-like; it was human.

And responsibility?

Dutch officialdom, on the whole, quickly fell into step.

Can we say why? Assigning motive is dangerous for observers — be they journalists, historians or philosophers. So can we guess and generalise in this case? Here is a tentative attempt. The co-operation and collaboration may not have been with especial glee or fervour, although some were certainly stirred. But there was a pettiness: a desire to lock sprockets in another machine. There was cowardice and comfort in this, in 'doing one's job' and confirming one's prejudice about the Jew. In Presser's words — speaking of the entire Nazi strategy: 'The extermination of the Jews was first and foremost an administrative feat — it was genocide by the civil service.' Hannah Arendt, writing at the same time, had more famously confronted us with the process by which the unthinkable became thinkable through *not* thinking. It led to her shocking, misunderstood apothegm: 'the banality of evil.'

She was writing about the Apex Bureaucrat, Adolf Eichmann. He was the small man with the very big job: systems manager for the cross-border wiping out of Jews. Arendt was covering his trial in Jerusalem in 1961, but she was also writing of everyone else involved in the process.

The idea that evil could be 'banal' was, of course, hotly contested. To Arendt, it was obvious, or rather, it had *become* obvious. Her reporting makes it clear: Eichmann's 'inability to think',[32] his ability to 'overcome his innate repugnance towards crime' and flip his conscience,[33] the 'ruthless desire for conformity at any price'.[34] She was *not* lessening the crime, or even the criminal. He was, she said, a new type of criminal: '*hostis generis humani*' (the enemy of mankind). In Eichmann's case, fundamental to its commission was 'sheer thoughtlessness…the strange interdependence of thoughtlessness and evil'.[35]

A postscript on the need to think, and the potentially terrifying implications of not thinking. I mentioned, at the start of Chapter Three, Frederick Douglass changing his mind on a grave issue – and the personal cost it exacted. Arendt endured something similar. Back in 1946, during the Nuremberg trials, she'd written to her friend Karl Jaspers to say that she was uncomfortable with him even calling the actions of the Nazis a 'crime'. Their 'monstrousness', she says 'explodes the limits of the law'.[36] Three months later, Jaspers quietly made his case: he was not 'altogether comfortable' with the idea that our legal system, our language could not encompass the guilt of the Nazis, because then it must take on 'a streak of "greatness" – of Satanic greatness'. Rather, 'it seems to me that we have to see these things in their total banality, in their total triviality… Bacteria can cause epidemics that wipe out nations, but they remain merely bacteria.'[37]

That was October 1946. In 1961, Arendt was observing the personification of that banality in a Jerusalem courtroom. In 1963, she responded to another old acquaintance – Gershom Scholem, who had been among those to criticise Arendt's thesis. 'Dear Gerhard,' she wrote. 'There are certain statements in your letter which are not open to controversy, because they are simply false.' She deals, at length, with those, before coming to the crux, 'the only matter where you have not misunderstood me… You are quite right: I changed my mind and do no longer speak of "radical evil"… It is indeed my opinion that evil is never "radical", that it is only extreme, and that it possesses neither depth nor any demonic dimension. It can overgrow and lay waste the whole world precisely because it spreads like a fungus on the surface.'[38]

All this would be to come, in the 1960s – this attempt to account for what happened, to consider its implications: the struggle, in other words, to acknowledge its uniqueness, but to place it in context.

And if there is to be an accounting, then we need to return to the 1940s and mark the thoroughness of the job the Nazis managed with Jechiel Roco's family. His son Isaac, the greengrocer, was murdered on the same day in Auschwitz as his – Isaac's – youngest brother, Abraham. He, like their nephew Joseph (whom we met above), was registered as deaf. Abraham had been at a special school for the deaf between the ages of four and fifteen, before enrolling at a school for furniture-makers. He was 'well developed and spoke rather well'.[39]

David Roco was the oldest of Jechiel's sons, born in 1901. He, his wife Aaltje (née Aldewereld), their 17-year-old son Jonas, 15-year-old daughter Sara, and nine-year-old daughter Rebecca, were murdered at Auschwitz early in the genocide of the Dutch Jews: between August and October 1942. Similarly, David's brother Philip: Auschwitz, 30th September 1942. His murder came four days after Commandant Rudolf Höss had received instructions to transform Auschwitz fully from concentration camp to death camp.[40]

~~~~

Joseph, Milka, Clara, Abraham, Willem, Elisabeth, Emile, Annette
<u>Scheveningen – Bergen-Belsen – Tröbitz</u>

[41]

A different place to be killed: Germany. And, it seems, a different class of cousin: middle, rather than working. Joseph was David Roco's second son, born in 1875. The undated photo, above, suggests — to me — a twinkle. He is well-dressed, well-groomed. The photographer has told him to hold that angled, over the left-shoulder look. If he were playing it straight, he might indeed be looking straight, away from the lens. But he cannot quite play the game: his eyes are gazing in our direction, appraising us. It could be rather intimidating, were it not for the amusement writ across the rest of his face: his lips pursed upwards, his cheeks dimpled; Joseph is feeling rather tickled.

He and his wife Milka (née Lisser) lived in Scheveningen, the coastal suburb of The Hague, whose big skies and wind-tossed seafront I would know well, 60 years later, as I followed the war crimes trial of Slobodan Milošević. Joseph was a salesman. The Dutch word *vertegenwoordiger* is as vague as the English: it appears to run the gamut from door-to-door salesman to agent in executive chair. Joseph's dress — and the way he tried to avoid death for him and his wife — suggests he was doing alright. Their granddaughter would recall, more than 50 years later, that 'their religion was bridge'.[42]

There is another reason to guess that Joseph and Milka were more middle than working-class. They were able to procure Honduran passports.[43] Early in 1943, the Nazis had announced that 'for obvious political reasons no disabilities whatsoever must be imposed' on a group of central and South American countries. The reason? 'Lest (they) be given grounds for submitting to the importunities of our enemies and make common cause with them against Germany.'[44] Word must have got out, or the realisation dawned, as this was not an order that the Nazis wanted publicised. Passports from Latin America were smuggled in from abroad or forged in the Netherlands. Hundreds of Jews holding Central American papers survived in Bergen-Belsen until the end of the war;[45] some were released in an exchange.

Joseph was not one of them. He died in the camp on 12th January 1945, three months before the British army arrived, and saw for themselves – heard and smelled for themselves – 'death and decay...corruption and filth...the world of a nightmare'.[46]

Milka managed, somehow, to make it to April, past the typhus epidemic that, among its thousands of victims, accounted, in late February or early March, for Margot Frank and her younger sister, Anne.[47] Indeed, Milka's record[48] states: 'Date of Liberation: 23 April 1945'.

The date provides the clue. She was not liberated in Bergen-Belsen, which the British had entered on 15th April, but more than a week later, by a Ukrainian division of the Red Army. She had wound up not far from the border with Poland, after a tortuous, looping train journey.

Close to 2,500 inmates had been compacted on to the transport. For the best part of two weeks, under SS command, it meandered east, searching for passage, it seems to Theresienstadt. Why? Different reasons are offered: perhaps to remove some of the living evidence from Bergen-Belsen;[49] perhaps to use as hostages, exchange material, later.[50] Typhus, hunger and thirst raged inside the carriages. The Allies repeatedly strafed the train.

The journey ended at the village of Tröbitz, 'in a delicate forest deep in eastern Germany'[51] where the Soviet soldiers took over.

Somehow – that word again – somehow 65-year-old Milka was not one of the hundreds to have died on board. But, in the end, the typhus won. Six days later – 29th April 1945 – she was dead.

Milka and Joseph had had two children: Clara and Willem. Clara was the elder: born in 1901, married in 1924, widowed on 24th September 1944, when her husband Abraham Vigevano was murdered in Auschwitz. Clara survived Auschwitz, one of the 6,000 to be liberated by the Soviet army. She would live another 40 years.

Released alongside Clara was her 40-year-old sister-in-law, Elisabeth (née Katan). She was the wife of Willem Roco.

Their story, and in particular that of their young daughter, Annette, is documented in detail in Annette's own words, on camera, in 1996.[52] Their story is a microcosm of the depravity, the betrayal, the resilience, the generosity and the damage.

Rotterdam – Scheveningen – Auschwitz – Warsaw

Willem worked in the stock market in Rotterdam. After the Nazis arrived, a business contact offered him a chance to escape with his family. Emile had been born in 1933; Annette in 1938. They could all have passage to the USA; they would go by boat from Portugal. It was tempting. But Willem, it seems, did not want to leave his extended family behind. He turned down the offer.

Instead, in 1942, Elisabeth and Willem agreed that – should they be ordered to 'work in the east', as the invaders and their local enablers euphemistically called it – and so should they need to hide, it would be better that the family split up. Willem asked his closest friend, whom he'd known since school, Wilhelm (Wim) Gieben, to take Annette and Emile in, if needs be.

Taking Jewish children to safe houses, though, was in itself fraught – open to suspicion and challenge. They could not be brought by a parent; it had to be a third party. And you had to be prepared to move at a moment's notice. You wanted to eke out the remaining vestiges of togetherness, you had to ensure that the place you were heading to was ready, but you also could not risk waiting for the round-up or the raid. And so, when Wim sent word to the Roco home, it was to say 'now': Annette and Emile had to leave immediately. Willem was not there; he was at work. Elisabeth managed to get a message to him. She, meanwhile, could not bear to take the children to the train. She had said goodbye at home, and left them to walk to the station with a friend, known to the children as Auntie Anna. Willem almost missed them. Annette recalls that as she approached the station, she saw her father haring down the street. 'He was in his raincoat…running, and running.'

Willem knelt to embrace his children. Annette was a little girl, no older than four, but she remembers her father's expression as he said goodbye to them. 'He looked totally bewildered.' Willem would not see his children again.

The little girl was bereft: she didn't stop crying. Her older brother, all of nine years old, did not allow himself to, at least in front of Annette. There was little time to settle. Wim and Serline, the family friends in the south of Holland who had taken in the siblings, had two children of their own, and Serline was heavily pregnant with a third. She gave birth soon after Annette and Emile arrived, but the baby died. It was, said Annette, 'the first blow', swiftly followed by another: Serline was diagnosed with breast cancer. She had a mastectomy.

After seven weeks, Emile was sent on to another family. Annette was 'devastated; I felt totally sick'.

She would stay for seven months. It would have been longer, but Wim was in the Resistance. They feared there had been a leak, some information had seeped out, and that – at any time – there could be a raid.

And so began a round of pinball. Annette careened at a few hours' notice from place to place, home to home, refuge to refuge. Once to Amsterdam, but the rest of the time around the villages and hamlets of South Holland. She would be conveyed by a stranger and deposited. She would be greeted, taken in, cared for. It was an act of bravery and some self-sacrifice, given the shortages, the need to divide the rations by one more. But Annette, aged four, five and six, learned not to trust: she never knew when she would be forced to move on. 'At a certain point, I didn't know what it meant to have your own mother. All I knew was (how) to adjust.'

Among those who showed kindness and courage were a couple in their early twenties, Jan and Franscina Schrier. They lived in a tiny cottage with no running water, no electricity. They slept in an alcove in the wall. Under that alcove was an improvised trapdoor leading to a shallow space below the floorboards; each time there was a knock at the front door, Annette knew to run to the trapdoor, and 'lie in my grave', sometimes for hours.

She would also be given a new name: Else Zonveld. In fact, Annette was told to forget her own. After the war, her mother would have a tough time finding her and her brother, because almost no one knew their real names.

In September 1943, her parents were caught. They had been hiding in IJsselmonde, south of Rotterdam.[53] Someone – possibly someone from the family – had betrayed them. Annette's mother, Elisabeth, had – despite the risks – kept a photograph of her children by her bedside. One of the Germans, accompanied by a Dutch collaborator found the photo, pocketed it.

Willem and Elisabeth were taken to the 'Oranjehotel' – the prison in Scheveningen. Willem was tortured, 'but he never said a word'.

The SS were not to be thwarted. There was a ticking biological timebomb to defuse. Unfound, unchecked, this small girl would become a fully grown Jew.

Shortly after her parents' detention, 'a big, black car' arrived outside Annette's latest hiding place – the farmhouse of Reinier and Jannetje Scheele. They happened to be out – dealing with a family issue in Rotterdam 'thank God' – but at home was a teenaged girl, Truus Groenenboom, who looked after the house and the Scheeles' baby.

Annette may have been only about five, but as she played at the window, there was something about that car – the way it drew up slowly, the men inside with black hats. 'So right away, I ducked.'

Truus answered the door. The men showed her the photograph. 'We're looking for this girl.' Truus didn't blink. She told the men to go to the barn, to look for Mr Scheele, to ask him. He wasn't there, of course. It was to buy time.

Enough time to push Annette into a back basement, to gather her clothes, her toys, all vestiges of her, and throw them down into the cellar. Truus slammed the door. There were nails on the outside, which she covered with clothes, to hide the opening.

Annette was left with the rats, in the dark, in standing water. She was crying. The men returned. Truus somehow persuaded them to go off again to look for Reinier Scheele. At which point she opened the basement door again. Annette recalls cowering, looking up at this silhouetted figure above her. '"You shut up," bellowed Truus. "If you make one sound, they're going to kill you." Slam. "Well I shut up, I shut up for hours."'

The Germans returned for a second time, pushed Truus aside, and turned the house upside down. They threatened Truus. She remained calm.

In the end the men left, having warned that they would soon be back again.

Truus – this young woman, maybe still even just a teenage girl – would show further, astonishing gumption. First, at nightfall, she took the baby on her back, on a bicycle, and pedalled off to find someone to look after it until morning. She phoned Rotterdam to tell Reinier and Jannetje not to come home. She then took Annette on the back of the bicycle, and set off again. There was a strict curfew. Each time a German searchlight swept the fields and the roads, Truus and Annette would throw themselves from the bike and lie as flat as they could.

No one wanted Annette. The last person Truus turned to was the minister. It took time, but in the end he was persuaded to have Annette for one night. Then a further three weeks at another farmhouse, a beautiful place, with peacocks. But the woman of the house spent those three weeks weeping in terror: the Germans might turn up at any moment, she thought, looking for this fugitive five-year-old.

Indeed, all doors closed in the face of this radioactive child. They knew her photograph was out there. Eventually, it was Reinier Scheele's parents who took her in – a granddaughter was the story, a daughter of their daughter Cordelia, who still lived at home. To add to the piquancy – that's almost certainly the wrong word – three German soldiers were also billeted to the Scheeles' house. From these Wehrmacht conscripts there was no hint of suspicion.

Annette stayed with the Scheeles until the Canadians liberated the south of the country on 24th November 1944. The rest of the country had to wait until 5th May the following year.

'Liberation'. It was that: it was clear-cut, at least in western Europe. Just as the war ended in victory for the Allies, it ended in defeat for the Nazis. But clarity didn't mean the light always shone brightly. How could it?

For Annette's parents, Willem and Elisabeth, after their detention in 1943 in Scheveningen, they had been sent to a Dutch internment camp. And then on, in one of the transports, along with her cousin Clara Roco and her husband Abraham Vigevano, in a wagon filled with the dead and the dying, to Auschwitz.

On arrival, the men and women were split up. For the women, a question: do you want to work, or do you want to go on the truck? 'My mother always liked to work,' recalled Annette. So, after three days on that transport, exhausted and weak, Elisabeth volunteered – and so saved her own life. All those who went on the truck were taken straight to the gas chambers.

Elisabeth's work would be special. She, and other women, were paraded in front of Josef Mengele. She made it through the audition. She was selected, and kept in the experimentation block. There Dr Mengele and his team performed their human vivisection.

In September 1945, Elisabeth talked about her ordeal. Her witness statement is held in the archives of Amsterdam's Institute for War, Holocaust and Genocide Studies. It is a profound disappointment, just two and a half typewritten pages: not only brief, but bare. Much of it is devoted to her recalling the names, the addresses even, of people with whom she was deported or incarcerated. Is that what her two male debriefers wanted of her? Were they overwhelmed by the information they were gathering, as the scale of the crimes was becoming clear, as the pieces began to be assembled? Did their task or perhaps their demeanour discourage Elisabeth from talking more about her 16 months in Auschwitz? Or was it she who was too spent, too traumatised to revisit the ordeal?

Most of the experiments performed on Elisabeth were through unnamed injections. Some women died. When she and her fellow guinea pigs had arrived, the fellow inmates of the 'experimentation block' said that 'there had been a lot of surgery in the past'. Elisabeth was spared.

Her release came with the arrival of the Red Army. But liberation came at a cost, hinted at by her daughter's testimony. 'The Russians were terrible. They were terrible.' Annette breaks off, rubs at a spot on her clothes. 'Can you imagine those people looking like skeletons? My mother says she looked like an 80-year-old man. And the Russians even came on to her.'

The survivors did not leave Auschwitz immediately. There had to be some recuperation, some treatment of disease, and the organisation of transport out. The Allies also began the process of questioning the inmates, gathering the evidence of the greatest crime.

Elisabeth was taken to the Dutch border; there was a further, short period of quarantine, for the scabies and lice. She contacted the Red Cross. As, previously, had Franscina, one of the tiny minority to know Annette's real name. The connection was made.

In southern Holland, Annette's pretend-mother Cordelia, knelt at Annette's side, and told her that her mother had returned. Annette heard the words, but 'didn't feel anything. For me, it was just another story. I had to wait and see what was going to happen.'

The day came. Elisabeth arrived by train, with a friend. It was the same woman who had taken Annette and Emile to the train station in Rotterdam, back in 1942. Anna or 'Tante Annie' as Annette knew her. The pair had a two-mile walk to the house – a long, slow journey for a woman just out of Auschwitz. Cordelia suggested to Annette that she go to meet her mother. She wore a new dress, new shoes even, all made by Cordelia for the occasion.

'I looked pretty. I walked down the dusty, curving roads of Zeeland. I walked and walked and walked. And I see these two people, far away. They were walking very slowly.'

On that country lane, they converged: two worlds collapsing back into one. It was Tante Annie who fell to her knees, to embrace Annette. Elisabeth was stiffer, in mind and body. She later told her daughter that she had been overcome with emotion when she had seen her seven year-old from afar, but had told herself not to upset Annette by being overwrought.

At the same time, the seven-year-old girl saw a woman with white hair who now, oddly, was quite fat: it was the oedema, the water retention of the starved body that has begun to take in food and drink once again. It was not a warm fat; it was the strange swelling where you pressed into the flesh and the depression remained. And she smelled, smelled so strongly of the tincture that was used to rid her of the parasites that had infested her body.

Annette recoiled. It must, she said, have been terrible for her mother. She remembers later, in the farmhouse, hearing Elisabeth crying in her room. She didn't cry in front of Annette.

And as for Willem: for years, Elisabeth, Annette and Emile waited. Then they heard, that after that separation at Auschwitz – men this way, women the other – Willem had only spent two weeks in the camp before he was sent to Warsaw to clear the rubble – presumably from what was left after the destruction and vengeance that followed the month-long uprising in the ghetto, in the spring of 1943. Within three days, Willem was dead. Many of the Dutch Jews who'd arrived as labour contracted a stomach virus. They couldn't work, at least not efficiently. So they were killed – almost certainly shot, either on site or at the KL Warschau, the concentration camp within the city. It didn't have gas chambers. But it did have machine guns.

Elisabeth, Emile and Annette moved to Amsterdam. At the age of seven, Annette started school. She did not make it to higher education. 'I was easily distracted. I was in my own world. Still am, I guess.'

The reunion had not been easy, and never would be. Fifty years on, Annette tries to cling to understatement. 'Something came between my mother and me.' Another attempt: 'We didn't have a great relationship.' Then the crack widens: 'She demanded a lot of attention. Whenever I did something wrong, in her eyes, I always had to hear that she'd survived Auschwitz. And so, it was – blackmail.'

But Annette remained, decades on, deeply grateful – to the point where her voice drifts off in wonder – for the generosity and fortitude shown by the non-Jewish families who took her in and sheltered her, the people whom she would forever consider her extended family, a balm for the gash left across her own family limbs.

She married at the age of 22; had a son swiftly after. She gave him the name – precisely the name – of his great-great-great-great-grandfather from Ancona: 'Rocco'.

Annette became a singer, different perhaps from her great-great-uncle Shimshon, but still a singer.

She released a few singles, was photographed in glamorous company. But she felt distanced. In 1996, in her late fifties, she spoke of herself, and of the displaced child:

'We were a family, and all of a sudden I was a refugee. And no matter how old you are you can definitely feel that. So I felt very remote. And that stayed with me…until now, I can feel very remote. Even now, that I'm speaking, I can hear myself.

'It programmed me for the rest of my life.'

~~~~

Salomon Roco's family

Shimshon Roco (my great-great-grandfather) had two brothers, you may recall. We have just read about the family of one: David Roco, 11 years older than Shimshon. Salomon was big brother to them both. He was a shoemaker. He, and his wife Rozetta had one child: Abraham.

Salomon's son, Abraham's family

Abraham was part of Amsterdam's intricate army of diamond-workers. In July 1889, at the age of 23, *diamantslijper* Abraham married 22-year-old *diamantsnijdster* Hannah Valencia. They had eight children. We will follow three of their stories.

Rosetta
Amsterdam – Westerbork – Sobibór

Their oldest, Rosetta, became a fugitive in her hometown. She, along with her husband, son and daughter-in-law, hid from the Nazis at seven separate addresses. In May 1943, they were betrayed by the brothel-owner who had arranged their safe-house.[54] Within six days, Rosetta and her husband Mozes had been killed at Sobibór. Their son, Raphael and his wife, Flora, lasted six months at the death camp, until it was razed. Without a gas chamber, they were probably shot in the back of the head. Ukrainian fascists were given that task.*

---

*Which means that Raphael and Flora witnessed, or took part in, the Sobibór uprising of 14th October and the escape of some prisoners. The incident led to the camp's closure. Another uselessly

Salomon
Amsterdam – Westerbork – Theresienstadt – Auschwitz – ?

Five years after Rosetta was born, Abraham and Hannah had their first son, Salomon. Along with his familiar name, a familiar trade: he was another *diamantslijper*, living a short walk from the Esnoga. So much, so normal. What would be janglingly bizarre was that – whether knowingly, or more likely, inadvertently – Salomon and his wife Engelina (née Bonewit) were enmeshed up in one of the more pitiful and largely futile attempts by 'Portuguese' Jews to stave off death. It was an episode which still perplexed Hannah Arendt 20 years later, as she covered the Eichmann trial. 'For God knows what reasons,' she wrote, in 1944 'some 370 Sephardic Jews remained unmolested in Amsterdam'.[55]

This is the reason.

Once the dominant force and number within the community, the *Portugees–Israëlitische Gemeente* were now a modest minority: 4,303 according to the census of October 1941.[56] Their days of clear separation, of cultural and familial heterogeneity had – by and large – long since gone. Untrammelled lineage from the Iberian Peninsula would, by the middle of the twentieth century, have been rare, very rare.

Still, some in the community with connections and, presumably, the money to commission the 'research', decided to try to play the system. In January 1941, the Germans had issued Decree Number 6. In which – Article 3, Part 1: 'Whenever there is a doubt whether a person must be considered a full or a part Jew...the matter must be referred for decision to the *Reichskommissar* for the Occupied Netherlands'.[57]

Members of the Jewish community compiled a 34-page report, under the auspices of the highly respected neurologist, anthropologist and – as we'll see – phrenologist, Professor C.U. Ariëns

---

partial synonym – 'closure'. The Nazis wanted to eradicate all trace of their death factory. They forced the remaining inmates to level the entire huge campus, and to camouflage as far as possible its interred remains. That work was done by mid-December. And so, by the time Raphael and Flora were murdered, they were probably nearing the end of their usefulness.

Kappers. It was entitled *Die Herkunft der sogenannten portugiesichen Juden* ('The Origins of the so-called Portuguese Jews').

The evidence included extracts from one of the seminal works of German nationalism,[58] the pungently anti-Semitic *Foundations of the Nineteenth Century*, by the British philosopher and natural scientist, Houston Stewart Chamberlain. His florid, exclamation-strewn revelations stretch across 900-plus pages, as he whirs himself into a frenzied apologia for 'the value of purer inbreeding'. Among his observations: 'the so-called "Spanish Jews"...can by purity keep (themselves) noble for centuries...(and) how very necessary it is to distinguish between the nobly reared portions of a nation and the rest...the so-called "German Jews"...for whom they (the Sephardim) have an almost comical repugnance.'[59] Chamberlain's gratitude to the 'genuine Sephardim' spurts across the page: 'This is....genuine nobility of race! That out of the midst of such people Prophets and Psalmists could arise – that I understood at first glance (at the Sephardim), which I honestly confess that I had never succeeded when I gazed, however carefully, on the many hundred young Jews – "Bochers" – of the Friedrichstrasse in Berlin.'

It gets even more bizarre in the two appendices[60] to the report.

The first is by Professor Kappers himself. To him, the task of setting out, using precise measurements, that 'Portuguese Israelites...belong to the long skulls. Jews on the other hand (sic) are decidedly short skulls.' The former also rarely have 'frizzy' hair, and the noses: very different. (Professor Kappers was also willing to sign off individual racial-exemption papers that had been compiled for dozens of Jews, in documentation which apparently saved them, and earned him a place in Yad Vashem's list of 'Righteous Among the Nations'.)[61]

The second appendix is the work of the academically decorated, royally knighted, Professor of Zoology, Comparative Anatomy and Physiology, J. F. van Bemmelen. He writes, he says, from a 'bio-genealogical point of view', and sets out nine ways in which the 'Portuguese' and the 'Ashkenazim' do not intersect. For example, Point 5: 'a large majority of the former were well-built with a distinguished appearance which was quite consistent with the civilised and more cultured class to which they undoubtedly belonged.'

It seems, from the underlining and marginalia that mark the copy belonging to the senior SS officer in the Netherlands, HSSPF Rauter,[62] that he might have approved of some of the arguments, if only on first reading. And that he did, at the very least, read it.

In what way were Salomon and Engelina entangled in this?

The circumstantial evidence is in the date of their deportation to Westerbork. The pseudo-academic reports and treatises and letters had bought the Portuguese Jews some time, although through much of 1943, there were repeated threats, by the SS, to 'inspect' this group. Indeed, at one point, the couple appear (along with Salomon's sister, Sara) on a list of *hartefälle* – 'tough cases' – from among those with Portuguese ancestry.[63]

The inspection kept on being delayed, but on 26th January 1944, *Sturmbannführer* Wilhelm Zöpf[64] ordered in any case that Portuguese Jews be included in 'deportation measures'. Many of them were rounded up, in raids on 1st February. The long-promised inspection of the Portuguese Jews finally took place on 20th February: 22 families, 273 people, paraded before three senior SS men: Zöpf, Aust and Gemmeker. Aust's verdict:[65] 'a sub-human race.' The officers agreed that the learned professors who had vouched for these Jews' difference had been duped. Zöpf suggested it might have been down to clever lighting effects in the photographs, and concluded that 'since these people were quite unfit for work (as a result of inbreeding and soft living) they would have to be put on the train for Theresienstadt that very week.'[66]

Philip Mechanicus, the gnarled journalist in Westerbork, learned of the news on Wednesday 23rd February. 'That was all (the Portuguese) got for parading last Sunday before the German authorities who were kind enough to take note of their cranial structure and their facial angle... What a performance! What grotesque lunacy!'[67]

And so, the Friday after that Sunday inspection, 308 Portuguese were deported from Westerbork to Theresienstadt, in the occupied Czech protectorate of Bohemia and Moravia.

On board were prisoner numbers 239 and 240 – Salomon and Engelina Roco.[68]

The couple stayed in the ghetto-cum-camp for seven months. Life was, overall – and this is a hazy, hesitantly offered generalisation – less gruesome than at other detention centres, the death camps in particular. In Terezin (to give it its Czech name), hunger and disease were the main killers. And through the summer of 1944, there had even been a lull in the deportations to the more lethal camps. But it was just a lull. On 28th September, Salomon was sent to Auschwitz. On 4th October, Engelina followed. There, two days later, she was murdered.

Salomon was not killed at Auschwitz. Rather, he died six weeks after the camp had been liberated, and two weeks short of his fiftieth birthday, on 28th February 1945. Yad Vashem marks the location of his death as 'Central Europe'. My best guess – my only guess – is that Salomon was one of the 60,000, battered and weakened from their time in Auschwitz-Birkenau, and in perishing temperatures, whom the SS had forced to march, westwards, away from the advancing Soviets. A quarter of the prisoners died en route, most shot for falling behind. Maybe Salomon made it to the city of Wodzisław, where he was to be put on an unheated freight train, to be deported to another concentration camp. Maybe…but enough.

Wherever he died, in whatever way he died, the fact of Salomon Roco's death remains, along with its cause: that the system demanded it.

Abraham & Sara
<u>Amsterdam – Theresienstadt – Switzerland – Amsterdam</u>
So what of Salomon and Rosetta's father, Abraham? He had been in his 75th year when the Nazis arrived in Holland. And, remarkably, he outlived them. (His wife, Hannah, had died, in Amsterdam, at the start of 1943.)

Abraham, like Salomon, had been deported to Theresienstadt – along with his daughter, Sara, now in her fifties. The camp would be liberated in May 1945. And yet the records show that he and Sara crossed into Switzerland three months before liberation, in February.[69]

They were two of 1,200 (433 of whom were Dutch) inmates to do so, in a cash-for-Jews deal brokered by the former Swiss president Jean-Marie Musy with Heinrich Himmler, no less.[70] The price was five million Swiss francs, placed by Jewish organisations in escrow in Switzerland.[71]

Salomon and Sara only learned two days before that some prisoners would be freed, let alone that they were going to be among those aboard the Pullman, as it eased out of the station at 4pm on 5th February on a 600-kilometre journey. H.G. Adler – the great historian of Theresienstadt – says that the top SS brass decreed 'no-one whose closest relatives had been deported to the East could go along'[72] (presumably out of some cracked fear that they might be more prone to blab to the busybodies at the Red Cross about rumours of genocide). But if so, the iron Nazi bureaucracy was beginning to rust, because Abraham's son Salomon had been deported to Auschwitz four months before. Perhaps the two Rocos qualified on the next criterion: 'no intellectuals or persons of high status were permitted'.[73] In his forties, Abraham had left the diamond workshops to become a synagogue caretaker.

It must have been the strangest journey – daring to dream of freedom, plunged into the shock of luxury. 'Ample food was distributed: bread, rolls, cakes, margarine, sausage, sugar, milk powder and vitamin pills. During the trip, marmalade, jam, and a large jar of Ovaltine was given out.'[74]

For father and daughter, the fantasy became reality just after midnight on 6th February, where the Swiss military took over the transport. 'From the border town of Kreuzlingen, where there was a magnificent reception, the liberated people arrived on the evening of February 7 in St. Gallen.'[75]

What happened next is less clear. From St Gallen, in the northeast of the country, Abraham and Sara are back on the books as 'entering' Switzerland on 3rd April – but doing so 'illegally'.[76]

Perhaps the Swiss authorities, who appeared to hope that these Jews would just have been passing through, en route to refuges elsewhere, had already lost patience.

In the end, though, Sara and Abraham wound back to the Netherlands. When, I don't know. What is certain is that Abraham lived until he was 91; Sara until she was 88. They are buried alongside their Portuguese Jewish ancestors, in the tree-lined, river-bound cemetery in Ouderkerk.

~~~~

The Rocos and the Chumaceiros

The Holocaust memorial in Berlin draws criticism as well as praise. That it is imprecise – in name as well as substance: a 'Memorial to the Murdered Jews of Europe' renders the killing passive. The grey concrete slabs are too anonymised, too easy for games to be played around, grinning selfies to be taken against.

But the power is there: the dipping cobbled paths, the reduction in perspective, the press of enormous gravestones, towering and tilting. And the fact that you wander in, the boundary unclear, and that many people do lounge or lark around it, underlines that this was no meteorite strike. This epochal crime grew and metastasised from a familiar environment. The responses then, our responses now, were not, are not, a given.

There was another redolence for me, and it came out of the memorial's discomforting geometries. That as I collated this research, light-leaching patterns surfaced. Cousins from separate branches of the Dutch family, who may never have met, but were all murdered on the same day in the same death camp. Or who, at another death camp, were murdered on the same day of the week, week after consecutive week. Or had families whose births and murders offered an epitaph of desolate symmetry.

My great-great-grandfather Shimshon Roco married my great-great-grandmother Simcha Chumaceiro in Amsterdam in 1869. They then moved to London. Their children and grandchildren survived.

Shimshon's nephew: 07-12-1942, Auschwitz
  Simcha's niece: 07-12-1942, Auschwitz

Shimshon had a brother who had ten children. Six lived until the 1940s; none beyond

Simcha had a brother who had eleven children. Six lived until the 1940s; none beyond

There will still be sketches of a family tree. But here, you get a mention if you happen to be murdered on a certain date, in a certain place.

Does a list help? Or does it dehumanise? Does it do some justice? Or does it just try to neaten the monochrome tumble of bodies?

~~~~

Auschwitz: 07-12-1942

Great-great-grandfather Shimshon Roco had a sister called Judith who had a son also called Simson (as it is spelled in the Dutch ledgers). It is a straight but knotted line. Judith had married her first cousin, Joseph. Judith and Rev. Shimshon's father and Joseph's father were brothers.

Until August 1942, Amsterdam contained 150 Jewish rest-homes. Judith's son Simson, born in 1870, and his wife Duifje (née van Moppes) lived in one of them. This made them, in Jacob Presser's unflinching words, 'easy prey'. 'What could be simpler than dragging off completely defenceless old people?'[77]

In June 1942, Eichmann had confirmed the plans for the Final Solution in the Netherlands, Belgium and France. Starting in July, 1,000 Dutch Jews between the ages of 16 and 40 were to be transported each week for 'labour' in Auschwitz. The trains ran so smoothly, that almost immediately, the target was upped to 4,000 Jews per week.[78]

A few months later, we could dispense with the fiction of 'labour'. Simson was 71 and Duifje 76 when they were both murdered in Auschwitz on 7th December 1942.

~~~~

THE LOST (PART I)

Chumaceiro Family Tree

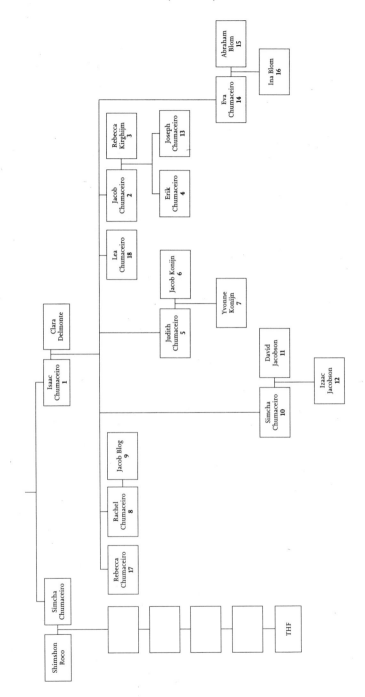

Great-great-grandmother Simcha Chumaceiro had a brother called Isaac ① who had a son called Jacob ②. Jacob was a barber. He married Rebecca (née Kirghijm) ③, a manicurist. Jacob died in 1934. Their older son, Erik ④, was sent to die at Auschwitz, on 30th September 1942, at the age of 15. Did his mother know? Rebecca was gassed at Auschwitz on 7th December 1942.

Great-great-grandmother Simcha Chumaceiro's brother Isaac also had a daughter called Judith ⑤. Her husband Jacob (Konijn) ⑥ sold stationery. Their daughter Yvonne ⑦ worked in a hospital laundry. Jacob was murdered at Auschwitz on 26th October 1942. Six weeks later, his wife and daughter were also killed in a gas chamber. It was 7th December 1942.

~~~~

May–June 1943: Sobibór
Maybe we just need to take a breath, as we recite each name. Take a breath, and dip a finger in the wine, mark a trace on the saucer. Keep them close. But don't let them bleed into each other.

Or maybe we should break the words of *Kaddish*, the mourner's prayer, with the names of the dead. An echo of André Schwarz-Bart in *The Last of the Just*,[79] damming the flow of that ancient Aramaic benediction — *yitgadal v'yitkadash sh'may raba* — with the twentieth century's monuments to genocide:

> 'And praised. *Auschwitz*. Be. *Majdanek*. The Lord. *Treblinka*. And praised. *Buchenwald*. Be. *Mauthausen*. The Lord. *Belzec*. And praised. *Sobibór*. Be. *Chelmno*. The Lord. *Ponary*. And praised. *Theresienstadt*. Be. *Warsaw*. The Lord. *Vilna*. And praised. *Skarzysko*. Be. *Bergen-Belsen*. The Lord. *Janow*. And praised. *Dora*. Be. *Neuengamme*. The Lord. *Pustkow*. And praised...'

And so as we have read, Saartje Roco and her son Joseph:
    14th May 1943, Sobibór.
And as we have read, Rosetta Roco and her husband Mozes:
    21st May 1943, Sobibór.

Now Rachel Chumaceiro ⑧ and her husband Jacob ⑨:
28th May 1943, Sobibór.

Her sister Simcha Chumaceiro ⑩ and her husband David ⑪ and her son Izaac ⑫: 4th June 1943, Sobibór.

Simcha's husband, David, was a barber. As was her brother, Jacob. We read about him on the previous page. He had died before the war. His wife, Rebecca, and older son Erik were murdered at Auschwitz. Erik and his younger brother Joseph ⑬ had been living in Megadlé Jethomiem, the orphanage which had been caring for Jewish boys for more than 200 years. Perhaps Rebecca's work as a manicurist had dried up; perhaps she could not afford to keep her boys. But her boys, in any case, would not be kept.

First Erik had been deported. Then Joseph appears to have been among the almost 100 other boys detained in the raid on the orphanage on 5th March 1943.

The Nazis had ordered the Dutch police that day to concentrate on the children. Their orders, indeed, were to allow the adult staff to go free. But the director of the orphanage, Saartje Hamburger, her deputy Ella Bing, and a trainee doctor Samuel Kops, all refused to leave.[80] They, and all the boys, were taken to Westerbork. None survived.

4th June 1943 was also when Joseph Chumaceiro was murdered at Sobibór. He was 12.

Rachel Chumaceiro had been gassed at Sobibór in May.

Her younger sister Simcha had been gassed at Sobibór in June.

Now their younger sister Eva ⑭ and her husband Abraham ⑮ were gassed at Sobibór in July.

Eva and Abraham's 18-year-old daughter, Ina ⑯, had been a clerical assistant in the Jewish Council in Amsterdam. She was murdered in October 1943, at Auschwitz. By then, more than five million Jews had been killed.[81] It was the moment for Himmler to speak openly to fellow SS officers about the matter which, hitherto, 'tact' had prevented discussion. 'I am referring to the evacuation of the Jews, the annihilation of the Jewish people... Most of you know what it means to see a 100 corpses lie side by side, or 500, or 1,000. To have stuck this out and – excepting cases of human weakness – to have kept our integrity, that is what makes us hard. In our history, this is an unwritten and never-to-be-written page of glory...we have carried out this heaviest of tasks...and our inward being, our soul, our character has not suffered injury from it.'[82]

~~~~

Auschwitz: 07-07-1944
What a family great-great-grandmother Simcha's brother Isaac had. His wife, Clara, bore 11 children. Clara was 43 when she gave birth to the youngest, Eva. Eva was murdered in 1943 at Sobibór.

Clara was 26 when their eldest, Rebecca ⑰ was born. The young family lived at 31, Weesperstraat. As it happens, you should be able to find Clara's name inscribed, just a few metres away. That is because directly across the road from their house is the *Nationaal Holocaust Namenmonument*, where the names of 102,000 people 'not given a proper burial' have been etched.

Rebecca never married. She was a seamstress. She may well have become part of that failed pseudo-scientific attempt to persuade the Nazis of Sephardi separateness – in which her cousin Salomon Roco also seemed to be caught up. Because like Salomon, Rebecca was deported from Westerbork to Theresienstadt on 25th February 1944.[83] Unlike Salomon, when she was taken from Theresienstadt, three months later, it was to head north rather than south: she was murdered in Auschwitz on 7th July 1944.

Rebecca shared that journey with her sister, Lea ⑱. She had appeared on list after list[84] of 'so-called' Portuguese Jews, as the Nazis tracked and catalogued and weighed what to do with this sub-group. Lea, like her sister, lived alone, although not in Amsterdam: rather, in The Hague, in a street of neat, terraced houses. Maybe she had that first floor room with the handsome oriel window, its creamy bas-relief tiles below, its italicised S-scroll wrought iron above. There is no place for such detail in the record. What there is, is her name on a telegram from *Hauptsturmführer* Aus der Fünten to *Höherer SS und Polizeiführer* Rauter, along with Lea's date of birth and – importantly – that address, Elandsstraat 22, Den Haag. The telegram was sent at 3.20pm on 1st February 1944. There was no time to lose. Lea was to be arrested, along with other Portuguese Jews across the Netherlands, at 11pm 'precisely'.

Sentence had been passed, in strips of capitalised letters. The next record shown is from 16th May 1944: Lea and Rebecca on transport 'Ea' from Theresienstadt to Auschwitz-Birkenau.

It was a time – the spring and early summer of 1944 – when 'Auschwitz was stretched to capacity and beyond by the most horrific and frenzied period of killing the camp would ever see.'[85] The mass deportation of Hungarian Jews, in their hundreds of thousands, had begun. The camp's crematoria, which were central to the capacity and efficiency of Auschwitz-Birkenau, had been expanded and refined over the years. But even they could not cope with the number of corpses. Pits were dug, bodies doused in oil, set alight. The smoke could be seen for miles.[86]

In July, Winston Churchill read a detailed account of Auschwitz based on the testimony of two escapees. He wrote: 'There is no doubt this is the most horrible crime ever committed in the history of the world, and it has been done by scientific machinery by nominally civilised people in the name of a great State.' Calls were being made, on both sides of the Atlantic, for the Allies to bomb the death camp.

On 7th July 1944, Churchill instructed his foreign secretary, Anthony Eden: 'Get anything out of the Air Force you can, and invoke me if necessary.'[87]

On 7th July 1944, the sisters, Lea and Rebecca, were gassed.

SEVEN

On Justice; The Lost (Part 2)

There was a question I asked towards the end of the previous chapter that was so hackneyed, you may have either sped past it, or paused only to roll your eyes. Could 'some justice' be served in organising those later murder files by geometry or chronology?

Of course not. In the literal sense, the question is ridiculously overblown. And yet journalists ask it the whole time. We ask it of ourselves. 'Are we doing justice to a story?' is shorthand for: what are we covering? And how?

I have said many brainless and bathetic things on air throughout my rich and diverse career. Few were quite as shatteringly vaporous as my last 30 seconds of broadcasting in Ethiopia.

It had been a very good trip. The back-story – this was early 2016 – had been the country's sustained economic surge, one that had prompted a senior official in the Foreign Office to tell me that Ethiopia could well be a 'test case for what successful development could look like'. But that long gallop towards middle-income status was built on unresolved questions: were these sectors high-growth in the long run? Would they satisfy an over-supply of impatient graduates? Would rigid state control have to loosen? And would that lead to a broader challenge to political repression? We had gathered some excellent voices: the brave, the hard-headed, the frustrated, and that eternal gift to broadcast journalism – the suave government minister offering steely assertions which, when prodded, prove rather tender: a democracy where there were no opposition MPs in parliament

('It's not for me to apologise for a decision of the people'); the new definition of 'terrorism' so broad it might include crimes against fashion, or sounding sarky ('I would make a friendly suggestion: why don't you go through the provisions of the legislation?' Unlucky: I have the key, sweeping clause ready to quote. What does 'intending to advance a political, religious or ideological cause by coercing the government...or destabilising social institutions' even mean?)

In fact, free speech was enshrined in the constitution. Of course it was. That piece of paper had not, however, protected 35-year-old Befeqadu Hailu. He was a blogger. That is not code for a paramilitary, or a militant. He was a blogger. In a subdued, level voice, amid the temporary protection of a noisy café, Befeqadu told me about his recent imprisonment: weeks without access to a lawyer; beaten on the soles of his feet with a cable; humiliation from his captors to the point where he was trying to work out how to kill himself.

We had also been able to head north, to Tigray. We had met some of the countless thousands of refugees who had crossed from Eritrea, a country whose suffocating, vicious, puritanical totalitarianism made Ethiopia's authoritarianism appear milquetoast. Hundreds of unaccompanied children languished in a UN camp. Most of them had been driven over the border by the prospect of extended conscription: the indentured labour which could stretch for 20 years or more. As we heard from the girl – one of many – who, at the age of 12, had left her mother in the middle of the night. She had given no warning; just slipped away. She feared that otherwise her mother might try to dissuade her. But she could not bear the prospect of inheriting her mother's life: a cook in the army, with a small plot of land that the People's Front for Democracy and Justice – let us just roll the irony filings of that name around our mouth – that the People's Front for Democracy and Justice had confiscated from her because of a perceived lack of enthusiasm at party meetings. It had been four years since the girl – she asked that we not use her name – had left. She had not spoken to her mother since.

It was a similar story in a boys' dorm. There, though, they were already planning what next. They would cross another border – and make the vast, perilous trek across Sudan, and then Libya, and then the Mediterranean. How, or when, they had no idea. But what else was there?

They may have been those with the least: the Eritrean children who had crossed into Ethiopia on their own. But the native children of Tigray, at that time, carried their own burden.

The region was wracked with drought. In the hamlet of Sheweate Hugum, the outer walls of the school-house still shimmered with energy, drawn from the murals of human anatomy, the periodic table, a *mappa mundi*, all garlanded with the dancing script of Amharic letters. Inside, the classrooms were bare, dusty and – in normal times – packed: an average of 55 to a room. These were not normal times. The drought meant the school had almost no sanitation, and barely anything to drink. Parents were keeping their children away, so that they could help with the increasingly time-consuming hunt for water. Those who made it to school often did so by lying to their parents – playing truant from home – and against insufferable odds. Takale was 16. His school run was exactly that: 15 kilometres each way, which he covered in one hour, in his cracked plastic sandals. He had one small bottle of water to sustain him the entire day. 'What can I do? I cannot abandon my studies. My studies are the only way to get on.'

All that was left, then, after several days of broadcasting, was for me to offer an aperçu of ringing inanity. I was doing a final two-way, as we call it – interview – with the smart, impish presenter in London. 'So Tim,' he began. 'You obviously briefed yourself before you went; read lots of books, spoke to people. What surprised you?'

I flannelled, flapped, and eventually amid a cloud of feathers, offered that I had been taken aback by my struggles with the language. That the most basic phrases had defied me.

Vacuousness of that profundity contains multitudes. The basest is that there had been an answer, and yet – subconsciously – I had stopped myself from saying it. I am all for a lack of guile on air.

But I did not want to appear ignorant and – I confess – unfashionable. The truth was that what surprised me was not surprising. Addis Ababa might have felt like a city in a hurry. But so much of the country was so bloody poor. Of course it was, you idiot. The overwhelming number of people lived off the land, from calloused hand to mouth. Driving through the countryside, you would pass them, walking vast distances, their feet churning through mile after mile.

Why does it matter? Because it was not just bone-headed, it was dishonest. And it was precisely these hard-hewn lives that made them all the more vulnerable to what would ensue four years later: the predations of a modern war pursued with medieval tactics.

Prime Minister Abiy Ahmed's 'law enforcement operation' launched towards the end of 2020 against Tigrayan rebels led not just to displacement, dispossession, rape and massacre, but hunger as a weapon of war and collective punishment. Hundreds of thousands were placed under threat of starving to death: a human catastrophe concocted and carried out with unequivocal intent by other humans. At least, that was what aid agencies and independent observers alleged. The Ethiopian government said that that was garbage. But then they insisted that no Eritrean soldiers were fighting alongside federal forces, before announcing that Eritrean soldiers would soon be withdrawing.

The depredations were not one-sided. Those school-rooms in Sheweate Hugum? Now filled with stinking corpses of Ethiopian federal soldiers. Those refugee camps filled with Eritreans – men, women and great numbers of unaccompanied children? Centres of mass rape, and mass expulsions back over the border into Eritrea.

A colleague and I wanted to get to Tigray. We pitched repeatedly, within the BBC. It could not be arranged.

But on *Newshour*, we came back to the story again and again. It may not have been as immediate, and as irrefutable, had we been there. But our job, if we can't rip the veil, is to bang on the outer door, and continue to shout questions.

If something seems hidden, we try to find out and find it; we ask and we ask. We don't assert. But we don't relent.

We may not be able to do a story justice. Who are we ever to suggest that we could? But we know that not to try: that might be an injustice.

~~~~

THE LOST (1940–1)
Part Two: Lithuania

> 'Literary historian and lecturer on Lithuanian literature and folklore at the University of Kaunas Juozas Ambrazevičius was appointed head of the newly formed provisional government on 23 June (1941). The provisional government was dominated by people with Christian Democratic leanings... The PG itself did not plan murders.'[1]

> 'Immediately during its first meeting, the PG (Provisional Government) sent an impassioned thank-you telegram to Hitler: "The liberating storm of war having passed through Lithuania, the representatives of the society of free Lithuania send You, the Führer of the German nation, our deepest and real gratitude for the liberation of the land of Lithuania from the all-destroying occupation of the Jews and the Bolsheviks and the liberation of the Lithuanian people, and express the hope that by Your genius the Lithuanian nation will be destined to take part in the victorious march led by You to destroy Judaism, Bolshevism and plutocracy."'[2]

The postcard reads like the opening scene in a disaster movie. We establish daily life. Something's gone wrong. Not really wrong. That will happen. But our distracted protagonist is dealing with a car accident or a divorce filed or a job lost. The scene cuts. A short way away, on the shoreline, the water thrums and bubbles and recedes. Cut. In the far distance, beyond the view of our hero, inexorably, a wall of water advances: the tsunami which will change everything.

The postcard is marked top and bottom, Wilkaviskis. In fact, at the bottom, it's become Vilkaviskis with a V. That's because Roman letters are less familiar. The rest of the handwritten text – close, neat, uncorrected – is in cursive Hebrew script. The language is klal or 'proper' Yiddish. The card has travelled from the centre of this western Lithuanian town to the centre of London.

Ya'akov has written a plea and a lament to 'my dear beloved sister-in-law' Tamar. He is still waiting for a response to earlier letters. 'Until last week, Miriam didn't know about our big loss – that you have lost your beloved husband and my Miriam has lost her good brother.' Miriam, it's clear, is Ya'akov's wife. Tamar is her sister-in-law, the widow of Miriam's brother, Herman. Herman had died in August 1939. The postcard is dated 30th May 1940.[3]

There had been five brothers and three sisters in this family. The brothers had all emigrated. As had one sister. That was Bella, my grandmother, who left for Britain after accepting a marriage proposal from a Lithuanian émigré in Manchester. The other two sisters stayed. Of them, one would be disappeared, the other murdered.

Great-aunt Miriam – she who will be disappeared – has been feeling ill since not hearing from her 'dear and beloved, dedicated, good' brother for such a long time. She has been fearing the worst; indeed, she's already lost 12 kilos. Last week, she learned the news. She is inconsolable. 'It's impossible to calm her down. She cries. She doesn't stop crying.'

Ya'akov begs – it's the word he uses – he *begs* Tamar to write to Miriam; Miriam regards her as a sister. Perhaps the children could send a message, too. After all, Tamar's oldest child, Lena, used to write much more often.

By the time the card had arrived in England, had been assessed, passed and stamped by His Majesty's war-time censors (did they have Yiddish-readers on hand?), and then pushed through the letterbox of Tamar's four-storey Georgian townhouse in Pimlico, Miriam and Ya'akov's world would already have changed. Two weeks after the letter had been posted, Soviet troops arrived. The end of Lithuania's latest, brief period of independence was marked. Two months later, it would be formally incorporated into the Union of Soviet Socialist Republics. That came, naturally, after elections in which more than 95 per cent of the electorate voted, and more than 99 per cent of them chose Communist-allied delegates.[4]

And now I will tell you a little bit about Vilkaviškis,* and about the Jewish population there, and the Holocaust. In a while, I will tell you about mead. Some scraps of memories will dance in the air.

But I can't tell you, with any certainty, what became of Ya'akov and Miriam. All I can do is infer. By one reckoning, between 1941 and 1944, 254,000 of the 265,000 Jews in Lithuania were murdered: almost 96 per cent.[5] Your chances were vastly lower even than those cousins in the Netherlands, where just one in four survived. Miriam and Ya'akov were never heard from again. And nor have I found trace of them. They are lost. They have been effaced.

For a time, I tried to weave a picture from the threads I had gathered. But it was — literally — displacement activity: a compensatory distraction for me, and off-centre from their lives. How useful would it be to draw a dabbler's historiography plotting the line from the Lithuanian massacres to the Wannsee Conference to the full savage machinery of the Final Solution? Not very, although I did find myself making detailed marginalia in an effort to do just that.

At the same time, the greater injustice may be to say that because I don't know for sure, because we as a family didn't or couldn't enquire too closely, or because we didn't tell the children so as not to upset them, and then they didn't ask, and then we died — that Miriam and Ya'akov have no memorial. In none of the family trees I have come across and asked about does Miriam or her husband even appear. My father only knew of one nameless aunt in Lithuania, who might even just have been an aunt by marriage. He certainly never said — and quite possibly never knew — that his mother Bella, who died when he was a young man, had had a sister. Let alone two sisters.

It was, in fact, Ya'akov who had married into our family. He was a barber, with a shop on Gedimino Gatvé, number 11.[6] There was a spruce parade of shops along the street: you can see them on a

---

*As it's now spelled in Lithuania.

postcard in the archive of the Holocaust Museum in Washington, along with another from Vilkaviškis showing the now-wonky stone table, shaded by a tree, at which Napoleon apparently sat in 1812. It was from there that the Emperor had declared war – 'glorious' war – on Russia.[7] The fields of Vilkaviškis would soon become larded with the corpses of the French, dying on their disastrous retreat from Moscow; 130 years later, those fields would consume a new, terrible cargo.

I have other postcards of a more limited run. On the back, in cursive Yiddish, a message 'from your sister and brother-in-law, Miriam and Ya'akov. We had our photos taken for Rosh Hashanah.'

The card had sat for decades, untranslated and unidentified, amid a jumble of photos and papers in a dented green laundry box in my parents' attic. Ya'akov, it's now clear from the two other photo-postcards I've matched of him, was a walking, coiffed advertisement for his business. All his neat lines will be undone in the ragged emotion of that postcard from 1940. Undone, and then rubbed out.

In contrast to her husband's German-inflected surname – Gelser – Miriam's family was more redolent of the Russian Empire. But the Pernikovskys* came from a small community teetering even closer to eastern Prussia, nine miles west of Vilkaviškis.

These days, in Lithuania, their home town is called Virbalis. Miriam and her family would have known it, in Yiddish, as Virbaln.† When they were growing up, it was – officially – Verzhbalove. Those four Cyrillic syllables spoke of its status as an outpost in what was then 'Russian Poland'. A postcard from 1904 shows the interior of the Customs Revision Hall: dozens of men in caps, tunics and imperial moustaches, surrounded by tall neo-classical columns. It was – at that point, at least – a 'first-class border station through which the Tsar's family often passed'.[8]

A family portrait from around the same time suggests that the Pernikovskys may not have been that well-off. The mother is in a sweeping black dress, the father in a frock coat and cylindrical black *kippah*; the three daughters are in pinafores; the five sons are in jackets. But peer closely at the creased and faded sepia, and you can see that the ground is rough, the boots scuffed, and they're standing in front of a rough-edged narrow building, propped on one side by a wooden pole.

About a third of the town's inhabitants were Jewish.[9] There were the poor, the poets, the pious, the students. But there were also the merchants and the smugglers. And the full spectrum of Jewish intellectual life – from the scholars of traditional rabbinic schools, to the *maskilim* – the followers of the Jewish enlightenment

---

*My father knew his mother's maiden-name as 'Rosen-Pinkovsky'. It wasn't really. Rosen became the family name for her brothers who had arrived in Britain before her, as the nineteenth century drew to a close. (They had followed the lead of their uncle, Morris: he had changed his name first to Rosenblum when he'd emigrated to Hamburg, and then shortened it when he'd moved to England.) When my grandmother was being courted by the man in England who will marry her, he sent letters via her cousin in the Prussian border town of Eydtkuhnen (present-day Chernyshevskoye, in Kaliningrad), and addressed them to 'B. Pernikovsky'. That became 'Pernicovsky' on her English wedding certificate. Her father, Jacob Aron, was Lithuanised in the state archives as Jankelis Aronas Pernikovskis: his appearance, in 1927, was to record his death, at the age of 70, from tuberculosis.

†In Yiddish, it would have been spelled ווירבאלן. 'Wirballan' is how her birth-place is spelled on her entry in the 1911 census of England and Wales.

— to the Jewish nationalists, the Zionists, the socialists and on. And why shouldn't they, like us, have had multi-faceted, shifting identities? The tight troika of small towns clutched around the border — Virbalis and Kybartai on the Russian side, Eydtkuhnen* on the Prussian — lent themselves to different pursuits: 'Should a Jew from Kibart wish to partake of a glass of beer or participate in a card game, he went to Eydkunen [sic] where he found what he wanted. If, however, he wished to hear a portion of *mishna* or a page of *gemara* or even to spend an evening in a spiritual atmosphere, one of culture, Hebrew, Zionism, Bundism and other ideologies, he had to go to Verzhbalove.'[10]

These communities were not — at least at the end of the nineteenth and the turn of the twentieth century — the shtetls of more recent history and legend, stricken by poverty, scourged by anti-Semitism. They had that.† But they also had grown out of the buzzing communities which had gobsmacked the imperial cartographers of the 1790s — Jews leasing mills, breweries, fish ponds, saltpetre factories and pastures from the town's landlords.[11]

From here it was a short distance to the Jews of pre-Great War Virbalis: farmers and craftsmen, yes. But also importers and exporters of grain, flax, lumber, pig-hair (the best for brushes), mushrooms, horses, crayfish, fruit, and millions upon millions of geese, ducks, chickens and turkeys, all driven flapping up the fowl-ramps of Eydtkuhnen, for transport across Germany.[12]

The third sister — the one we have yet to meet — lived barely a mile from Virbalis, in the small community of Kybartai. Simcha (also known as Sonia) married Avraham Bromberg, a manager at the *folksbank* — the mutually owned institution, similar to British building societies, which provided loans to the middle and poorer, working classes.

They had two children, Frieda and Herman, whom everyone called Herschke.

---

*See footnote on previous page.
†Including — in Virbalis — its own blood libel, leading to the execution of a Jew, in 1790.

It may well have been Simcha that my father was recalling as his only aunt on his mother's side, because he also had an evanescent memory of a visit from some Lithuanian relatives to his home in Manchester, when he was very small, in the 1930s. He recalled that one of them might have been something to do with a bank. It may have been they, then, who brought a miniature, toy *Sefer Torah* for him – Dad – to parade around his shul in Manchester on *Simchat Torah*. There was also a set of tiny *chumashim* inscribed on the inside front cover in Yiddish. A stronger memory for Dad was that these visitors from Lithuania had brought mead.

The Jews of north-eastern Europe were bee-keepers and inn-keepers. True to form, their abilities and the proliferation of Jewish-run taverns were both welcomed and deplored. The tradition of mead-making could be traced back to the founder of Hasidism himself, Israel ben Eliezer, the *Besht*.* He was an erstwhile tavern-keeper; he could also, it seems, hold his drink. All, of course, for a good cause: 'the Besht...was reputedly able to outdrink gentiles by recalling his awe of God, and achieve sublime

---

*The acronym of Baal Shem Tov (Master of the Good Name) c.1700–1760.

mystical heights while imbibing liquor on the holiday of Simchat Torah.'[13]

When my father moved from Manchester to London in the early 1960s, he took with him a bottle of that mead. It was precious – a vestige of a time and a side of the family which had gone. But the seal was not hermetic. The mead evaporated, the empty bottle mislaid.

~~~~

Ya'akov had given no clue in his postcard to Tamar from Vilkaviškis, but beyond the private grief over the bereavement, and the trembling adjacency of Stalin's Soviet Union and Hitler's Nazi Reich, life was already tough: a new railway line was by-passing these border towns; the brush-trade had collapsed, the flax business monopolised. To the west, Virbalis and Kybartai – the two smaller settlements on the frontier with eastern Prussia – had only recently re-built from the ravages of German occupation in the Great War. Now, although the German town of Eydtkuhnen lay just over the Liepona – not even a river, more a rivulet – there was barely any trade, barely any contact.

Most people felt poorer. The Brombergs were not insulated in Kybartai. An earlier letter from Avraham to Newcastle, to Simcha's brother Bert, is shot through with carefully calibrated anguish. It was April 1939. He – like Ya'akov writing to Tamar – had not heard anything from Bert since he and Simcha last wrote, 'a year and several months ago'. (You hope – you hope – that it was because the letters from England never made it, rather than they were never written.) It had been a year when 'everything changed for us so much, that I don't really know what to begin to write about.' We're all well, he says. It is one of those pinched definitions of 'well' to imply only that you've lost none of your limbs. Until now, Avraham says, he's made a decent living. Until now. 'Now we carry on living only through the hope that a miracle can occur, that we may somehow be able to carry on existing. Unfortunately, however, we severely lack a belief in miracles.'

Was this just despair about livelihoods shrinking? Or were there even deeper fears, about where this might lead? As the economy shrank, so anti-Jewish venom spread. And then the Soviets came and Lithuania ceased to be. Jews were spat out: their organisations dismantled, their lay-leaders arrested and deported to Siberia. Almost precisely a year later, the Molotov–Ribbentrop pact collapsed. On 22nd June 1941, the Nazis invaded. The tsunami thundered towards the shore. The first wave of the Final Solution was about to break.

The Jews of Vilkaviškis or Virballen or Kybartai ended up caught in the paradigm: if they were not world-controlling capitalists, then they were communist insurgents fomenting rebellion – a charge especially potent given the local Jewish history of organised labour and socialist cultural groups. As one of the most penetrating analysts of the Holocaust, Timothy Snyder, writes: 'Lithuanians quickly grasped that the Judeobolshevik myth amounted to a mass political amnesty for (their own) prior collaboration with the Soviets, as well as the general possibility to claim all of the businesses that the Soviets had taken from the Jews.'[14]

From theory, to practice.

By the year's end, 80 per cent of the country's Jews were dead. They had been murdered by Nazis and Lithuanian 'partisans', organised into the 'Labour National Guard'. The work was not spread equally. For the smaller communities, such as Simcha and Miriam's, Lithuanians did most, if not all, the abuse and killing. Indeed, the historian Dina Porat points out that despite the pressure on the members of *Einsatzgruppe A** to display their 'determination and devotion' to the mission in their reports to German headquarters, they could not but 'testify to the eagerness the Lithuanians demonstrated'.[15]

What happened in Vilkaviškis was this. In July 1941, most of the town's male Jews – several hundred of them – were taken to a barracks on the town's outskirts. They were ordered to dig two pits. The following day, 28th July, standing in those trenches, they were

---

*The *Einsatzgruppen* were the Nazis' paramilitary death squads.

shot. In August, the Jewish women and children of Vilkaviškis were moved to the barracks. The day after *Rosh Hashanah*, 24ᵗʰ September, they too were massacred: shot dead in pits, more than 3,000 of them.

Great-aunt Miriam and Ya'akov don't appear on the kill lists from Vilkaviškis. By whatever permutation you make it, combine it, comb it through the databases: they are lost. At least to me.

Great-aunt Simcha, Avraham, Frieda and Herman do appear on the death register from Virbalis and Kybartai. The murdering was even more efficient in these twin neighbourhoods. Days after the first Nazi units had crossed the border, a group of Jews was ordered to dig their own mass graves in a nearby sand quarry. Then: hand over your money and valuables; undress; line up, backs to the trenches; face us; be shot. A second massacre and then a third, on 11ᵗʰ September 1941, after the remaining women and children had spent a month in what had become the Virbalis Ghetto.

One field. Two thousand Jews.

'There were no Germans present during the shooting,' a non-Jewish eyewitness testified. 'They just drove up in a car and filmed everything the Lithuanians were doing.'[16]

Pause

I referred at the start of Chapter Six, the first of the two chapters on the Holocaust, to 'our catastrophists'. We have no monopoly.

Jean-Paul Sartre diagnosed the enduring appeal. The gift of having another. The irresistible smallness of it. 'Réflexions sur la Question Juive' was written in 1944, just as France was readying itself – like so many other liberated countries – to paint its role in the war in the neat colours of victimhood and resistance – barely stained by collaboration, tacit or active. Time to move on. Sartre disagreed; he barged through the doors of the asylum where the default alter ego – the anti-Semite – had been hastily shut up. The philosopher dragged the embarrassment out and performed a public pathology. 'Anti-Semitism isn't a Jewish problem,' he announced. 'It's *our* problem.'[1]

It is also jolly useful. Another Paris-based intellectual had spotted this more than a century before. Of his fellow Germans, Ludwig Börne wrote: 'Some reproach me for being a Jew; others forgive me for it; the third even praises me for it; but they all think of it.' It was a bottomless resource. His compatriots were hooked, obsessed: they drew such comfort from the fact that whatever oppression constricted them, at least they weren't Jews.[2] What was petty solace for nineteenth-century Germans, Sartre turned into a *weltanschauung* for the contemporary French. 'The anti-Semite is afraid of discovering that the world is ill-constructed; because then it would be necessary to invent, to modify and man would find himself master of his own destinies, saddled with a harrowing and unending responsibility.'[3] But having The Jew around absolves the need. 'Anti-Semitism is, in a word, fear in the face of the human condition.'[4]

Sartre's short book is sharp, confrontational and insightful. There are moments which have me nodding – about the endless second-guessing, the endless interior dialogue about motive (in my case, particularly, over the discourse around Israel and Zionism). W. E. B. Du Bois may have already given us 'double consciousness', the sense of looking at ourselves through the eyes of others. Sartre put it rather more dramatically: the Jew is 'over-determined' (a bad place for an existentialist to be) – 'his life a long flight from others and from himself…reduced to pursuing the impossible dream of universal brotherhood in a world which rejects him.'[5]*

But Sartre also carries the curse of the clever person: he's got our attention, his tone is confident and declamatory, and so when he starts banging out tunes which are a bit off, he doesn't notice and we start wincing. In this tightly cast opera, the anti-Semite needs the Jew to save himself from the need to act. The Jew needs the anti-Semite just to exist.† The Jew is trapped in the dialectic. The Jews have no place in history beyond their history of martyrdom.‡ There is *something* here: that for some Jews, their Jewishness may amount to little more than what an acquaintance once dismissed as 'Holocaust-Bagel'. But to theorise, as Sartre did, that that is *all* there is (minus the bagel), is painfully ahistorical, incurious and illogical.

But if he's wrong – and believe me, he's wrong – what do we do with anti-Semitism?

---

*Sartre does give one painful and plausible example: paying tribute to the founding role of Jews in the Resistance, he says that some hesitated because although they wanted to fight back, they feared that the Resistance would be *too* clearly of benefit, ultimately, to the Jews. So they were left second-guessing their own rationale. 'They wanted to be sure that they were not resisting *as Jews* but *as Frenchmen.*' (p.117)

†'The only ethnic characteristics of the Jew are physical' – something which, apparently, 'we have accepted as incontestable'. Have we? (pp.144, 123)

‡He generously name-checks Hegel for the original slur, made of Africa in his *Lectures on the Philosophy of History*. Although Sartre argues that the Jews are even more ahistorical because there's just nothing to their collective being, beyond persecution and passivity. (pp. 80–1)

Sartre says there is such a thing as an 'authentic' Jew. But that means someone prepared to out themselves and stand up for themselves, just as the worker who achieves class consciousness: theirs is the prelude to the revolt which will abolish class; so the authentic Jew rejects assimilation today, in the hope that the 'radical liquidation of anti-Semitism'[6] will allow the gift of real assimilation to the next generation. In other words, as Karl Marx had argued, Jew-ness becomes redundant. It can, like anti-Semitism, be liquidated.

Sartre was writing in late 1944. Some months before – in April – Hannah Arendt had published *The Jew as Pariah: A Hidden Tradition*. She, too, had anatomised Europe's emancipatory bargain: 'that the Jew might only become a man when he ceased to be a Jew'. Not much of a deal, she concluded. Hers, though, was a rather more open-ended call to arms. Sartre wanted to show us systems. Arendt was less interested in proving where everything would inevitably end up, and more in how we should think and act. '(E)very pariah who refused to be a rebel was partly responsible for his own position and therewith for the blot on mankind which it represented.'[7] She was writing about the French Jewish polemicist Bernard Lazare writing about Jews; but it feels like we are seeing her own flint core.

Arendt sets an exacting standard. I'm not sure I'm up to it. Maybe a contemporary philosopher offers me another way. Judith Butler has said that 'failure of determinism is the space for freedom'.[8] She was speaking on a podcast, so I hope she won't mind if I play with the aphorism. There are times when the catastrophists *are* right, when determinism is imposed by the power of the state; the space for freedom closes, utterly. It is rather where the grip of the given, of the thing that everyone knows – where that relents, for whatever reason – maybe in part because we are resisting – that there the space does lie.

And it is how, perhaps, we can begin to turn from the Holocaust. What follows is all about how we bend the lines which describe us.

EIGHT

On Trust; The Immigrant

It seems strange, I grant, to talk of trust. Us hacks: our eyes are hooded, our language gruff, our questions curt. You assert; we push back. Or maybe we take a beat, our gaze level, our mouth a line; we blink, and ask another question.

That's the fantasy, anyway – occasionally summoned, even more rarely attained.

The greater truth is that we *do* trust. One of the eternal verities of a foreign correspondent's life is that you're only as good as your fixer/translator/producer. You can set the tone in your search for the story – with enthusiasm and clarity and occasionally, maybe more than occasionally, with steaming frustration and monomaniacism.

But it is they who will often find you the places and the characters and the events. They will take you there, and be prepared to walk with you – incognito – through the doorway in Athens. The two of you stay shtum as one of you doesn't speak Greek; she can, and so only will if needs be. You walk past the baseball bats that aren't used for baseball, up one flight of stairs past the shop selling attractive hardback editions of the speeches of Adolf Hitler, then up another flight to join what's meant to be a closed meeting of a powerful and increasingly popular neo-Nazi group.

They are the people who will head with you across this hot strip of the Middle East, towards the smoke, towards the phut and clatter of weapons, along the road scattered with bodies. They will place a hand on your shoulder and tell you that the farmer has said don't step off the road, that field is mined. They will guide you through the refugee camp to meet the cleric who is sending young men across the border to fight and to die. It is they who will squeeze their contacts in Latin America or in Africa, to get you to the minister or the militant whom you can interview as hard and forensically as you can muster. Easy then for you to walk away; they may have to stay in-country and take their chances.

I have leaned on them, and on the most golden of calling cards. The BBC is an accident of history whose reach and reputation has been built, carried and extended by thousands of thoughtful and brave journalists. There are plenty who hate us, or say they do. But they understand that we matter. And that our job is to ask. To find out how we got to this point. To wonder where we might now go.

~~~~

THE IMMIGRANT (MARRIED 1921)

'And he lay the palms of his wide-open hands on my head
with the Yom Kippur blessing: Honour, love, that thy days
may be long upon this earth. And the voice of my father —
white as his hair. Then he turned his face to me one last time,
as on the day he died in my arms, and said, "I would like to add
two more commandments:
the Eleventh Commandment, 'Thou shall not change,'
and the Twelfth Commandment. 'Thou shalt change. You will change."
Thus spoke my father, and he turned and walked away
and disappeared into strange distances.'

YEHUDA AMICHAI[1]

The name, I know. It's mine. The place: that's another story. A skein of stories.

I remember nothing of my grandfather. I remember clambering stairs — interior, institutional; my stubby three-year-old legs found it hard going. Dad and I were going to see him in what I now assume was a hospital or a nursing home, in 1971. That's it.

My father always said that his father was tall. His hospital record from World War One has him at five foot eight-and-a-half. Even back then, not that tall. Another memory falters.

What there were, were splenetic running rows, sotto voce Yiddish, and the most painful silence parents could impose.

So what do we know?

Leon Hyman Franks came to England as a child: yes.

Actually, not quite – the boy who immigrated came to be known as Leon Hyman Franks.

He came from Oryol[2] in Russia: sort of.

He went to Lithuania after World War One to bring his wife to England. But how they first met: an utter mystery.

One thing, at least, was certain. He said prayers of mourning for a son who was still alive.

~~~~

'Whereas Leon Hyman Franks, an Alien, residing at 213 Darlington Street East, Wigan, has presented to me, the Right Honourable Winston Leonard Spencer Churchill, one of His Majesty's Principal Secretaries of State, a Memorial, praying for a Certificate of Naturalization, and alleging that he is a Subject of Russia having been born at Sivakie Suvalskie in Russian Poland on the 14th January 1885; and is the son of Ezekiel and Minnie Franks both subjects of Russia – a General Dealer – is unmarried, and that in the period of eight years preceding his application he has resided...'

It was 31st March 1911. Leon, aged 26, was swearing by Almighty God that he would be faithful and bear true allegiance to His Majesty King George V. Leon was becoming British.

It had been a long journey, made as a bare teenager – possibly even as young as 11. He had been born in whatever it was the Justice of the Peace in Wigan had transcribed for the attention of the Home Secretary, the Rt. Hon. W.S. Churchill: the cursive handwriting offers us 'Sivakie' or possibly 'Suvakie' or 'Swakie'. It was what the Jewish community at the time would have called Shaki; what Lithuanians now call Šakiai. It was a small town in western Lithuania. Ten miles from Prussia. 1,250 miles from Lancashire.

Except, Šakiai to Wigan was only part of the epic. Before he became Leon, he'd been recorded in the imperial Russian birth register as **Хаимъ Лейбъ Франкъ** – Haim Leib Frank* – his given names connoting 'life' in Hebrew and 'lion' in Russian.† And the boy's odyssey was mythic not simply because of his redoubtable name – or his age – but because he and his family had first headed more than 600 miles *east* – to the oblast of Oryol, due south of Moscow. That was where his younger brother – 'John', as he'd be re-named in the UK – was born in 1891.³ It was the place-name my father heard his father talk of, and repeated to me, when I began asking where the family came from. Not 'Shaki'. Not Lithuania. Oryol, in Russia.

But why? It was so far away (in the wrong direction), Oryol was not even in the Pale of Settlement, where Jews were, by and large, allowed to live by the grace of the Tsars. It was only in 1876 that the Jews of Oryol city had been granted permission to build a synagogue.⁴ That meant that the Franks had moved from a small town where they had ancestral links going back to 1760,⁵ with a reputation as a centre of '*Torah* and wisdom',⁶ and in which three out of four of the population were Jewish,⁷ to a medium-sized city where only one in 40 was. And Leon's was a profoundly observant family: religious practice did not slot into what we might loosely call daily life; daily life waited patiently for the spaces around the ritual.

This great, eastward feint remains, for the moment, a mystery.

The murk doesn't clear even with the suggestion that, in any case, the family had returned to Šakiai by 1896. That was where

---

*Assuming the clerk recorded the name correctly, I don't know when or why Frank became Franks. It may have changed with the siblings' arrival in Britain. 'Franks' has an extensive Ashkenazi pedigree. In the London of 1761, Aaron Franks – no relation, sadly – was signing humble representations to the court of King George III. There's even a 'Ffrancks' counted among the Jews in the city's 1695 census.

†Although 'Leib' appears a corrupted transliteration of the Russian for 'lion' (*Leb*), the name used to address Leon in all formal Jewish settings – from synagogue to grave – was, unmistakeably, Haim *Aryeh* – the Hebrew for 'lion'.

the youngest child, Ettie, was born, in 1896 — at least according to a handwritten account by her daughter (and Leon's niece), Rivelyn.[8] If so, we're told they didn't stay long: Rivelyn wrote that when her mother was three months old, 'by edict of a Pogrom the family was ousted from their home and journeying across Russia in the bitter winter Yechiel David (the father) caught cold and died.'

And yet I can find no record of a pogrom in Šakiai in 1896. The carefully curated rampages against the Jews which had begun in the 1880s, and became internationally familiar by their Russian name, had yet to visit western Lithuania. (The Jews of Šakiai would be attacked en masse by retreating Russian soldiers during World War One; far worse would follow within 40 years from Nazis and local nationalists.)

The question remains, then: why emigrate? Perhaps it was that the family would now have been hearing from pioneer relatives and acquaintances — in England, in the US, even Australia — that not just economic opportunity but religious Orthodoxy could exist beyond the shtetl. And Josef Rosin, in his exhaustive history of Lithuanian Jewry, says that whatever spiritual attractions Šakiai may have offered in the nineteenth century had gathered dust by the start of the twentieth: 'religious fanaticism, boorishness and superstitious beliefs still dominated the community, with only a few reading books other than religious ones and very few studying in the Russian High School in Vilkavishk (Vilkaviškis), about 50 kms away. Only one Jewish family in Shaki subscribed to a newspaper.'

One cloud had, without doubt, been hanging low. Rivelyn has her own imagery. 'The boys,' she writes, 'were interesting fodder for the military might of Holy Russia.'

An account from the nineteenth century offered no such understatement: indeed, 'not even a brush full of black paint could put such horror on canvas'. It was 1835. A young man who would become one of Russia's great essayists, an 'amateur of genius',[9] had been sentenced to exile in Siberia for the crime of lèse-majesté. As Alexander Herzen left Perm amid an unceasing downpour, a kindly escort offered him a cup of tea, and introduced him to his commanding officer. Herzen asked this 'unintelligent, good-natured "old" soldier': "Whom are you taking, and where to?"

'"Oh, don't ask; it'd even break your heart. Well. I suppose my superiors know all about it; it is our duty to carry out orders and we are not responsible, but, looking at it as a man, it is an ugly business."

'"Why, what is it?"

'"You see, they have collected a crowd of cursed little Jew boys of eight or nine years old[10]... Not half will reach their destination... A Jew boy, you know, is such a frail, weakly creature, like a skinned cat; he is not used to tramping in the mud for ten hours a day and eating biscuit – then again, being among strangers, no father nor mother nor petting; well, they cough and cough until they cough themselves into their graves."'

'They brought the children and formed them into regular ranks: it was one of the most awful sights I have ever seen, those poor, poor children!...

'Pale, exhausted, with frightened faces, they stood in thick, clumsy, soldiers' overcoats, with stand-up collars, fixing helpless, pitiful eyes on the garrison soldiers who were roughly getting them into ranks. The white lips, the blue rings under their eyes bore witness to fever or chill. And these sick children, without care or kindness, exposed to the icy wind that blows unobstructed from the Arctic Ocean, were going to their graves.'[11]

The incentives for grandfather Haim Aryeh to leave – the disincentives to stay – were there.

Whenever he and the rest of his family set out for England, whether together or apart, whether from Russian Poland or Russian Russia, it would have been no easy journey. Procuring exit papers from the late nineteenth-century Russian state was cumbersome and expensive; it was also utterly unreliable. Many tried to avoid the cost and the gamble. But then it was a different risk – to rely on false documents, possibly corruptible border guards and people smugglers. If you managed to make it to the Baltic coast, 'an army of parasites was assembled to batten on the innocents'.[12] You might lose your luggage or your money, or be sold a ticket to the wrong destination. The crossing to England – Leon landed at Hull or Grimsby – took up to three days. In steerage – and it would have been steerage – it was a jammed, grimy passage.

So I don't know exactly when they crossed the North Sea, but certainly, by the turn of the century, as the record-keepers for the 1901 census were making their diligent way along England's streets, Leon, three of his siblings, his mother and a boarder were already in the two-up-two-down at 28 School Lane, Wigan.

~~~~

In 2010, under a broiling sun, after a lunch of beans and rice, I had my mind cooked by one of Microsoft's top executives. We were sitting outside, in the UNHCR quarters of the Kakuma refugee camp in north-west Kenya. He was doing some good works. I was waiting to travel up into what was then, still, just southern Sudan, not South Sudan. He was patiently trying to explain to me the idea of the cloud. (Never catch on, I thought to myself, though was too well-mannered to say.) One part of the conversation was comprehensible: the idea – the fact, apparently – that the amount of data being created was rising super-exponentially: we were spewing, and storing, more information in months than we had done in centuries.

I clearly won't now say anything tired or predictable or old-fashioned about the amount of dismal daily guff people feel the need to catalogue for public edification. No. But what I will point to is the aching contrast with the indurate desire of the immigrant to move on and away. At least, those immigrants, then. Why dwell? The decision had been taken; the journey made. If you're going to keep a memento, make it useful, like a silver spice box for *Havdalah*. But documents, diaries, recollections – what purpose do they serve? The driving force now was to cleave to observance of the religion which had become increasingly dangerous in the old country; to overcome poverty; and to ensure that our children had it better than us. Eyes locked forwards.

That desire to move on can also be twisted into an etiquette which, several decades later, would be furiously lampooned by Hannah Arendt. She had just fled Germany and then France for the refuge of the US, and hers is the 1943 equivalent of a Shouty. Social. Media. Post (i.e. a short essay, entitled 'We Refugees', in the American–Jewish intellectual journal, *Menorah*). She comes out blasting. 'In the first place, we don't like to be called refugees.' She gives you a few lines to recover, then serves the explanation, dressed in vinegar. 'Before this war broke out we were even more sensitive about being called refugees. We did our best to prove to other people that we were just ordinary immigrants. We declared that we had departed of our own free will to countries of our choice, and denied that our situation had anything to do with "so-called Jewish problems". Yes, we were "immigrants" or "newcomers" who had left our country because, one fine day, it no longer suited us to stay, or for purely economic reasons. We wanted to rebuild our lives, that was all. In order to rebuild one's life one has to be strong and an optimist. So we are very optimistic.' *[13]

~~~~

My grandfather may not have talked much – at all – about why he moved. So what clues remained about his entrée into Britishness? The year after I learned about the scale of our current, accelerating data splurge, the National Archives cracked open its titanium-lined vaults, and allowed access to a few bytes of information about Leon. The label affixed in 1911 to this 'Alien's' application for naturalisation had read: *Closed Until 2011*.

Among the drab jewels allowed air after 100 years, there is a letter from Detective Inspector Christopher Wills to the Chief Constable of Wigan. The D.I. respectfully reports that he has made careful enquiries about Leon Hyman Franks. He is able to speak, read and write English very well; what is more, 'I, personally, have

---

*From the same essay, her sardonic dismantling of 'patriotism' and the refugee appeared in Chapter Four – with the row over Shimshon Roco's immigration to London.

known the above-named for the last 5 years, and consider him a very respectable young man.' Elsewhere in the sheaf, a further four men attest that they have known Leon Hyman Franks for eight years. Henry Barton, John Barton, Thomas Woods, Matthew Nolan can all 'confidently vouch for his loyalty and respectability'.

It works. In March 1911, Leon becomes British.

He will cement that attachment abroad, on the Western Front. Leon had not been conscripted. But when his younger brother John was called up, Leon – as was permitted by the authorities – had enlisted in his stead. In June 1916, at the age of 31, he joined the King's Own Royal Lancaster Regiment.

Four months later, Leon was embarking from Folkestone to France. He was heading for the war's most blood-soaked, mud-caked course, the 15-mile front in the Somme. Across the '141 days of horror'[14] between July and November, the British had advanced at most seven miles, at the cost of well over 400,000 men. But by luck, four days before Leon was posted to A-company and the field of battle, General Haig had decided to suspend the offensive in order to re-group.

Leon's time on the front line was brief. That winter was exceptionally bitter. So much so, one non-commissioned officer recalled, 'I felt like crying. I'd never felt like it before, not even under shell fire.'[15] Just over three weeks into his deployment, Leon was in the field hospital with trench foot.

There was no quick cure. Treatments varied widely – foot washes of lead and opium, oil of wintergreen, powder of boric acid, among others. Leon spent more than a year in hospital in Manchester.[16] The doctors could not stop the big toe of his right foot sloughing with sepsis. In September 1917, they amputated. He was allowed out of hospital in February 1918, released from further military service in March.

The army awarded him a small pension, and a lapel clasp – the 'Silver War Badge', issued to those honourably discharged for wounds or sickness. It was designed to be worn on civilian clothes, to forestall the often open abuse from others, who might see a fighting-age man without an obvious debility, and decry him as a malingering coward. After the war, while the beribboned active service medals were kept in a rigid leather folder, the silver badge nestled, along with two tiny photographs, in a silver-plated clasp purse. Even today, when you open it, a faint, powdery scent of rose rises from inside. The purse belonged to the woman whom, before the war had ended, Leon was wooing.

~~~~

There is an anachronism that in my coarse youth – let's say from school to my mid-forties – I used to greet bug-eyed or sniggering when I came across it in a pre-modern novel: the characters in conversation as stiff as their corsets, 'making love'. How on earth had the author smuggled *that* on to the page?

Maybe it's we who are guilty of the circumlocution, replacing mention of sex with a more seemly-sounding activity. But there's also something wonderfully evocative about the phrase as it was: the idea of a couple making – constructing – a tie, or tangle, a relationship of love; or, more tantalisingly, a suitor whisking up a sweet soufflé, hoping to tempt, but risking deflation should their ardour remain unrequited.

In Leon's case, another image works better, especially amid the sparse, dry landscape of official records which mark out his life to date. It is that now, as he makes love, the words gush. Where there was an absence – of documents, of a sense of a voice – now there is a torrent.

He may be appalled that his letters have been read by his grandson. He may take some comfort in that it was his beloved Bella who could not bear to part from them, and kept them in their small, delicate envelopes.

Leon is in wholesale clothing. His partner is his older brother, Lazar Arnold, a forceful, dominant figure – according to his nephew, and his partial namesake, my father. For a time, they have a business together on Miller Street, in the centre of Manchester – the city to which the family has moved before the Great War has ended. 'Franks Bros.' purveys 'Gents' Shirts, Collars, Pyjamas,

Handkerchiefs, braces, Etc., Etc.' The brothers are not just partners; they are neighbours: Lazar at 213 Cheetham Hill Road, Leon at 211. 'The rowing,' my father recalled 80 years later, 'was monumental'.

Business is tough. Leon's letters, even when he is courting, speak of a thin existence, built on insecure foundations. He travels the north of England and into Wales. There are wan attempts to sound upbeat. In 1921: 'Things look very black at present. The miners are on strike and we are expecting the transport workers also to come out, but while there is life there is hope, so it is no use meeting trouble halfway.' My father was born in 1930, the youngest of three, and he remembers nothing different: his father on the road, trying to sell cloth, scraping pennies together, pouring what little was left over into the children's education.

For decades, though, there was a puzzle. How had Leon and Bella met? He was a poor boy from Russia, who had immigrated to Lancashire. She was a girl from Lithuania who had first come to London, and then returned to the home-country, before being brought, by her fiancé, to Cardiff for their wedding in 1921.

The first clue lay in the belated unearthing of Leon's 1911 naturalisation certificate. He may have lived in Oryol – that city in Russia proper which my father recalled – but Leon was born in Šakiai. That was in 'Russian Poland'. It is present-day Lithuania, and just 27 miles from Bella's birth-place, Virbalis, and – according to Leon's imperial Russian birth register – the hometown of his father.

It still seemed a stretch: even if the teenaged Leon had visited Virbalis before emigrating, Bella was only born in 1896. She was 11 years younger. Friendship, let alone burgeoning love, was inconceivable by the time he left. Nor would there have been a match arranged so far in advance.

The answer came when, just a few years ago, my father gave me the trove of letters, bound in an ancient, barely elastic, dark brown rubber band. One of the letters, on vanishingly light paper, folded and re-folded inside an envelope marked 'für B. Pernikovsky', was dated 31st October 1920. 'Dear Cousin', it began.

I can trace no line on the family tree which joins Bella and Leon. Nor had my father any recollection. But another person, who has yet to be properly introduced in this story, told me even more recently that he, as a child, had been told, yes, Leon and Bella were second cousins. He had given it no further thought, until I had brought it up, nearly 90 years later.

Leon and Bella had met when she first came to England. She appeared on the census of 1911, aged 15,[17] a 'tobacconist's help', living with her older brother, Herman, his wife Tamar, and their infant daughters Lena and Queenie.* Bella was still in England in 1918, because the first surviving letter is from 30th June that year: 'Bell…I may possibly be in London this week and no matter whether you like it or not I shall come to see you, Kind regards, Leon.'

And then: a shock.

It is June 1920. Leon is 'very much surprised to hear that you have gone back to well…can I really say you have gone back Home?' This is the first letter to be addressed to Eydtkuhnen in Eastern Prussia. It is not, indeed, Bella's home. But it is, as we saw from the previous chapter, very close – just a few miles from what she knew, growing up, as Wirballen, what present-day Lithuanians call Virbalis. The town was all-but destroyed by fire in the Great War, and most of the population left. The German army was not evicted until the beginning of 1919.[18] Bella, it seems, was staying with family in Eydtkuhnen. The 'Herr Braustein' on the envelope is clearly the Poste Restante for this small border settlement, as all future letters to Bella have the barest address: his name, her name, the town's name, *Ostpreussen*.

Summer turns to autumn, and with it comes the 'Dear Cousin' letter, and a suggestion of the distance yet to travel, and the desire to make the journey. In a note on the back, in different-coloured ink, Leon asks Bella if she is also called Clara. (She was.) He's just noticed the name on her letter.

He also calls her 'dearest'.

---

*Tamar was the woman to whom Ya'akov Gelser, husband of Herman and Bella's sister Miriam, had written that pleading, pre-Holocaust postcard from Lithuania, in Chapter Seven.

Three days on, and panic. Leon's just received a letter from home, 'Shaki',* informing him that she's expected to become engaged.

'<u>Is it true?</u> Bella dear are you sure you will love the lucky man? Please dear cousin forgive me, if you was in England no doubt you would say to me mind your own business, and there might be a great deal of truth in your remark. I must be an idiot my interpretation of love is quite different to other peoples, to me love is not a pation (sic), to me it is more than that, it is friendship, comradeship, something besides a wife (perhaps this is why I have not married I never wanted a wife) but a real companion, a true and devoted couple devoted to each other, real pals, do you think this is possible? Or is all utopia? Well Bella, I think I let my thought carry me away too far. Will you write to me after all this, Leon.'

That was 3rd November. As the week wears on, the weather forecast in the *Manchester Evening News* warns of a depression, a cold front.

15th November. A reply has come. Leon writes back, reeling in relief. 'To (sic) proud to ask, Well Bella you make me laugh. No darling, it is <u>not</u> pride, it is cowardness, it is the fear, that perhaps I would not be all that the Girl would like me to be, or that I may not be able to give the Girl all I would like to do, that made me afraid to ask, Bella! If the Girl I marry would not be happy and contented with me, it would make me wish I never returned from France at all... Do you honestly and truly love me a little?... Will you try and develop this to a mutual love between us, so that it would grow from day to day ever so much, much much bigger than anybody else's love, I think you will think I am talking like a schoolgirl, but I AM WRITING THE TRUTH.'

Within two weeks, Leon tears open the letter 'for which I have been waiting almost three years. Bella you say that you do love me, Bella listen this word to me is like sunshine in the grayness of my life.'

The wedding is set for the following year, 1921. Across the ensuing correspondence, there is a stream of spooniness and

*I.e. Šakiai.

neediness. In January 1921, Bella is to visit Vilkaviškis. It's only nine miles from Virbalis, but Leon opens the throttle: 'you will perhaps think me silly but...when you say you are going away I seem to feel as if you are leaving me'.

Even though we only get to eavesdrop on one end of the conversation, it's clear that both lovers are in thrall, impatient and insecure. They need frequent declarations of love. Bella's clearly taking some heat back home over the age difference, and the fact that her 'young man' is in England.

It is May. The wedding is two months away. Leon is heading to London to obtain all the visas. He is on a fast thrum. 'I went three times already to the passport office and tried the door although I knew perfectly well that they would be closed on Sunday and to day Bank Holiday.' He's hoping to arrange a journey which avoids Poland. The visa costs a whacking '£3-1-3 and to tell you the truth I would begrudge the Poles a 1^d of my money, they do not deserve it'.

At last Leon has his passport. He is coming to collect his fiancée. He would like to see Kovno,[19] then the capital of Lithuania, and a great entrepôt of Jewish life. He must visit 'Shakie' for a day or two 'then I would like to spend two or three days in Berlin'.

On a sun-drenched day in July, Bella and Leon marry. The *chupa* is in Cardiff, home to two of Bella's brothers.

~~~~

There were three children. Leonora was born in 1922, David in 1924, Arnold – my father – in 1930. All of them studied dentistry. David became a community orthodontist. His beat was the schools of Lancashire. He fell in love with his practice nurse, Doris. In 1953, as his younger brother was taking his final examinations at Manchester University, David told his parents that he was going to marry a woman who wasn't Jewish.

Their lives – his parents' lives, and those of their whole extended family – had been cemented in the daily demands and expectations of a traditional Jewish faith: the rules, and my goodness there are many rules, were all kept; shul – it would never have been called synagogue – was attended frequently and regularly, and seats on the executive taken; tefillin were laid every mandated day. Cement is the wrong word. This was your circulatory system, as essential and as complete and as intricate as arteries, veins, capillaries. This is the way it was, and this is what you did.

And the other thing you did, when a child married out, was to treat them as if they were dead. It was binary. There was one course of action. You could either take it or not. Intruding emotions – of love, grief, fear, loss – were immaterial.

It was the last time David and his parents spoke together. Because how could his parents talk to a dead person? And so Leon and Bella sat on low chairs for seven days, and recited the shiva prayers. The simplest flow diagram of the lot was thrust – probably wordlessly – into my father's young hands. It didn't need saying: you were either loyal to your parents, or you weren't. You chose. It was one or the other.

David stayed in Lancashire. Dad moved to Birmingham. The rupture lasted beyond their mother's death in 1960, their father's in 1971. David had sent a card in 1964 when he learned that his brother had had a daughter. For Dad the wound, be it self-inflicted or not, was still too near the surface. He, we didn't talk about it. No one talked about it. I knew I'd had an uncle. But I was unsure of his name, and thought he was dead.

On 8th December 2017, Mum phoned me. She was in a tizz. By mistake, she'd opened an envelope which she realised had not been addressed to her and Dad. It was just addressed to Dad, and Dad was out, and the card was from David: to say hello, to say he'd discovered* Dad had recently moved; to wish him well in his new place.

Nine days later – 64 years after – Dad and David spent an hour together, just the two of them, in David's retirement flat in Wiltshire. They then joined us in the pub close by. David was a widower now. But we also got to meet one of his sons, Nigel, and a daughter-in-law, Ana.

At our next meeting, I gave David a copy of my notes about his father's letters. David, aged 94, says yes, now you come to mention it, when he was a small child, perhaps only five or six, he remembers his sister saying that their parents were second cousins.

Less than a year after our first reunion, Nigel and Ana were taking seats in the row behind me in our synagogue in London, as my youngest son had his bar mitzvah.

~~~~

This had been a story, so nearly, with a different ending, had that leap of trust not been taken.

David died, aged 96, in 2021. Dad died, aged 93, in 2023. At Dad's shiva, I talked about the astonishing distance travelled in space and time and times from his parents' lives to his to ours. And I talked about my three sons – there in the living room with us – and the changes and choices which they and their possible descendants will make: changes and choices and lives of which I, too, can barely conceive.

The story is never complete.

---

*It later emerged that while noodling on the internet, David had gone to the open electoral register, and discovered Dad's change of address.

NINE

On Joy; The Artists

The story is not complete. It is never complete. And now two more things this story is not.

It is no longer chronological. We're going to return to where we began, to the time of the elusive refugee from Inquisition Lisbon, Ester Orobio Furtado. She is the blank template – a name, a birth-date, a birth-place, a marriage – from which so much of this book has been spun. Her times, and the family she joined, will bookend our story.

And this coda will play out in a different key. So many of these stories, especially over the last century, have been told in slate-grey tones and minor keys. It was the century my mother lived through, and you'll meet her, albeit as she's dying, in the epilogue. But she deserves a mention now because, as she was dying, she had two requests for the funeral. The first – I wrote this down, ever the journalist, as she and I talked over the phone: we had to check she was 'well and truly dead'. The other was that after the liturgy and the eulogies, after her coffin had been lowered and we had recited *Kaddish*, that we play out – the funeral would be on Zoom – with the aria *Va Tacito*, 'Go Silently', from Handel's *Julius Caesar*. If possible, sung by Janet Baker. It was possible, and it was the perfect, horn-garlanded F-major coda to a beautiful service.

Through these pages, we have heard some stories set in the bleakest registers, their themes worked through dark developments. Hannah Arendt lived through the darkest. And yet she remained, as one brilliant recent account of her put it, 'an expert at inhabiting moments of wonder'.¹ In fact, it was fundamental to her view of life. Hers, and Mum's.

So now, let's approach the end in a rich blare of major. Jewish major.

~~~~

ON JOY

It is the listeners' lament. Why can't you do more cheerful stories? There is an answer, but I'm not sure we ever give it. That even the meat and potatoes are, indeed, all about the pursuit of happiness, at least in the form of its pre-requisites: dignity, justice, freedom and safety. Why else bother?

It was where I also occasionally disagreed – let's say, in emphasis – with some of my colleagues in the sports department. Perhaps it could be traced back to names: I was never quite sure, because the BBC was never quite sure, whether we were Sports Correspondents or Sports News Correspondents. Yes, there were times when we quite rightly suited up and plunged into stories about racism, homophobia, corruption, drug abuse. But fundamentally, even atavistically, we care about sport because we revel in play.

And sport deserves its place on the news menu – normally as dessert – precisely because of its lack of importance. It may come sauced in joy or anguish. Both are guilt-free thrills. I would say ephemeral – but then there was Róbert Gunnarsson, his six-foot-three frame sagged to my five-foot-nine, as he leaned his head against the wall of the corridor on 8th August 2012. He, along with his Icelandic handball team-mates had just come off court, having lost by the narrowest margin to Hungary in the second period of extra time of their quarter-final match at the London Olympics. Handball mattered back home. The team's silver medal at the Beijing Olympics four years before had been hailed by the President as the country's greatest ever sporting achievement. Róbert was a big man, crumpled. 'How long will it take to recover?' I asked. 'Call me in a month,' he said.

Happiness, pain – and wonder. And therein can be the task. Sport is like music. How do you convey what you just saw or heard? Especially on TV – when the viewers can see what you can see, and given the brevity that broadcast journalism always demands. So in Andy Murray's tough, tight first set of his fourth-round match, we showed a rally with him flung and frazzled around the court by his elegant opponent. My voice-track, over the pictures: 'for a time, Gasquet played with verve, and élan, and other French words'. Sometimes there would be fights I would lose. Rafa Nadal, all snarl and triceps, was thrashing his way back into a game. We had a close-up of him narrowing his wrath towards the small, furry sphere that had the temerity to be boinging back towards him as he wound up to unleash his Hammer of Vengeance. So: 'Nadal began to hit the ball as if it had been rude to his sister.' The TV news editor made me cut the line. I sulked. He went on to join the board of Ofcom.

My bigger problem – I dare say, my bosses would argue one of my many bigger problems during my two and a half years in the department – was the dead zone between those hulking hard news stories about FIFA and PEDs and hooligans, and the frothing emotion of watching people running and jumping and kicking and hitting. Was Chelsea going to sack Rafa Benitez? Live from Stamford Bridge, our Sports or is it Sports News Correspondent Tim Franks. Live, but barely, from the fish counter, our stunned brill, grey eyes glassy, mouth agape, his mind a void.

I had had an early warning of my unsuitability. One of the worst – I mean buttock-crampingly bad – questions I ever asked someone, was that which I'd lobbed at a sporting supernova a decade before. I was on a brief tour of duty as Washington correspondent, in the six months after 9/11. The bulletins were full of Afghanistan and anthrax and Enron. Somehow, I persuaded the bosses to send me to the Super Bowl in New Orleans. I cranked out a piece about the security around the biggest set-piece sporting event since the attacks. I also fulfilled a schoolboy dream of watching the Super Bowl. It was a magnificent game, won on the final play by the underdog New England Patriots and their barely-known back-up quarterback, Tom Brady. The St Louis Rams were piloted by their all-conquering League MVP, Kurt Warner. He was the chiselled star.

After the game, I hung around the kishkes of the Superdome, as the players wandered out of their changing rooms. In a small, subterranean space, lecterns had been arranged in a stiff square. A Ram or a Patriot would stand behind one, the hacks would gather, and ask their urgent, detailed questions. Eventually, the league's most famous, most garlanded star – Mr Warner himself – appeared. It was late. Most of the reporters had gone. Only a bare handful – I think maybe four plus me – clustered close. The questions were desultory. The answers from the dethroned king were polite, brief. There was silence. I felt I needed to justify my presence. That was the first mistake. The second swiftly followed. 'Mr Warner, what's that (gilt-edged, leather-bound) book you're holding?' 'It's the Bible. I lead prayers before every game.' 'So was today a bit of a faith-shaker?'

Somehow, sport has remained a meadow in which to frolic.

There were other flickers of joy to be found on the BBC News website, in a regular 'Jerusalem Diary' – words which are all the harder to write as I do now, in the throes of the latest catastrophe. Monday, 14th April, 2008: 'Until the end of last week, I had thought it was difficult to have strong feelings about lettuce. It is true that Ian, one of the BBC bureau's two Australian cameramen, has always been an open enthusiast. Lettuce features strongly in his salads, and at times he talks almost emotionally about the leaf.' Together, Ian – Drucey, in truth; no one called him Ian, except when he was being told off – and I had visited the 14th Annual Festival of Lettuce in the Palestinian village of Artas, just south of Bethlehem. Certainly, there was also a story to be told about farmers unable to sell their goods because of Israeli checkpoints – of the unceasing, unpredictable, growing constriction of life under occupation. But as we arrived in the village, the first thing we saw were men, eyes misting, mouths tearing at clumps of long, green leaves. By the end of the piece, I was happy to confess my conversion. 'I had thought that the point of most lettuce was to sit at the bottom of the salad bowl, pushing the more interesting ingredients to the top. At our Saturday lunch, I gave the Artas lettuce nowhere to hide. I served it unseasoned and undressed, just chopped and washed. It was a triumph: sweet and juicy, with a magical top note of dill. Ian would have been thrilled.'

Sometimes, it is true, the joy needed to be smuggled on air. That was fair enough: we are publicly funded, and I was Europe correspondent, not Arts correspondent. But it was clear to me which of the two reports I was more interested in, out of Austria. One, from Vienna, was an earnest, bloated piece for Broadcasting House, about the future of the proposed EU Constitution as the Austrian government assumed the presidency of the European Council. The other came from Salzburg. It was for Today. A much crisper cue for the presenter to read. 'In ten days, we will be celebrating the 250th anniversary of Mozart's birth. But are we guilty of drowning him in a sea of bad-taste memorabilia?'

Getting the commission was only half the sweat. What music to choose? To begin, the twirl and mysterious chromatic scale at the start of the A minor piano rondo, K.511. Then, croaking: 'I feel sick.' A beat. 'Is it because, in this Salzburg café, I've eaten half-a-dozen Mozart chocolate balls, or because I've eaten half-a-dozen Mozart chocolate balls?' Over the pulsing Adagio dissonance that opens the string quartet K.465, a recitation — in crotchet then quaver beats — of some of the Mozartiana on sale: 'lighters — sausages — matches mugs meatpies teatowels umbrellas aprons thimbles golfballs ashtrays - - ponchos'. The interviewees hit all the right notes. From the mayor of Salzburg confessing that he could stop municipal tat, but not commercial: 'This is somewhat embarrassing. In German, we call it kitsch.' To the music director of the Salzburg Festival saying the commercialism is inevitable but 'there's this wonderful French word: it's dégueulasse.' Throw in the Soave Sia Il Vento trio from Così Fan Tutte. Acknowledge that Mozart was no snob: he spent his life composing on commission, and knew the importance of commercial success. Stress that nothing can bury his artistic achievement. Close with the thought that if you're unmoved by this, you've probably been dead for several months, as Alfred Brendel plays the last few bars of that magical A minor rondo.

Except. The meat-heads in the *Today* studio didn't bloody wait for the final two pianissimo chords. They closed the fader and green-lighted the presenter. The Brussels bureau was used to my coloratura swearing. But that morning I occupied all available sonic frequencies. I demanded – I promise you this is true – I demanded of the *Today* editor that he play the final two chords at the next available opportunity, with an on-air apology. He actually said yes, but I think it was just to get me to leave him alone. That's the bastard thing about spreading joy. Get it wrong, and it hurts.

We will get on to Jewish joy in a moment. But a final word on joy in journalism and the joy of journalism.

First – flip the concept. Most people, you might think, want just what you and I want: security, companionship, a reasonable living, a sense of worth, liberty. It is their absence that we spend most of our time reporting and investigating. Yes, we flock to things when they're going wrong. That, though, is because they signal an absence of happiness.

And 'the joy of journalism'? Easy enough to understand when fossicking among music, or sport, or food. But given our usual unlovely stamping ground, it may sound odd, tactless, even tasteless to talk of joy. But hear me out. Journalism gives us a reason to go to places, speak to people, and then tell others about what we've seen and heard and found out. How good is that?

~~~~

THE ARTISTS (PLAYED 1660–1799)

'Ya que os produce las flores,
de compuestos ramilletes,
agradeced sus saynetes,
que juzgan bien de colores'

(*As he produces flowers, set in bouquets, cherish his vignettes, well-judged in colours*)
ABIGAIL DIAS DE PINA FONSECA[2]

THE ARTISTS

*'It is always interesting when Jews become artists,
given the conventional wisdom that they are not cut out for it.'*

ANTHONY JULIUS[3]

Everywhere, in this book, lines.

The gimcrack pipework of power and patrimony described by Cousin Diz; the severe confines of Victorian convention, the rules and placement which polite society implied and which were you to defy or simply miss would unfortunately only underline your unfitness. Thus can the plot of a novel or the appointment of a cantor be fouled up.

The circles around the key points on a map; the arrows directing the massed forces; the angles calculating the shell-fire which will kill great-uncle David. All that, you imagine, in 9H pencil. Yet the mark that lasts the longest comes from the soft script of his letters home.

A letter from a group of young men, two centuries before. These are lines of denunciation; lines and lines of them winding around the 'noxious weed'. The conclusion is neat. But would it be fairer to see the rigid Orthodoxy of great-great-great-great-great-great-grandfather Abraham as a layer in a palimpsest, underwritten by where he came from, superimposed by where he then settled?

Two chapters of redaction. Names blacked out. Lives circumscribed. Families scored through. Some so thoroughly obliterated that the page of the ledger has been ripped, the identities disappeared.

More letters, drawing two immigrant lives together. Thirty years later, the parents will cut out and cast off a child. Another 60 years, and that snapped line will begin to rethread.

Over 53 days a ship ploughs from the old world to the new. And this family will, down the generations, test and break boundaries of convention. Some of the battles they will choose to fight; at least one is a choice embraced only with reluctance. The question, always: on whose side do you line up?

And now, to end, the lines drawn by an artist, in a family of artists.

~~~~

Ester Orobio Furtado was the woman in her twenties we met in Chapter One. Born in Inquisition Lisbon, she had made passage to Amsterdam early in the eighteenth century. I imagine her assaulted on arrival, her senses bombarded by the maelstrom of the dockers yelling, the cargo of weapons, grain, luxury textiles and sugar unloading, and by the blasts of smell: tobacco, bay leaf and fish. Was there someone to meet her, to accompany her south from the reeking wharves on the IJssel? To navigate the network of canals and bridges and passageways; to negotiate the clotted, guttural consonants?

She had arrived on one of the streets within walking distance of the great Esnoga. Now, her pulse was slowing. But the shock was about to deepen. We cannot know the psychological landscape of the Lisbon she left behind: whether there was terror or repression or merely self-censorship. We can be certain that her Jewish identity was not on display, let alone an object of public celebration. It had to be there, though. Otherwise, she would not have been able to make her mark, that five-legged X skidding below the zephyr-born ribbons of 'Josseph Siprut Gabay', in Amsterdam's municipal wedding register, that August day in 1736.*

Why the shock? Because until she stepped ashore, her Portuguese Jewishness could only have been a pale root in stony ground. Now, in the Dutch Jerusalem, it could erupt in a garden of colour — tended by her husband.

*See the illustration on p.14.

Great-great-great-great-great-great-grandfather Joseph Siprut de Gabay was a man of many talents. An illustrator, a poet, a calligrapher, a belletrist, a teacher, a chiseller, a kabbalist, a friend who delighted in the company of others. He was a serious artist, in the un-serious, but substantial sense. He was the professional who was an amateur: he exuded love for his craft. He was also, in his way, the very image of a modern Jew. His image, unlike his pictures, we will need to assemble from a jumble of tesserae. But the impression they will leave is unmistakable.

Was it him, or was it Amsterdam? His parents, remember, were the *belogrados* we met in Chapter Four – down-at-heel Orientals, just immigrated from an increasingly hostile Constantinople. His father, Rabbi Abraham, had required welfare in the form of a blanket in 1696, the year after Joseph was born.

From the earliest age the boy had been embedded in Jewish learning. His name appears dozens of times, and several ways – Joseph Josseph Siprut Shiprut Chiprut – in the clergy's class registers, bound in dun canvas and deposited in the municipal archives. He's there, in his mid-teens, jostling for space among dozens of classmates, under the tutelage of the leading Hebrew grammarian, Rabbi Selomoh Judah Leão.[5] By 1718, in his early twenties, he had ascended to one of the most advanced Ets Haim yeshiva classes.[6] The pot was about to be stirred. His teacher was a highly controversial figure: the associate rabbi, Solomon Ayllon.

Ayllon was a major enough figure to warrant a portrait by the pre-eminent Dutch engraver of the eighteenth century, Jacobus Houbraken,[7] who declared him 'the most learned and skilled theologian' (*doctissumus peritissmusque theologus*). Others were not so kind. The rabbi had previously been the *Haham* in London, laying the foundation stone of the synagogue at Bevis Marks,[8] but resigning before the building opened its doors. He had been subjected to a 'virulent attack'[9] by a congregant – another rabbi – who accused him of having been an acolyte of the most outlandish Sabbateans, and bringing with him from the east (possibly Palestine, possibly Salonika) the stench of exotic licentiousness. According to an unremittingly unflattering account in *The Jewish Encyclopedia*,[10] the *mahamad* – the governing council of the London synagogue – 'caring more for its dignity than for the truth, endeavored to suppress the scandal'. But the congregants had lost faith in their senior rabbi, and he headed off to Amsterdam where, almost immediately, he wandered – or blundered – into another pyroclastic row over allegations of false-messianism, heresy, academic credentials and synagogal *amour propre.* They were still venting in 1718, the year Ayllon was teaching Joseph. The young man must have known: the students, the community would have been abuzz. What lesson did Joseph take? It could have been: eyes down, draw inwards. Everything that follows, suggests otherwise. It was not that Joseph took sides. But that he was unconfined by sides. He was head up, eyes wide, hunting light.

And maybe those juices were already fermenting. Joseph had wed two years earlier, in 1716, at the age of 21. His first wife was another Ester, 17-year-old Ester Semah. In the municipal marriage register, there is our first tiny clue of a calligraphic talent in bud.

11

Ester – typically, and like the second Ester whom Joseph will marry 20 years later – had not learned to write. Hence the circle. Ester Semah would have had little time for her letters, and probably less encouragement: she had been an orphan these past eight years. Her mother Ribca (who *could* write)[12] died when she was nine. Four years before, her father Manuel had abandoned them – mother and child – skipping town, maybe ending up in Paris.[13]

Another scrap of information, then: Joseph's first marriage, arranged and approved as it would have been, does not suggest the Siprut de Gabays were sniffy – or could afford to be sniffy – about the faultless bride's bad-luck back-story. And that extended beyond Ester's parents: her mother's maiden name, unsteadily inked in the marriage register of 1695, was Levi de Barrios. Ribca's father, Ester's grandfather, was the astoundingly colourful troubadour, Miguel Levi de Barrios.

There, in 1673, sits Miguel with lute and family. Feeling the weight beneath those fine-toned calves is a vanquished dragon, gasping the tribute *'dan a Miguel la voz, y a mi el tormento'* ('Give voice to Miguel, and torment to me'). With cruel irony, Miguel's infant daughter Ribca — she who will be abandoned by her husband and die when her daughter Ester is just nine — is mid-air, cherubically brandishing the power of love.

It is a mise-en-scène worthy of Miguel's life. Born near Córdoba in 1635, his family are pursued by the Inquisitors. A relative is burned at the stake. He gets slashed in the face in a knife-fight. Most of the family flee to Algiers. Miguel winds up in Italy, in Livorno. He has himself circumcised, and adopts the name Daniel Levi de Barrios. He marries and departs with his first wife for the Caribbean. She dies. He returns to Europe. He splits his time between Brussels, where he is a cavalry captain in the Spanish army, 'outwardly a conforming Christian',[15] and Amsterdam, where he has re-married and is a practising Jew. He is renowned in both cities as a poet and a playwright. So famous that it may be we get to see his gorgeous tresses again.

16

The Rijksmuseum, which holds Romeyn de Hooghe's drawing of the 'Circumcision Scene', identifies that baby with the strangely miniaturised head as Simon Levi de Barrios – in other words, Miguel's son. The scholarship has wobbled over time. Some of the more extensive research, by the art critic William Wilson,[17] does not mention the de Barrios, and reasonably points out that the room is so large and posh and the commission would have been so costly, that it must have been at the behest of a merchant family like the d'Acostas. But he concedes he can't be certain of the baby's identity. No such cavilling from Jacob Zwarts — one of the few published art historians also to have been a shochet* and a cantor. In an essay from 1929, Zwarts insists that Miguel's wife, Abigail de Pina, came from a very nouveau riche family, that the baby is Simon — 'obvious' he writes,[18] and that on his left, is his father. If so, what a portrait of Miguel that is: the pose all dash, his lips suave curves. He proffers the tray at a relaxed angle; it bears not canapés, but the instruments of circumcision.

Zwarts then encourages us to follow him into the clouds — or, these days, the Gallery Of Honour in the Rijksmuseum. There, in the far corner, is Rembrandt's masterpiece, The Jewish Bride. The models for the gently amorous duo are, says Zwarts, Miguel and Abigail. He's backed a few decades later by the historian and collector Mozes Gans, who suggests that 'Rembrandt must have known them well, for not only did he paint them several times (my emphasis) but he also gave his imagination free rein with their costumes.'[19]

It's the sort of pub talk — sorry lads, I mean erudite enquiry — that you can imagine filling the evenings in Amsterdam's bruine kroegen. More recently, as the pints — I do apologise, the academic papers — have flowed, the louder, or at least the more numerous, voices have been the sceptics'. The couple's identities, say the cognoscenti, are either uncertain or unknowable. But there are two specialists, Kenneth Brown and Francisco Sedeño, who feel that the weight of evidence is that Miguel and his talented, handsome poet of a wife, Abigail, were Rembrandt's models. They have many arguments. I will pick one. It is this:

---

*Kosher slaughterer.

There: you can see it clearly in the de Hooghe etching. The lesion on Miguel's left cheek, from that brawl and slashing he suffered as a 22 year-old in his native Montilla, either during or shortly after a violent robbery of his parents' haberdashery/gambling den.[20] The scar, they say, is also visible in *The Jewish Bride*. 'Rembrandt began to scratch a scar on Miguel's left cheek with his artist's knife.'[21]

With the impeccable timing that has marked much of my journalistic career (colleagues in several bureaus have found their leave cancelled should I be flying out of the country, away from them, on the grounds that my departure tends to coincide with the eruption on their patch of a bulletin-hogging disaster), I only read Sedeño and Brown's research two days after I'd been standing, mesmerised, in that corner of the Rijksmuseum's Gallery of Honour. I hadn't noticed a scar. I *had* thought that the man — may I now call him Miguel? — looked familiar; this husband's features chimed with those other depictions; his expression here was gentle, fond, worn — the face, perhaps, of a young parent.

Enough. Time to haul myself away from the canvas, because we're barely through Act Two of Miguel's theatrical course. He becomes an avowed follower of Shabbetai Ts'vi, and a founder-member of two salons of the arts (*The Academy of the Thirsty*, and *The Academy of Flowers*). His work is baroque in form and content, 'larded with references to classical mythology'.²² He is lauded, sought after – and chastised. The *mahamad* in Amsterdam frown on his published work and his private life. He is forced to stand on the naughty step in the synagogue and publicly recant.* Eventually, the tabloid eddies of approval and disapproval prove too much. Mental illness and poverty overwhelm him. As the years stack up, the balance reads: 'a life of brilliance, but even greater misery'.²⁴

You may reasonably argue that, lovely though Miguel's Sephardi soft-wave is, I am stretching the bounds of family to include him in Joseph's story. But this is more than gratuitous sleb-spotting. It sets the tone for Joseph's immediate family and broader milieu. His union with Ester had embraced another familial line, full of kinks and question marks at which others may have balked.

Indeed, that line will take a further twist given that Ester and Joseph will have a son who – up to now – has not been outed as theirs. He is a man who will gain renown, internationally, for his creative output – and for being, in England at least, bang in the middle of some salacious company that *everyone* was talking about. We will meet him later, but Joseph has been waiting patiently for us to turn our gaze on him.

Even now, two generations on from the troubles endured by the grandfather of his first wife, Joseph's own artistry – and in particular his poetry – would be practised in an environment where yes, the arts were celebrated, but the rule-makers and arbiters and patrons could suck their teeth and cause no end of trouble, especially to those not financially independent. And who, but a gilded coterie of merchants, was? Fall foul of the gentlemen governors, and you will be cancelled.

It began slowly for Joseph. There were scraps of work, or at least evidence of a scrap: in 1724, Joseph got 3 guilders for inscribing 26 names.²⁵ The first major project came in 1729, as he co-translated an Ottoman rabbi's 165-year-old 'Guide for Life'. There was a glittering subtext: 'that Jewish moral philosophy cannot be understood

---

*Miguel would have known the potential cost: everyone did. He had 'picturesquely but unmistakably' referred to Spinoza as a 'thorn' (in Spanish – *espino*), consumed by the fire of true faith, amid which Spinoza and another accused of impiety strove still to shine.²³

outside the context of European culture and that the creativity of Jewish philosophy in the 16th century is to be found in ethics'.[26]

But the pickings remained thin.

Amsterdam, remember, had been in the grip of a *furiosa Epidemia* that we read about earlier: Joseph's younger brother, Isaac – he, who would become Disraeli's great-grandfather – was summoned to the synagogue to blast the alarm calls of the *shofar*. Opportunities for a skilled craftsman such as Joseph would have been limited: the city's guilds remained closed to Jews until the very end of the century. Into the 1730s, into his late thirties, Joseph was still relying on welfare.[27] His wife Ester died in 1735; nine months later he registered his four children with the *weeskamer*, the Orphans' Chamber.[28]

His art refused to suffer. Joseph maintained the reputation of being 'one of the best calligraphers that Amsterdam ever had', writing 'in a very beautiful hand'.[29] We see it – in its romanised form, at least – in the signature recording his second marriage, in 1736, to Ester Orobio Furtado. Joseph was also taking time to teach, nurture, and influence a young talent, 18 years his junior.[30]

David Franco Mendes was, in the words of his not uncritical biographer, Jozef Melkman, 'one of the great figures of Hebrew literature'.[31] The historian J. S. da Silva went so far as to call him 'the soul'[32] of the Jewish Enlightenment in Amsterdam. Franco Mendes' first collection of verse, *Kinor David*, begins with a poem and a tribute from Joseph – saying how impressed he is by the precocity of his young charge.[33] (Franco Mendes, in turn, composed two poems dedicated to Joseph.)

Of particular significance among Franco Mendes' voluminous output are his collections of Hebrew verse. One of the 'most important'[34] is *Emek Hashirim*, described in the catalogue of Amsterdam's great Ets Haim library as including 'music and melodies, lamentation and wailing, responsa, letters and riddles'. The anthology was collated long after his mentor Joseph had died, but includes two poems by him. Indeed, they occupy prime positions – opposite the title page and the first leaf of the volume.

Above the billowing silken threads of Joseph's sign-off is a 'psalm of David'. It's a panegyric to his protégé, written – it seems – in the style of the medieval, 'Golden Age' of the Spanish diaspora. Joseph sings of David Franco Mendes' ability to weave poetry, beauty and scholarship – akin to the mystical power of the breastplate jewels worn by the ancient priests. Difficult to top that compliment – but it's the line before that couplet that arrests me: that David's artistry – his rhymes, his arrangements, his tributes to the people who are his historical lodestars – captures that all is 'connected, traversing, every one is connected'. These are four words which – at least in my fond imaginings, borne of little understanding and less Hebrew – in their compressed, switchback form convey that sense of link and flow: of faith, woven.

I am playing for time. My most frequent self-criticism – on air, at least – is that I fail to ask the crisp, pointed question. So here are two: what else is he saying? And what is its worth? And like the most infuriating interviewee, I will duck and swerve. I can offer you this: Joseph was well-known as a poet at the time.[35] That suggests he was held in some contemporary regard. His 1748 'Signs of Love' wedding poem, displayed at the start of the chapter, seems to include a touching image of the couple's children in the years to come, as fruitful and rooted and long-lasting (and Levantine) as an olive tree.

But I agree: I appear to have mounted an exhibition where the pictures are small, blurred copies; more prominent are the curatorial notes offering insights such as 'Look! Isn't it nice? Yup, dunno!' Let me try to whisk you past and onwards to some grand conclusions. I did promise that the impression Joseph left would be unmistakable. Here is why, in three parts.

~~~~

1. The company he kept.
Take the more celebrated (and studied) output of David Franco Mendes, whose formative years Joseph helped shape, and whose fellowship he held until the end of his life. Franco Mendes revelled in a catholic mélange of styles. He translated works from across the European canon, starting with extracts from the Portuguese national

epic, Camões' *Os Lusíadas*, and going on to include, more than once, Voltaire, poor chap.* Classical references garland his own poetry, in the vein of Miguel de Barrios. 'It may,' his biographer Melkman suggests, 'sound strange in our ears that a pious man...should talk about Apollo, Daphne and Calliope'.[36] There was comic verse, about a 'stuttering poetaster' and 'a sneezing apothecary',[37] alongside poems of proto-Romantic anguish. There are risqué pastiches.

A cousin of Joseph's, and another member of his and David Franco Mendes' salon – the *Mikra Kodesh* – was the bibliophile Isaac Cohen Belinfante. In 1764, he translated a Dutch poem, *The Scholar in his Study*, into Spanish and Hebrew. It is, according to the description in the Ets Haim catalogue, about 'a wise man who had renounced the worldly pleasures to devote his life to science'. To science. And it's surmounted with an illustration of *putti* – naked, as *putti* tend to be – disporting themselves as librarians. As Melkman says of other illustrations to be found in Franco Mendes' *Kinor David*, 'we find all sorts of symbolic figures (such as skulls and crossed bones, a little angel with an hourglass) which one would never expect from a pious Jew.'[38]

There seems to be a hunger among these friends – and they were friends – to sample all that they can. They are eighteenth-century chefs strolling through markets, filling their baskets, whipping up dishes for the delight of each other. It reached one riotous apogee with their 1767 'five-minute *Haggadah*'† – a tumble of Spanish, Portuguese, Dutch, transliterated Hebrew, and drinking songs; there's even a parody of the traditional *Seder* song '*Dayenu!*' ('It would have been enough!') with new lyrics wishing that our forebears fleeing Egypt had been able to take with them more than the bread of affliction – i.e. the dry, tasteless, gut-binding *matza* that we all eat over Passover – and that instead God had provided all sorts of not-necessarily-kosher delicacies. '*Abastáranos!*' [39]

---

*Voltaire presumably would rather not have suffered translation into Hebrew. After all, 'C'est à regret que je parle des Juifs: cette nation est, à bien des égards, la plus détestable qui ait jamais souillé la terre.' (Philosophical Dictionary, 1769)

†A *Haggadah* is the story of Passover, read around the family table, on the first night or nights of the festival. The *Seder*, as the story, songs and meal is called, takes all evening – and for many, on into the early hours.

All of which leaves that further, indelicate question: is this stuff any good? The response lies in a word I did not initially know how to pronounce, let alone define. 'Epigone' rhymes with 'stone', and connotes a sense of a mediocre, second-class follower or imitator, in art or philosophy. Shlomo Berger and Irene E. Zwiep's essay *Epigones and the Formation of New Literary Canons: Sephardi Anthologies in Eighteenth Century Amsterdam*[40] now has, the authors may not be tickled to hear, its own epigone: me.

The key, say Berger and Zwiep, is to see the forest, not the trees. The anthologies are, textually, a great clump of nothing very significant, of 'no more than moderate…talent'. The key is the shift towards modernity, to a 'new, more rich and varied Jewish literary canon in which the historical and the contemporary, the religious and the secular would be preserved side by side.'[41]

All this, say the authors, implies a new confidence in Jewish creativity. 'Rather than feeling they were admitting foreign flowers into their garden, the Sephardi *literati* of Amsterdam ventured into their neighbours' garden to plant a Hebrew rose in its midst.'[42]

Which image brings us back to Joseph.

[43]

~~~~

2. The Jewishness of his work.

By which I do not mean to ask whether a poem in Hebrew or an illustrated *Omer* counter can be categorised as Jewish art. Nor to weigh how 'Jewish' is Joseph's work. Pissarro and Chagall – both Jewish artists. But which one is Jew-ish? I will leave that ontology to the academics and the spirit of Lenny Bruce.

Rather, the question is: what can we learn from Joseph's evocation of Jewishness?

It was the sweeping proscription on representative imagery in the Ten Commandments[44] that led to the assumption, as Anthony Julius put it in the epigraph at the start of the chapter, that Jews simply don't do visual arts. Or, in the more forceful words of the – Jewish – art dealer and critic, Bernard Berenson: 'There was the fanatical hatred of the anti-Hellenic Jew against everything that might entice him away from his bleak abstractions and the passionately fervid, aggressive, and exasperated affirmation of his monotheism.'[45]

Joseph's riposte was not just in his handsome letters and flowers rampant, but the spirit in which he and his friends created their works. Their identifiably Jewish and identifiably non-Jewish influences did not run on parallel tracks. They did not exist *despite* each other. This was *and* rather than *but*. They don't seem to be the 'contested souls' that they've been labelled elsewhere.[46] To invoke a word we'll wrestle with in the epilogue: if you had suggested to this group that this somehow meant they were *inauthentically* Jewish, and then allowed them a little time to translate that into Spanish or Portuguese or Dutch or Hebrew or whichever of the myriad languages they knew: they still would have blinked at you in incomprehension.

In the last decade of Joseph's life, he and Franco Mendes were at the forefront[47] of that salon, the *Mikra Kodesh*. The name is a nod to the 'sacred convocation' God ordains for the start and end of Passover.[48] Melkman insists the name 'can hardly mean anything but *hevrah* (society) for the study of *Torah*',[49] and is incredulous that earlier historians could have described it as a 'literary society'.

Perhaps. But this feels like a distinction with little practical difference. These artisan cosmopolitans surely did not think of their religious study and literary leanings like sets of kosher cutlery: one for the meat, one for the milk, always to be housed in separate boxes, never to mix.

They were creating a new Jewish aesthetics, as the eighteenth century would redefine that word: the idea of the science of sensory perception. These Jews were sensation-seekers.

To that end, Joseph was prepared to venture out of his salon, beyond his paid commissions, and into the deepest and most opaque realms of Jewish mysticism. He aimed to draft the circles of the universe. Christian mystics told you about their voyage to enlightenment, lower-case.[50] Joseph would not have approved of the personalisation. It would not have figured in his work or his world-view. Jewish mystics, *kabbalists*, saw themselves as more objective, mapping 'the topography of the divine'.[51]

Professor Yossi Chajes came up with that delightful wording. He also happens to be an expert in *ilanot*: trees. Joseph, as we've seen from the wedding poem, among other work, can draw flora. These trees belong to a different kingdom: they are the schemata of the cosmos.

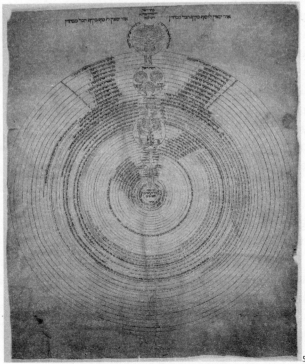

52

And intriguingly, these drawings play with the fire of a highly combustible messianism. Shabbetai Ts'vi and his chief apostle, Nathan of Gaza, had the previous century, swept the Jewish world with messianic fervour. It was an episode of protracted hysteria which ended with the protagonists cast out, disgraced, the movement vilified. But their mystical explorations had seeped far into kabbalistic roots. In another of Professor Chajes' punchy phrases, Joseph's *ilanot*, like others of his time, 'bear witness to the domestication of deviance'.[53]

So to survey the breadth of Joseph's work — as with his collaborators — is to see an equal celebration of Jewishness and the arts, with radical messages in both. To those within the Jewish community fearful of contravening the prohibitions on graven images from Exodus or Deuteronomy, or of breaking the rules of the establishment, and to those non-Jewish religious authorities who saw the experience of the sublime as their preserve, Joseph and his confrères were cheerfully announcing that they would not be constrained. They would define it their way. And it would not be esoteric. The illustration and calligraphy, the ornamental title pages, the luxurious bindings, the riddles and belles-lettres, and the fact that many of these volumes were placed in the library of Ets Haim all meant that their many pursuits were intended for public edification.

In form and content, I keep returning to a musical image: irrelevant for you, perhaps; insistent for me. The music critic Charles Rosen observed that 'the eighteenth century was cultivatedly self-conscious about the art of conversation: among its greatest triumphs are the quartets of Haydn.'[54] That is precisely, synaesthetically, how I hear the work of Joseph and his band: as the wide-ranging, close-knit, ground-breaking conversation of Haydn's chamber music. And what I can deduce from Joseph's own works feels like that composer's triumphant *Creation*: a biblical oratorio that is also a secular oratorio, and one where, as Alfred Brendel described it, 'chaos and darkness are annihilated by light'.[55]

~~~~

3. His heroic disposition.

I am over-doing it. Joseph was not Shelley or Schumann. He was not the artist in spite of life's slings.

But he does stand out. There was of course a cultural elite drawn from the Amsterdam Sephardi aristocracy: a small circle of bom judesmo, whose wealth and power insulated them from censure.[56]

Joseph was almost certainly not among them.* In wealth, in family background, and in exposure to the temper of the times, his paid work and lay musings were not made from plumped cushions. Joseph may not have even made enough to pay tax; few belogrados did.[57] There's no record of him giving money to the synagogue: he was not even assessed for the lowest level of finta – membership dues. Whatever he earned for his gorgeous Love Tokens wedding poem, he was in a different world to the families of the bride and groom. In 1743, Teixeira and Levi Ximenes were listed among the richest Sephardi names: families with an annual income of 16,000 guilders.[58] In 1745, Joseph was paid just 20 guilders[59] to write a book of escavot (special prayers for the repose of the soul of the dead).[60]

He scratched out extra work inscribing tombstones, teaming with François Absiel, a stonemason from Liège. Again, there was a commission from the Levi Ximenes family: in 1746, he received 22 guilders and 10 nickels for carving Abraham's epitaph.[61] These earnings suggest Joseph was not impoverished.[62] But nor does his craftsmanship appear particularly well-remunerated: in 1751 he worked on the slab for Hana Alvares. Chiselling 275 letters brought in 34 guilders and 10 nickels.[63]

So middle-aged Joseph was not rich, perhaps barely what we would now call middle class. His new wife was a refugee from a land simmering with accusation, betrayal and death. And his own country – the seven provinces of the Netherlands – was weakened: burdened by debt, exhausted by the wars smashing up

---

*Consider also how Miguel Levi de Barrios ended up – a 'schnorrer' according to his biographer Wilhelmina Pieterse. And as for Joseph's protégé and friend, David Franco Mendes, Melkman refers to his weak health, depression, loveless marriage and financial troubles later in life.

Europe, losing maritime trade, and riven internally. A contemporary Yiddish chronicle of the 1740s, forgotten for two centuries, re-discovered and translated into Dutch after World War Two, was published with the title *The Seven Provinces in Turmoil*.[64]

A man such as Joseph could not have been insulated from these harsh times. And yet he did not shrink into his coat.

There is a psalm – number 103 – which we sing in a quiet E minor swell on the High Holy Days. It warns about the frail, short span of life. A man's days are like grass; he blooms like a flower of the field; the wind passes over it, and it is gone. Joseph alighted on a similar image, redolent of brevity as much as beauty: cut flowers, in their scarlet, vermillion, indigo, pink and yellow. They won't last long. This was, after all, just an illustration to mark the passing of one day, on an *Omer* calendar.* But the artist insisted that we not sigh. Or if we do, it is with pleasure.

~~~~

My abuse of musical analogy is about, at last, to be less otiose.

Abraham Chaim Braatbard, that Yiddish-speaking chronicler of the turmoil-lashed Netherlands, writes wide-eyed about a competition in 1743 to find a new *hazan* – cantor – for Amsterdam's Sephardi community. The idea of a *hazzanic* talent show was not new: open auditions and voting had been used earlier in the 1700s. This contest would mirror great-great-grandfather Shimshon Roco's experience 140 years later, in London:[65] six entrants, filthy politicking, and 'a huge ruckus among the Portuguese'.[66] The other contemporary historian, David Franco Mendes, furnishes further details: the *mahamad* felt compelled to issue instructions to the congregation to stop making such a racket during the auditions, not to applaud or heckle the contestants excessively, not to solicit votes for their favoured candidate, and not to place bets. The auditioners were also warned that before they went up to take their position in front of the Ark in

---

* See illustration on p.239.

the synagogue and perform their audition, they too shouldn't be 'taking offers'.⁶⁷

As for the contest itself, 'the rivals, seeking to impress their audience, looked for unpublished poems which their friends, the local poets, were only too happy to provide.'⁶⁸ Among them – indeed, according to the musicologist Israel Adler, one of the 'better-known' – was Joseph.

The verse was sufficiently sought-after to be printed as broadsheets.⁶⁹ The music appears to have been composed by one of the most famous and prolific Dutch Jewish composers of the time, Abraham Caceres.* Another manuscript of Caceres' survives, re-using the melody – albeit transposed down a tone, and setting a different text.⁷⁰ No matter: now we can hear how Joseph's words were performed. When *Shabbat* went out, his lyrics – along with the other works in the hazzanic contest – were sung as 'new quartets'.⁷¹ It is not just the arrangement (in this case, two voices harmonising, two unison violins and a bass). It is the style: a sarabande.

And it is the accompanying silence. There is no account of the disputatious Portuguese disputing over such a form. The idea of setting a prayerful Jewish text in the contemporary, secular style was not new. The experimentation had begun in Renaissance Italy. But in the great span of Jewish worship, that still counted as recent. And fights had flared from the start.

Obscene! Lewd! Rabbi Archevolti of Padua had railed, in 1602.⁷² To which Rabbi Leone of Modena† had icily retorted: 'I do not see

---

*Who also set the work of Rabbi Moses Haim Luzzatto to music. See Chapter Two (p.30).
†The man who would be my choice in the non-existent parlour game, 'Which clerical figure from the past would you most like to meet?' According to his entry in *The Jewish Encyclopedia* (1904 ed.), 'at the age of twelve (he) translated into Hebrew verse the first canto of Ariosto's *Orlando Furioso*, and about a year and a half later he wrote his dialogue against gambling, which passed through ten editions and was translated into Latin, French, German and Judaeo-German... Besides preaching and teaching, Leon exercised not less than 26 professions, but all his resources were swallowed up in gaming... The community of Venice in the seventeenth century must have been animated by a spirit of tolerance, for Leon continued to remain a member of the rabbinate until his death.' It is his proselytising on music which makes me swoon. According to Franz Kobler, *Letters of Jews Through the Ages* [Ararat, 1952] p.400, Leone benefited from his father's desire 'to give his son the exquisite and many-sided education characteristics of the Italian Jews of the Renaissance...(so that) in his youth he was a skilled singer, dancer and musician who once even conducted an orchestra.' As a

that anyone who has a brain in his skull would cast doubt on praising God with music in the synagogue... Would it be better to bray like an ass...to shout to the Lord like a dog and a crow?'[73]

So Amsterdam's raucous cantorial competition of 1743, replete with fresh text and a contemporary musical setting, should be seen as a burst of confidence and energy. Joseph's poem may have been sung in A minor, but I am still placing it in the key of Jewish major.

These were Jews unbound.

Joseph died at the end of 1766.[75] Perhaps, then, the previous year he'd been able to attend one of the recitals in Amsterdam comprising solos and concertos, bridging the late baroque music of the

---

rabbi, he championed music in prayer and in services; he brought polyphony to the synagogue in Ferrara in the early 1600s.

cantorial competition and the early classical music now in vogue. Joseph might have had a particular reason to go to the concert: the notices in the *Amsterdamse Courant*[76] said that the performer and composer was the London-based, 'M. Siprutini'.

Up to now – as far as I'm aware – the 'excellent violoncellist' Emmanuel Siprutini has not been outed as anything other than the son of a Dutch Jew.[77] But the evidence[78] is that Emmanuel was a.k.a. Manuel – the son from Joseph's first marriage to Ester Semah (Miguel de Barrios's granddaughter), born in either 1728 or early 1729. In which case, Joseph could not have seen his boy for a while: Manuel had headed to London where one of the pioneers and popularisers of the newfangled violincello was Giacobbe Cervetto – an immigrant Italian Jew.[79] Cervetto had changed his name from Basevi, and perhaps, along with lessons, Manuel decided that an Italianate stage-name would be more of a draw. The young man had another reason to be in London: he had an uncle in town. We met Isaac in Chapter Four as the increasingly well-to-do younger brother of Joseph, whose daughter Sarah would marry Benjamin d'Israeli. (And their son, Isaac – Dizzy's father – would marry Maria Basevi – from the same family as Giacobbe.)[80]

By 1758, 'Sig. Siprutini' was performing at the Great Room in Dean Street.[81]* Within two years, he was an impresario as well as musician, at some of the higher-end London venues.[82] In 1761, the astoundingly colourful – that's a euphemism – singer Mme. Pompeati (a.k.a. Mme. Trenti, a.k.a. Mrs Cornelys, a.k.a. Mrs Smith)[83] performed for his 'benefit'. In January 1764, Emmanuel was initiated into the Masons, on the proposal of 'Mr John Soafany'.[84] Theirs would be a fateful friendship.

That same year – 1764 – London resounded to the plinking prodigies as the Mozarts arrived on the latest leg of their grand European tour, Dad Leopold marketing – milking, really – eight-year-old Wolfgang and 12-year-old Nannerl. Respite for the kids

---

*Also in 1758, Manuel Chiprut Gabay appears in the accounts book for Bevis Marks Synagogue – albeit with his membership dues not yet paid. (LMA 4521/A/04/01/074)

from the constant parading and performing came when Leopold was under the weather. In July, he was struck by 'astonishing pain' in his stomach; it lasted for days, he drifted 'in a stupor...unrecognisable...exhausted'. His wife made warm broth; doctors fussed and prescribed. None of it worked. But then, 'a friend of mine, called Sipruntini (sic), a Jew by birth, brought along a doctor who is a Portuguese Jew,[85] and he came with powdered rhubarb, mixed with stomach-fortifying substances, and gave me a mild evacuation'. 'Hebrew medicine,' Leopold called it – and it worked magnificently.[86]

Emmanuel was more than a friend. He was also 'a great virtuoso on the violoncello' – which from Mozart Sr was high praise. And he was that intriguing sort: a Jew. But not, implicitly, like the Jews back home. This lot were *herrlichen* – 'marvellous'. Instead of beards, they sported velvet clothes and stiff wigs. 'What's more, when the Portuguese Jews go to their synagogue[87] they went in all their finery, like the French; you'd never think they were Jews, to look at them.'[88]

Of course, the real advance would be to reject Judaism altogether. Leopold thought highly enough of his friend Emmanuel to try to help him over the line. He believed he was close: Emmanuel, 'having travelled through Italy and Spain, finds the Jewish faith laughable. So he's abandoned the faith.' In Leopold's assessment, from all that Emmanuel said, it was clear he believed in one God, and that he must love his neighbour like himself, and to live as an honest man. (*Note to Leopold: that's what Jews are supposed to believe.*) Emmanuel agreed with him, Leopold, that among the Christian faiths, Catholicism was the best. 'I shall make another *attaque* next time: one must proceed gently. Patience! Perhaps I'll become a missionary in England.'[89]

Perhaps, Leopold. Perhaps you can also imagine Emmanuel, who quite possibly wasn't the most devout, observant Jew, smiling and nodding as his friend sawed away. They were discussing big things; the biggest of the lot, really. Leopold believed his Catholicism was the one true expression of the one true faith. Emmanuel sat – however lightly – in a tradition which does not seek to convert.

And documentary evidence, from the end of his life, suggests that that was indeed where he remained.

Emmanuel was also about to be associated with company that I can't quite believe Leopold would have approved of.

At the end of 1765, the Mozarts moved on from London to the Netherlands. Emmanuel had preceded them, earlier that year, giving recitals in March, April and July in Amsterdam[90] – maybe, I fondly imagine, re-uniting for a final time with his father. There, Emmanuel also joined the great retinue of an Englishwoman on a grand tour. She was not just any aristocrat: Elizabeth Chudleigh, as it says on the cover of a highly entertaining 2021 biography, was 'The Woman Who Scandalised A Nation'.[91] She was sensationally glamorous; a courtier whose first, rushed, secret and unhappy marriage to the heir to the Earldom of Bristol was followed by a second marriage to the Duke of Kingston. She had a reputation for many things – much of which was fuelled by gossip, jealousy, hypocrisy and chauvinism – but she was, without doubt, a woman who took hosting and entertainment immensely seriously. Music was integral to that.

And Emmanuel seemed to have been more than a session musician. More than two centuries before Paul Burrell, there was Thomas Whitehead. He'd been the long-serving valet to the Duke from before the romance with and marriage to Elizabeth. Whitehead clearly loathed Elizabeth's entrée into his master's life. After her death (12 years after she'd been unanimously convicted of bigamy by the entire House of Lords), Whitehead published a scurrilous tell-all.[92] He recorded his mistress's routine and company: among the regulars was 'Sip*****i, a performer on the violoncello, since turned wine-merchant.' The musician was among a group of gentlemen whom 'it was observed, might have done well enough for a cobbler, not for a duke.' Whitehead confirmed that Emmanuel travelled abroad with Elizabeth 'for a few years before', along with 'E***s, an apothecary'. They 'were very necessary attendants'. Evans would induce vomiting after Elizabeth over-ate. 'The Jew musician used to attend her Grace after an extra glass in the afternoon, while she dozed on the sofa.

She had an excellent strong tone through her nostrils when asleep, which overpowered his instrument.'[93]

Whitehead then 'cannot help mentioning' a story from the Duke and Duchess's country seat, Thoresby, in Nottinghamshire.

'Sip*****i had a very pretty wife, whom Zop***i, a portrait-painter, was very fond of.' (This was the celebrated German painter and Royal Academician Johan Zoffany – the man who'd proposed Emmanuel for the Masons back in 1763.) 'They were invited to spend a few weeks at Thoresby-house. The Jew and his wife came first. In about three days the painter arrived. The room was shown him where to sleep. Some time after supper, when the ladies were withdrawn, he told the Duke he was much fatigued with his journey, and begged his Grace's permission to retire to bed. The servant was called to light him to his chamber. He took the candle; said he would not trouble the servant, as he could find the way himself. The gentlemen made the poor Israelite who remained quite mellow, he being fond of his glass. At 12 o'clock he took leave of the company, to go to his pretty partner: but you may guess, Sir, his disappointment when he found her door fast. He knocked several times, and was answered at last by his wife, that he could not sleep with her that night, as Mr. Z— was there; he must therefore go to his room opposite.

'This did not please poor Sip–i: he still kept thumping, and made such a noise that several of the footmen came out of the servants-hall, which was at the bottom of the stairs, near the Jew's apartment. They listened, and heard the Painter give him a good drubbing, compelling him to retire to the other room; which when effected, Z–i returned to the beautiful Jewess for the remainder of the night. It was supposed, by the Jew's taking this affront so quietly, that he had been used to such disappointments by more of Hagar's offspring than the Painter. The neighbourhood soon heard of the affair: it became the tea-table conversation; not without some additions, as stories of this kind seldom lose by travelling. The discovery soon roused the Jew, his Wife, and the Painter. In a few days they set out for London.

The Duke's good nature ordered his post-chaise and four to take them to Nottingham, which was 23 miles over the forest. The post-boys declared the story had reached the Black-moor's Head (the inn the Duke used to put up at) before them: here they took the stage, and pursued their journey home.'[94]

Whitehead may not be the most reliable witness. But I, too, 'cannot help mentioning' one further morsel, not out of prurience – moi?, but because it at least suggests another, more assertive side of Emmanuel. After he had accompanied the Duchess on her successful trip to Dresden at the invitation of the Dowager Electress of Saxony, the pair had returned to Thoresby. There, 'they had some high words'. Elizabeth sought her husband 'to tell him of the Jew's ill-treatment of her'. Whereupon – and again, these are Whitehead's quotation marks, best handled with tongs – Emmanuel replied: 'D——n ye madam. You know that I know you well. I will inform the Duke of your tricks abroad.' Emmanuel stalked off to another part of the house, the Duchess racing after him, incensed, only then to realise it would be politic to make her peace. And lo, 'at supper that night there appeared as much cordiality and good nature between them as ever'.[95]

Whitehead mentioned – probably snidely – Emmanuel's second career as a wine merchant. And this was how he re-appeared, in Belgium. Since 1781, Emmanuel had been doing 'considerable' business, especially in wine.[96] In 1786, he petitioned to become a member of the *bourgeoisie* – so to gain the full rights to ply a trade. Emmanuel was requesting, in effect, what still was prohibited of him and his Amsterdam relations – to join a guild.[97] In August, Emperor Joseph's plenipotentiary in the Austrian Netherlands, the Count of Barbiano and Belgïoïoso, granted Emmanuel admission to the *bourgeoisie* of Brussels. The certificate emphasised, though, that this was '*despite* (my emphasis) him being of the Jewish Religion'.[98]

Emmanuel did not forego music altogether. In January 1799 he applied for two passports – for him and his wife Maria (their marriage having clearly survived the attentions of Johan Zoffany). He had composed a cello concerto, and wanted to have it printed, published and performed in Holland.* There's the eighteenth century equivalent of a mugshot for him and Maria: the application form stating that he wears a wig, has brown eyebrows, brown eyes, a long nose, an average mouth, a wide chin, an oval face and an ordinary forehead. He and Maria are short, even for the time: four foot ten. Maria's nose is normal, her chin round. Emmanuel's age more or less tallies. Maria appears to have shed a few years. It says she's 52.[100]

Theirs is an incomplete duet. I can find no burial records in London, Brussels or Amsterdam matching their multiple names. Emmanuel does reappear in 1903 though, having somehow blagged his way into the most stunning company: Novello And Company had re-published 12 transcriptions for two violins and piano. *The Musical Times* said that 'the contents are well selected from works by Gluck, Corelli, Leclair, Handel, Haydn, Siprutini, Schubert, Beethoven and Mendelssohn.'[101] In 1979, the cellist Nona Pyron tells *Early Music* magazine that she's looking forward to reviving music such as Siprutini's, 'which hasn't been heard in modern times'.[102] In the 2020s, Claudio Ronco and Emanuela Vozza record 24 of Emmanuel's cello sonatas. Struck as Leopold was with Emmanuel's talent, says Claudio in his sleeve notes, the Mozarts certainly possessed the sonatas. Indeed, he says you can find 'traces and fragments in the best-known works of Wolfgang Amadeus'.[103]

Maybe. (That word again: how often has it appeared in this book? Probably almost as often as 'perhaps': the BBC lifer's cell-level aversion to sounding doctrinaire.) What I can say with greater certainty is that this clutch of artists – Miguel, Abigail, Joseph, Emmanuel – *are* exerting an influence now, at least on me: their traces, unearthed, pored over by a weekend archaeologist. I may

---

*Would it have been a risky journey? Back in 1773, in Amsterdam, Jean Jaques (sic) Le Febvre & Sons had signed a power of attorney for two men in London to 'pursue implead seize sequester arrest attach imprison and to condemn' Mr Emmanuel Siprutini over unpaid debts. [99]

only understand them imperfectly, but the impression they leave is marked, in colour and adventure. These were Jewish lives with the doors flung open.

We may not all have their craftsmanship. There is still a pen on the table. So tell me: what comes next?

Epilogue

Birmingham & London (2020)

'Aware now that amid all that blab whose echoes recoil upon me I have not once had the least idea who or what I am.'

WALT WHITMAN[1]

'Oh, I forgot to tell you that, in order to write, one must have something to write.'

PRIMO LEVI[2]

An echo from two earlier episodes, writ across my face. This is less dramatic than the Venezuelan cavalryman cousin, cheek scarred by a Spanish sabre in 1823, or Miguel de Barrios, knifed lip-to-jaw in 1657. Unlike them, I imagine this will be temporary. I have a beard, or my longest ever beginnings of one. Ten days ago, my mother died. I intend not to shave until her *yahrzeit*.*

This morning I visited her grave for the first time. It lies in grounds which are kempt, huge, and in the way of Jewish cemeteries, stark and spare, at least in the graves and pebbled paths around them. Mum does not have a headstone yet. We wait about 11 months after burial, before the ceremony of stone-setting. So there's just a small, plastic marker jammed in to the earth: Esther Franks it says, awkwardly. Esther on her birth and now death certificates. At every other point in her life, Tessa.

*The anniversary of a death. It follows the Jewish, lunisolar calendar.

It was grey, gusty and mild this June day. I had forgotten my *yarmulke* and *siddur*. The prayer halls were locked shut, of course, so I wheeled back to the superintendent's small office: locked too, but through the open window I asked him if he had a prayer book he could lend me, along with that thin black *yarmulke* I could see balancing upside down on a top shelf. He had a face mask slung under his chin: no, no prayer books; and we're not allowed to give them out anyway at the moment. No bother, I said. I'll get *Kaddish* up on my phone. You can keep the *yarmulke*, he said.

I passed just three people on the long walk to HHH-177, a workman next to his small flatbed truck, and a late middle-aged couple, arms around each other as they stood halfway down a row. Mum's right at the back. I notice that she is a few along from our rabbi's recently dead grandfather. In the years, probably decades to come, she will be more in the middle, as this great Hertfordshire field fills.

I edge down her row. The spacing appears uneven. It isn't. Mum is just on the left-hand side of a double burial plot. Next to her, in time, will lie Dad. There is no stone: that will be inscribed and erected in another 11 months or so, as is tradition in the diaspora. I recite *Kaddish*, holding the phone in landscape. It is Aramaic, not Hebrew, and that often comes less easily to our European tongues: I remember stumbling over a prayer once, as a child; Dad quoted the part-time prayer-leader at our Birmingham shul saying 'you could break your teeth' on Aramaic. *Kaddish* is the exception: it is so full of familiar words, its lines set to a rocking, incantatory rhythm. Still, the words do this morning clog in my mouth. Over the rumble of M25 traffic, muffled by the thick tree-line, I say it twice. And then I stare at the rocks and earth and the green plastic oblong collar which marks the circumference of the grave. And then I chat to Mum.

My last decent talk with her had been 13 days before. She was receding, physically. She had been for two months, and it was no gradual decline. The virus had dumped her off a cliff; flattened, battered, wrecked her. It had wrought less damage against her acuity, wit and strength of character. The doctors who'd bent the rules to allow what they – and so I – thought was a final visit in March 2020, five days after she'd tested positive, had probably not got the full measure of the gasping elderly woman behind the oxygen mask. Chances were, they had not recalled the 1992 interview with her in *The Birmingham Post*, previewing her exhibition of 'miniature rugs' at the Botanical Gardens. Early on – para two – the 'Lifestyle' editor has a reader advisory: 'Tessa Franks is a lady who likes to push the limits of a situation.' Para six, direct quote: 'I don't like anything safe or predictable. Anything airyfairy like bowls of fruit or landscapes.' Closing para, direct quote: 'Some of my friends don't understand the carpets at all and view my work as brutal, ugly, challenging and hostile. But I don't care.'

It took her a further nine weeks to die – this talented, outspoken, tough and loving woman ebbing from Urgent Care to side room to hospice to nursing home.

By the Thursday before last, it was clear her body was running on fumes. So at one point, I offered to talk at her. I told her where I had got up to in some research about the younger Abraham Mendes Chumaceiro and his nineteenth-century championing of black civil rights, and about his brother Joseph Hayyim and his appeal to those with God on their side not to believe that their God-given perspective gives them the right to sit in judgment on other conceptions of Divinity. I sketched Joseph Siprut de Gabay, the artist-hero of the previous chapter. I rattled on for perhaps 15 minutes. I drew breath. Mum turned her head on the pillow, gave me a skewed grin, and said something very, very nice which I will not repeat but which will stay with me forever.

She loved that I was uncovering this shrouded gallery. Less than a month before she was felled, I gave her a version of David Van Ryn's story. She rang me to say that she had read it through twice. She had wept. Tender and angry, I think she said.

There will be no full chapter on Mum. My sister Annabel and I each delivered a *hesped* – a eulogy – at her funeral; I spoke that night at the *shiva*, and again, two days later, when I talked about her relationship to the *Torah*, to the covenant we were celebrating, and about which I was going to *leyn* that *Shavuot* morning. And none of these is the last word, or sufficient words about Mum. But they are a start, and they are written down.

And Mum – and Dad* – are pulsing throughout this book. In the family tree they are in the trunk, in the gnarled and complex roots, in the secret communications of the mitochondria, in the twigs that sprout. We can branch in wilful, countervailing ways, but even as we grow apart, we remain bound.

Perhaps a 'tree' is the wrong metaphor. It would be more accurate and more liberating to say that we are seeds, cuttings – transplanted into environments that change with time and place.

But the tree is more than just a useful schematic and an appealing symbol. It conveys nature and nurture and maybe the wide intersection between the two, if the mysteries of epigenetics ever begin to clear. The complexities of the branches – even if in the case of Mordechai and Juan, they are ancient lateral shoots out of reach in next door's brambled garden – is part of the wonder.

In that sense, getting to Mum's story couldn't be more straightforward. But it's still problematic. Helpfully problematic.

Because I blithely suggested at the start that this was a book about Judaism and journalism, and how an understanding of the underpinnings of both – or at least my construction of them – could proffer a way to think about identity. That will happen.

There's a basic question I've failed to address, though. What do I mean by Judaism, or Jewishness?

Even if we discard Sartre's sterile and anachronistic dialectic – that the Jew only exists because of anti-Semitism – you can remain trapped in a circularity: Jewishness exists because it matters to me and it often matters to others, and confusingly my estimation of how much it matters to others may be warped by my projections, which might be inaccurate. *Cogito*, as well as *cogitant, ergo sum*. What's more, those others may be – to use the neologism – Jew-identifying, or clearly not so. And these groups may view Jewishness as mattering in a positive and negative sense. Even if I

---

*Who died in 2023. I wrote a brief obituary for the *Guardian* www.theguardian.com/education/2023/nov/09/arnold-franks-obituary

– and you – just accept that it is enough that it matters to me, then as the author of my identity, how far am I making a choice about how much it matters? Am I, to use an irresistibly inappropriate term of Sartre's, just acting in bad faith?

One easy, but satisfying answer is that 'to struggle' is authentically Jewish. Far greater philologists and theologians than me – in the sense that they, unlike me, are actual philologists and theologians – have pointed out that the original biblical use of the word 'Israel' conveyed the sense of struggling with, maybe even against, God.

(That hasn't, of course, stilled the seething struggle, the endless windmill of fists among Jews themselves. One rabbi in Jerusalem told me, early on in my posting, that he wished earnestly to make peace with the Palestinians not simply because it was a moral imperative, but so that we could get on with sorting out the conflict between Jews, within the Jewish state.)

Struggle is good, then. It conveys an idea of action. Action is where we will end up.

But there was a word three paragraphs back which I just realised I skated over: 'authentically', as in 'authentically Jewish'. One of the lessons from my journey across continents and centuries in the company of my ancestors is that any definition of authenticity comes freighted with implications: the risk of judgment passed, an excluding order served. A search for authenticity can fast shift into a demand for purity.

At its most jarring for my family it has underpinned those hideous skull measurements used for my cousins under Nazi occupation. It spurred the demand from an ancestor in 1725 that an alleged apostate be ripped from the community's midst, and the decision by my grandparents to sunder their own family, to mourn a son who was still alive. Less frightening, but no less powerful, it has fuelled the ageless clerical clashes over tradition and reform, and the arguments over the place of Jews within non-specifically Jewish environments. It has even, and now we're entering the more relaxed world of pub chat, raised a question as to whether that maternal-first-cousin-of-the-wife-of-my-third-cousin-seven-times-removed, the sword-slashed Bolívarian horseman Juan né Isaac de Sola, counts as Jewish (cf. Disraeli) or even family (viz. common sense).

I am much more of a consistently observant and engaged Jew at my Reform Synagogue than I was at the Orthodox shul in which I grew up. But to some, that very sentence is a contradiction; the suggestion that I may now be more deeply Jewish, a howling offence. As I was leafing through an ancient photo album of Mum and Dad's before the funeral, I came across a picture of Rabbi Louis Jacobs speaking at their wedding reception in December 1962. He had married them, at Dad's request. He was perhaps the greatest British Jewish scholar, teacher and theological thinker of the twentieth century.* He had also, shortly before, been declared the proponent of views which were *haram, treyf*, Beyond the Pale. Those views – about the *Torah* and the Jewish people's relationship with it – had in fact been set out in a slim book a few years before. It had barely gained any attention on publication, but when Jacobs appeared the shoo-in for a subsequent academic promotion, some of the more rigidly Orthodox high-ups around the Chief Rabbi had demanded that the appointment be blocked, and that Jacobs be made to recant. The book title, *We Have Reason to Believe*, appeared no defence.

Six months before he married Mum and Dad, Louis Jacobs spoke in public for the first time since being disowned by the establishment for, among other transgressions, investigating human involvement in the writing of the Bible. He gave a lecture to more than a thousand people; scores had to be turned away. Jacobs spoke without notes for almost 90 minutes.[3] He took on those who said that any challenge to the traditional reading of revelation was, *a priori*, wrong. 'Yet people who say (this) claim sometime to speak as representatives of scholarship. I prefer the Lubavitcher Rebbe, who rejects all science, to that kind of people.' In other words, it is fine to disagree with his approach. But please don't pick and choose

---

*Actually, scrap that: a 2005 poll of *Jewish Chronicle* readers on the 350th anniversary of Cromwell's permission for Jews to re-settle in England had him way out in front for Greatest British Jew Ever. To which the modest Mancunian said he felt 'both embarrassed and daft'.

your ahistoricity and objections to science and study. Your coherent world-view places you with the eighteenth-century *Hasidim* of the Russian empire.

The argument over authenticity percolates as I sit, for the last times, next to my mother. Mum did not have a simple, or at least comfortable, easily-delineated framework of Jewishness. She was, I said in that Shavuot *d'var Torah*, Jewish, very Jewish – although I was unsure whether 'Jewish', like 'unique', should ever be qualified. But her relationship with our central tenet, *Torah* and a covenant with the Divine, was not one of particularly warm embrace. If others insisted on treating the text and the covenant as a monolith – a huge, unyielding, unchanging presence – guarded, sometimes polished, but mainly just guarded, by concentric circles of men, often with beards, then she was not going to hold her tongue and make the tea.

And it is one obvious lacuna in what I've been able to gather in this story – so glaring that it is all too easily overlooked: that much of Jewish history, like much of History, has been written by men about men. It is they who have filled the leading roles in community and country, and they who have hoarded the ink. (That includes Joseph Siprut de Gabay, whom I'd love to place in a baroque tableau entitled 'Progress'. While his wedding signatures are festooned with swirls, decades later his daughter Ester's remains bound by the womanly lexicon of noughts and crosses. It is only in 1792 – the year that Mary Wollstonecraft published her *Vindication of the Rights of Woman* – that Joseph's granddaughter, Ribca, is able to write her name into the marriage register.) The books and the archives have brimmed with Abrahams, Isaacs and Jacobs. Rarer have been the Sarahs, Rebeccas, Rachels and Leahs.

So the women who have appeared here remain vastly in the minority – even if they provide some of the strongest characters, from the burning indignation of Sarah Siprut de Gabay to the astuteness of Annette Roco. It has been towering figures such as George Eliot and Hannah Arendt who have guided me. The absences, too, have seared: Ester Orobio Furtado started my search. In her company that search ended. Her life must have been marked by extraordinary, wrenching change. But of these, and of her, I can only imagine.

This is not just about a numerical correction. It can't entirely be coincidence that the observations of the women who do appear, while no less acute, can seem qualitatively different. They often seem more approachable, less demotic. If they are pointed, it is probably because they are puncturing the huffing, snorting self-regard of a herd of males, hooves stomping the same old dusty paddock.

I'm still embroiled in struggle, aren't I? Maybe the philologists are right. Or maybe I'm making it sound too heroic. I could just be thrashing around. Flailing, either through a lack of insight, or because the critics have been right: I'm locked, unwittingly or not, in my slanted perspective. As the minister pointed out to me: 'Your views are extreme and radical.' As @amerimutmann14 asked, after accusing me of 'dissing Franco' on air: 'Are you Jewish?'

We have reached the point where both deserve to be answered. Sadly, there will be no checklist of insights on carbon pricing, Palestinian statehood, religion – on balance a force for good?, welfare entitlement, synthetic embryos, even the removal of Generalissimo Franco's remains from the mausoleum in what had been called The Valley of the Fallen.

The correct response is the one given by a rabbi who's written several books: among his peers, I am definitely not. I was musing to him that it might be useful for fumblers such as me if there were a single guide to Reform Jewish Theology. The rabbi roared with laughter, and mimed handing me a slim volume. 'Here's the Good Word,' he said.

Fair enough. Hannah Arendt, I think, would have appreciated the gesture. And so I continue to vibrate between the poles of acknowledging self-evident certainties and understanding how little we may know.

Maybe it will help if I come from a different angle. How *useful* is the idea of Jewishness?

Let us imagine that there can indeed be a definition – an agreed standard of Jewishness – acceptable to a majority of Jews. How useful is that inside and outside the walls of the synagogue or the *Beit Hamidrash* or the home? Is a compendium of Jewish thought just stuff that Jews happen to have come up with? Or is there a type of thinking which, were you to taste blind, you could roll around your mouth and say, ah yes, that's a Jewish vintage? Equally, when I, the layest of lay leaders, stand on the *bimah* near the start of a Rosh Hashanah or Yom Kippur morning service, and introduce a 'study passage', I should probably choose a text that reflects on one of the themes of the High Holy Days: awe, humility, responsibility, community, introspection, even – dare I say it – God. None of those is unique to Judaism. Yet there is a certain expectation – which I have sometimes confounded – that I pick a Jewish writer. Why?

Perhaps an answer lies in the smudged snapshots, the frayed and faded threads that run through this story. That I am an accidental Jew. Some of what stirs me – words, rituals, questions, tradition, struggle, family: again, none of those is unique to Judaism. They are, though, where I come from. You may say – quite reasonably – who cares? As Iris Murdoch pointed out, 'the self, the place where we live, is a place of illusion'.[4] We draw lines and then draw ourselves within them. I can understand the eye-roll of those who see only self-regard, self-aggrandisement in a search for a storyline to encompass ourselves, maybe our family, maybe humanity.

But equally, I'm not sure I want to strip all that away to search for the authentic me. That sense of authenticity has the stale tang of 1970s self-help books, curling on the 50p shelves. Beyond my discomfort, there's something rather distasteful in me announcing on the book tours to come: 'Here I am, naked before you.'

So no, there's no authentic me. Not one I can find, or rather, more accurately, one I think it's worth finding and embracing, let alone revealing. I'm happy to end my search at contingent me. Again, I imagine Hannah Arendt – and her impatience with the self-absorption of some existentialists – might approve. 'Men's lives must be nominal, not exceptional.'[5]

At least, for the time being. There are contemporary philosophers and polymaths who argue that we don't own the patent on consciousness and that authenticity is a delusion. That we'll soon be as writable as algorithms. Data will rule. Literally. We'll be as obsolescent as the carthorse. Our replacement will just be one more evolutionary judder.[6]

To which – fine: you may well be right; you are certainly way cleverer and better read. I will nod and close your books and replace them on the shelf and put on some music. It is not that I am giving up. I like attempting to open my mind, to listen to others, to garner new experiences and maybe gain new understanding. It is one reason why I like my job as a journalist. But I have also come to accept – on the whole without too much anguish, maybe just an inward sigh – that some things lie beyond my comprehension.[*] That is not just indolence or crabbed ambition. It also may be that they are, in fact, unknowable. At least now. I take some comfort – entirely self-servingly – when I happen across writers from previous centuries – George Eliot, implicitly; Montaigne, explicitly – who ask us to think about how much we *can* see. Nor is that a charter to hedge, however tiresome and discordant the one-toned barkers and purists may be. Some stories deserve our full restless outrage, to pursue and rip open. But as I have suggested elsewhere, we will recognise those all the better if we begin sceptical of our abilities, our limited vocabulary and partial taxonomies; if we are self-aware and sensitised; perplexed, even. We should be held back by questioning ourselves; hurled forwards by our desire to question the world, our desire to know and to tell.

I understand, as well, the outward danger of this self-questioning, this introspection – the exploration of Jewishness, the questioning of authenticity, the striving to understand how identity can be defined and built. Kenan Malik warned of it in his book *Not So Black and White*. 'Like racial thinking, the identitarian perspective fractures civic space and fragments the political sphere. Once we accept that social conversations can be limited by one's identity,

---

[*] The other day, en route to work on the Northern Line, I came up with a haiku. I called it 'Philosophical Me'. If you'll allow me:
Spinoza and Kant:
spines of books about books cracked;
pages dense, face blank

we begin fencing off the common pastures of society... "Stay in your lane" is the antithesis of politics.'[7]

So we must resist subsiding into aggressive defensiveness. This is not a new thought. 'The fact still remains,' wrote Frantz Fanon in the 1950s, 'that certain individuals endeavour to enter into pre-conceived categories, and we can do nothing about it. Or rather, yes, we can do something about it.'[8]

Of course, just as much as we can embrace an identity, we can reject it. What we may not be able to do is to ignore, or remain impassive. The history of the Jew tells us that even if we choose to disengage, others may stay all too keen to tell our stories on our behalf. So we are not cilia vibrating in the wash of history. Maybe nerve terminals tingling.

Indeed, there could be a rather modern first principle to be invoked: the idea that properties of things – in this case, *Torah*, rituals, family, community, et al. – attain values from our consideration or, to further the physicists' metaphor, from our measurement. It may be misleading even to think of an absolute value. An ancient and sometimes mind-bending set of traditions can be given the treatment by a modern and mind-bending branch of science. Call it quantum Jewishness.

That is not to suggest that these values remain entirely beyond our grasp. Shot through this haphazard parade of partial, and partially re-imagined stories from a happenstance family, the same lessons emerge.

The need to be defiant, outward-looking, questioning, self-questioning, risk-taking, tickled by the beauty of things, troubled – really troubled – by the wrongness of things. To be capable, however jaded we may feel, of wonder and humility. To be aware of what has passed and how we got here; aware of how much more is to come. We are just a point on a continuum. But perhaps by the choices we make, what we say and do, we can stick a boot in the water and help direct the turbid flow.

And this, for me, is where it comes together. Conjuring with Jewishness, with identity, with agency, has been akin to the practice of journalism, albeit in a different conjugation: how come, who can tell me about it, what does it mean? But then – not what are you going to do about it; rather, what am I, what are we – as loosely or broadly defined as you wish – going to do about it? In Fanon's stunning language: 'like a splinter – to force, if needed, the rhythm of the world's heart.'[9]

So yes, we can retreat into our boxes. But my, the geometry is dull.

Am I talking about my journalism or my Jewishness? Exactly. Jews might frown in incomprehension that my day-job at the BBC could teach me anything about our faith, our practice, our culture, our history. Journalists might frown in horror that I could think it fit to bring my identity into work. Those are fundamental rules of belief and behaviour, and for years I have convinced myself I am doing all I can to adhere to them. Now I understand. Those lines I draw: they are not of separation, but of connection.

Acknowledgments

These circles overlap. But they're also far too tightly drawn. I apologise to all those whose names deserve to be here, and are not.

Thank you to the academics, archivists and amateurs who have helped apparently gladly, certainly selflessly, and many repeatedly: Heide Warncke (the curator at the Ets Haim library in Amsterdam ticks all three adverbs), Ton Tielen, Steve Brummel, Philippe Pierret, Alistair Malcolm, Nancy Henry, Tirtsah Levie Bernfeld, Ralph Salinger, Miriam Rodriguez-Pereira, Rachel Montagu, Bart Wallet, David Jacobs, Nava Benyamini, Bernard Benarroch, Abigail Levene, William Gross and Yitzhak Melamed. David Runciman, through his podcasts and writing, has been brilliant at opening doors. There have been countless others whose work I've drawn on and often relied on. I know this is often formulaically recited, but I promise you it is meant: the ensuing mistakes and misunderstandings are all mine.

Rabbi Michael Marmur, Rabbi Howard Cooper and Peter Hyman all read drafts and offered comment. For that I'm grateful: I'm more grateful for the example that they set, in many ways.

Lucy Atkins provided wise and patient advice in what I delicately call 'the early years'; Doug Young, at PEW Literary, gave me the mallet to beat my thoughts into shape. Rabbi Tony Bayfield and Robin Baird-Smith saw something and were kind enough to lead me towards the magnificent team at Bloomsbury: Tomasz Hoskins, Octavia Stocker (the best sort of editor – sharp, smart, well-read and kind) and the splendid Sarah Jones, among others.

I hope this book is about more than family. But family is at its core. As with weddings and other *simchot*, there's a risk with trimming the invitation list: but special thanks to my sister, Annabel, and my recently discovered first-cousin Nigel. If much of life is an attempted flight from parents, I haven't gone far: it is they who steeped me in music, in Jewishness, in books. I'm only sad that they never got to read this one.

My boys. Can I still call Leo, Harry and Aaron that? My men, really, except I'm not Genghis Khan on the field of battle, and they are their own people. And that is the point. They are restless and inquisitive and fired by a keen sense of justice. I don't know how they will write the next chapters. But I know that they will be trying to weigh on the balance for good. They are an unending source of wonder and pride and love.

And none of this – none of it – would have happened without Sarah. Practising Jews may shudder at my metaphorical sacrilege, but the truth is, she *is* my rock and my redeemer. (Lower-case 'r', if that helps.) There's no other way to begin to thank her for lighting the path, and letting me accompany her. All the way from Jericho.

Glossary

Ashkenazim   Jews of northern and eastern European lineage (compare *Sephardim*).

Bar Mitzvah   On turning 13, a boy becomes an adult with all the accompanying rights and obligations (as does a girl through a *Bat Mitzvah* in progressive communities). Often used to refer to the ceremony in synagogue when he reads for the first time from the *Torah*.

Beit Din   Literally, House of Law: a rabbinic court for religious or civil adjudication.

Beit Hamidrash   Study hall. Usually attached to synagogue.

Bimah   Platform and/or lectern from which the *Torah* is read.

Chazzanut   The vocal arts of a *Hazan*, in reciting, chanting and singing.

Chumash   Five books of the *Torah*, normally bound in one volume.

Chupa   Canopy under which couples are married.

D'var Torah   Short speech introducing that week's *parasha*.

Dayan   'Judge'. i.e. member of a *Beit Din*.

Gemara   The commentary on the *Mishnah*.

Haggadah   The Passover story (with songs and blessings) read at the *Seder*.

Halakha   The rules of Jewish behaviour.

Haham   Rabbi, especially a senior rabbi, in *Sephardi* Judaism.

Havdalah   Brief ritual at the end of *Shabbat*.

Hazan   Cantor.

Kabbalah   Jewish mysticism, embodied in a vast collection of literature and lore.

Kaddish A prayer of praise to God. There are various forms, including the 'Mourner's *Kaddish*', recited to mark or commemorate a bereavement.

Kashrut The set – the very long set – of dietary rules.

Kiddush Brief ritual to mark *Shabbat* or festivals.

Kippah Head-covering worn always by strictly observant men; by others when involved in any Jewish ritual.

Kol Nidre The evening service at the start of *Yom Kippur*. The name comes from the prayer at the start of the service.

Leyn Recite, in a chant, from the *Sefer Torah*

Mahamad The governing council of a *Sephardi* synagogue.

Marrano A 'hidden' Jew of Inquisition-era Spain and Portugal – many of whom might have ostensibly converted, but continued to practise in secret.

Mishnah The founding text of the *Talmud*.

New Christian Those who converted (often under duress) during the Inquisition on the Iberian peninsula.

Omer The seven-week period between Passover and *Shavuot*.

Parashah The *Torah* is divided into 54 *parashot*, and read weekly over the course of a Jewish (lunisolar) year.

Parnasim The executive officers of a synagogue.

Pesach Passover.

Rosh Hashanah Jewish New Year.

Seder The evening service for the first two days of Passover, involving a meal, a story, ritual, singing. Often held in homes.

Sefer Torah The scroll which contains the entire, handwritten *Torah*.

Sephardim Jews whose ancestors came from Spain and Portugal (compare *Ashkenazim*).

Shabbat Sabbath (Friday sunset to Saturday sunset).

Shavuot Festival, seven weeks after Passover, celebrating God giving Jews the *Torah*.

Shiva Seven days of mourning after the death of a close relative.

Shul Synagogue (though not a term that tends to be used by *Sephardim*).

Siddur Prayer book used for everything other than big festivals.

Simcha Celebration, party.

Talmud The great volumes of Rabbinic commentary begun early in the Common Era. A.k.a. 'The Oral Law' – compared to 'The Written Law' of the *Torah*.

Tefillin Phylacteries. Which is a word no one ever uses.

Torah The first five chapters of the Bible, a.k.a. 'The Five Books of Moses'. Can also imply a wider body of traditional Jewish learning.

Treyf Not kosher.

Yahrzeit The anniversary (according to the Jewish calendar) of a bereavement.

Yarmulke see *kippah*.

Yehidim members of a *Sephardi* synagogue.

Yeshiva A seminary or academy for higher Jewish learning.

Yom Kippur The Day of Atonement.

Notes

ABBREVIATIONS

EJ: Encylopedia Judaica (2nd edition, 22 Volumes, Thomson Gale, 2007)
JC: The Jewish Chronicle
JHSE: Jewish Historical Society of England
JQR: The Jewish Quarterly Review
JR: The Jewish Record
LMA: Bevis Marks Synagogue Archives, held in London Metropolitan Archives
NIOD: Institute for War, Holocaust and Genocide Studies, Amsterdam
SAA: Stadsarchief Amsterdam (Amsterdam City Archives)
SR: Studia Rosenthaliana
JE: The Jewish Encyclopedia (12 Volumes, Funk & Wagnalls, 1901–06)
OT: The Origins of Totalitarianism, Hannah Arendt (Penguin ed., 2017)
USHMM: United States Holocaust Memorial Museum
YV: Yad Vashem

CHAPTER 1

1 The Human Condition, p.178 (University of Chicago Press, 2018 ed.)
2 George Eliot, Daniel Deronda p.682 (Penguin, 1967)
3 Albert Hyamson, The Sephardim of England p.206 (Methuen, 1951)
4 Joy Oakley, Lists of the Portuguese Inquisition Vol.1, pp.246–7 (JHSE, 2008)
5 'The New York Gazette' No.67 (1726–7), reprinted in Publications of the American Jewish Historical Society No.22 (1914), pp.180–2
6 First published 1748. This translation from the 3rd edition, 1762. Vol.2, p.149
7 Michael Geddes, Miscellaneous Tracts, Vol.1, 'A View of the Court of Inquisition in Portugal', p.518 (1714)
8 Ester Semah, 1699–1735
9 SAA 5001-722-108

CHAPTER 2

1. George Orwell, *Homage to Catalonia* p.195 (Penguin ed., 2020)
2. Spinoza, *Theoretical-Political Treatise* 20:35 (from *The Collected Works of Spinoza*, Vol. 2 – tr. & ed. Edwin Curley)
3. '*depradadas opiniones*' – 'depraved opinions' – LMA 4521/A/03/02/001/009/A
4. '*arancar planta tan mala y perjudisial*' (at least that's how I decipher the cursive script)
5. '6 Elul 5485' in the manuscript
6. Moses Gaster, *History of the Ancient Synagogue of the Spanish and Portuguese Jews 1701–1901*, p.129 (private publication, 1901)
7. 'Vault' is Robert Alter's translation. More common is 'firmament'.
8. Israel Solomons, *David Nieto and some of his Contemporaries*, JHSE Vol. XII, (1915), p.60
9. A.P. Arnold, *A List of Jews and their Households in London 1695*, JHSE Miscellanies VI (1962). And their number was growing rapidly. A.S. Diamond (JHSE paper, 1962) estimates that by 1720, there were 1,050 Sephardim in London.
10. TE, Vol. IX, pp.302–3
11. Solomons, p.1
12. Gaster, pp. 116–17
13. David Ruderman, 'Jewish Thought in Newtonian England: The Career and Writings of David Nieto (in memory of Jacob J. Petuchowski)', *Proceedings of the American Academy for Jewish Research*, Vol.58 (1992), p. 201. (London may have been one of the easier places to be a Jew: there was still anti-Semitism. In 1732 a man called Osborne published leaflets alleging that Jews had burned 'a bastard child begotten by a Christian on the body of a Jewish woman'. London Jews were assaulted. Osborne was found guilty of libel, in a precedent-setting case. *Hate Speech and the Constitution* Vol.1 pp.1–3, ed. Steven Heyman [Garland, 1996])
14. The issuing of a ban – a *herem* – was not that unusual. But the curses which accompanied Spinoza's were unprecedented. And strangely, it was handed down in 1656, years before Spinoza produced his key works. The chances are that the young man had already started expressing his unvarnished opinions. (See Steven Nadler, 'Why Spinoza Was Excommunicated', *Humanities* Vol.34 No.5 (Sept/Oct 2013). There's also a theory that this was more a political than philosophical dispute, as José Ramón del Canto Nieto suggests.
15. Hyamson, p.90 and ff
16. D. Nieto, 'De La Divina Providencia' (1704) pp.5–6, quoted by Jonathan Israel in 'Philosophy, Deism and the Early Jewish Enlightenment (1655–1740)', from *The Dutch Intersection: the Jews and the Netherlands in Modern History*, ed. Y. Kaplan, pp.189–90 (Brill, 2008)
17. José Ramón del Canto Nieto, 'Natura naturans y natura naturata en Spinoza y en David Nieto, Haham de la comunidad sefardita de Londres a prinicipios del siglo XVIII', *Anales del Seminario de Historia de la Filosofia*, Vol.27 (2010), p.186

18 'D'Argens', *Lettres Cabalistiques*, Vol.7, p.123 (1741), cited by J. Israel op.cit., p.191
19 Yitzhak Melamed, 'Cohen, Spinoza and the Nature of Pantheism', *Jewish Studies Quarterly*, 2018
20 Which began in 1714, with the coronation of George I.
21 Israel, p.183
22 as Yosef Kaplan terms it
23 SAA 5001-704-146 (30-05-1704)
24 Henry Kamen, for example, argues in *The Spanish Inquisition: A Historical Revision* that by conjuring a 'historical Godzilla' of the era, the past may be distorted and present threats unrecognised (pp.392–3). Simon Schama, in his technicolour histories of the Jews *Finding the Words*, and *Belonging* does not, in any way, downplay the devastation of the Inquisition – but nor, I think, would he suggest it was an aberration, setting it in the blood-soaked tapestry of anti-Jewish violence. Take the upheaval, in Spain, a century before: 'The annihilations of 1391 had torn Sefarad into three parts, each perhaps of 100,000: the first were the dead; the second the converted; the third, those who somehow decided to remain Jews whatever the oppression that lay in store.' (*Finding the Words*, p.389 [Vintage, 2014])
25 Schama, Finding... p.396
26 Daniel Swetschinski, *Reluctant Cosmopolitans: The Portuguese Jews of Seventeenth-Century Amsterdam*, p.60 (Littman, 2000)
27 Miriam Bodian, *Hebrews of the Portuguese Nation: Conversos and Community in Early Modern Amsterdam*, p.13 (Indiana UP, 1999)
28 Grandfather Abraham's second marriage, to 26-year-old Benvenida Jessurun (Jacob's step-mother) was in Amsterdam in 1693. SAA 5001-698-201.
29 Swetschinski, p.120
30 Alistair Malcolm, *Royal Favouritism and the Governing Elite of the Spanish Monarchy, 1640–1665*, p.76 (OUP, 2016)
31 ib., p.78
32 Bodian explains the migration from Portugal to Spain pp.12–13
33 Cecil Roth, *History of the Marranos*, p.136 (Jewish Publication Society of America, 1932)
34 Alistair Malcolm – correspondence with me.
35 James Casey, *Family and Community in Early Modern Spain: The Citizens of Granada 1570–1739*, pp.172–3 (CUP, 2007)
36 Miguel (aka Daniel) Levi de Barrios, *Triompho del Govierno Popular*, p.554 (pencil page ref online via Google books, pub. 1683)
37 'Wayward New Christians and Stubborn New Jews: the Shaping of Jewish Identity', *Jewish History*, Vol.8 No.1/2 (1994). Swetschinski bridles a little at the 'New Jew' tag: anachronistic hints of split consciousness, he says. But he allows the connotation that 'Amsterdam's Portuguese Jews were modern Jews without ever having been medieval Jews.' Nice.

38 Jonathan Israel, chapter in *The History of the Jews in the Netherlands* p.114 (Littman, 1996)
39 Judith Belinfante, *The Esnoga: a monument to Portuguese–Jewish culture*, p.32 (D'arts, 1991)
40 SAA 334-223-115. There are examples of compound family names being abbreviated elsewhere in the register.
41 David Sclar, *Adaptation and Acceptance: Moses Hayim Luzzatto's Sojourn in Amsterdam among Portuguese Jews*, Association for Jewish Studies Vol.40, No.2, (Nov. 2016), pp.335–8
42 EH 48 D 34, EH 48 D 10, EH 48 B 21
43 He was born in 'Leghorn', i.e. Livorno, Tuscany, in 1797. The one oddity appears to be the second name – 'David Meldola'. David was Abraham's brother, as far as I can see. Abraham's father was Raphael, who was elected *Haham* of the Spanish and Portuguese Jews of Great Britain in 1805, and then brought his family over from Livorno.
44 There's a fearsome collection of bullet-pointed denunciations from Padua and Venice held in the Ets Haim library (EH 47 D 37)
45 '...deeming it just enough to retain a fresh understanding of *mitzvot* (commandment or good deed) without abandoning his primary focus of *devekut* (spiritual adherence to God).' Sclar, p350
46 Luzzatto stayed in Amsterdam for ten years, in all. But around the mid-1740s, his re-kindled love for *Kabbalah* drew him to emigrate, to Safed. Then, as the *Jewish Encyclopedia* elegiacally puts it: 'in the midst of his plans for the future he, together with his wife and son, died of the Plague in his fortieth year, and was buried at Tiberias beside R. Akiba.'
47 *Jerusalem: City of Mirrors* (Fontana, 1989). Amos Elon is unsparing of Mea Shearim, as he is of so much of the city. It is still, even now, a book that fizzes.
48 David Franco Mendes, '*Memorias do Estabelecimento e Progresso dos Judeos Portuguezes e Espanhoes Nesta Famosa Citade de Amsterdam*', p.117 (1769) Reproduced in SR Vol.9 No.2 (July 1975)
49 www.dutchjewry.org/P.I.G./image/01544301.jpg
50 They married in Bevis Marks on 28th August 1730, their names recorded as 'Abraham de Jahacob Mendes Chumasero' and 'Lea de Castro Lara'. (The Decastro/Decastor/Decastros name had a London pedigree: ten of them, from four addresses, appear in the 1695 census.)
51 His name is recorded as Hisqiau Aron on the register of the Beth Haim cemetery. He signs himself plain 'Aharon' on his wedding register.

CHAPTER 3

1 *Poetry Notebook 2006–2014*, p.120 (Picador, 2014)
2 *An Apology for Raymond Sebond*, pp.151–2 (Penguin, 2006)

3   *My Bondage and My Freedom*, pp.317–18 (pub. 1855; this from the Yale UP 2014 publication, ed. David Blight)
4   Frontispiece, *Afscheidsrede over Genesis XXXII:27 door A.M. Chumaceiro, Predikant bij de Ned. Port. Isr. Gemeente te Amsterdam, beroepen tot Opperrabijn bij de Port. Isr. Gemeente te Curaçao* (1856)
5   Bart Wallet, 'Religious Oratory and the Improvement of Congregants: Dutch-Jewish Preaching in the First Half of the Nineteenth Century', SR Vol.34 No.2 p.191 (2000)
6   JE Vol.4 p.77 (1903) – co-author of entry: Joseph Hayyim Mendes Chumaceiro
7   www.joodsamsterdam.nl/uilenburg-geschiedenis/
8   Wallet, pp.178–9
9   ib., p.171
10 Isaac Emmanuel, *History of the Jews of the Netherlands Antilles*, Vol.1 p.353 (American Jewish Archives, 1970)
11 R. G. Fuks-Mansfeld, *The History of the Jews in the Netherlands* p.225 (Littman, 2002)
12 ib., pp.122, 177–9
13 OT, pp.79–80
14 *Tweede Zestal Leerredenen door J.v.J. Ferares, D.L. Cardozo en A.M. Chumaceiro* pp.106–7 (Amsterdam, 1843)
15 Fuks-Mansfeld, p.191
16 Wallet, p.191
17 Chumaceiro, p.105
18 Fuks-Mansfeld, p.202
19 Emmanuel, p.359. 'Exceptionally liberal for his day, he did not grow a large beard.'
20 Both sons will have their own separate mentions, below.
21 Dr B.I. Ricardo, writing in the *Nieuw Israëlietisch Weekblad* of 1st June 1934 (in a long piece celebrating the 300th anniversary of the community in Curaçao) says the visit was 1854. He confirms the other details of who and what was involved, and the effect that it had.
22 If he were indeed 'King' Pedro at the time of his visit, then it must have been 1853, the year he ascended to the throne, at the age of 16. His *NewYork Times* obituary, just eight years later, ('at the age of 24 the young Portuguese monarch…now dies of a terrible disease' – probably typhoid), says that his tour of Europe, including Holland, was 1853. In his reign, he won the reputation of a moderniser, and a calming influence on a restive country, and was nicknamed *o Esperançoso*, 'the Hopeful'.
23 My great-great-great-grandfather (Simcha's father).
24 I.e. president of the synagogue, Dr. Sarphati.
25 Now known as 'The Winter Synagogue', within the grounds of the Esnoga
26 Presumably the writer means Luís I, who had many names – namely, Luís Filipe Maris Fernando Pedro de Alcântara António Miguel Rafael Gabriel Gonzaga Xavier Francisco de Assis João Augusto Júlio Valfando – none of

which appears to be Alphonso. He did have another rather catchy nickname, though: in this case, *o Popular*.

27 Most closely, his great-grandmother, Ester Orobio Furtado, born in Lisbon in 1708 (see Chapter One).
28 Cardozo de Bethencourt, 'The Jews in Portugal from 1773 to 1902', TJR Vol.15 No.2 (1903), p.270
29 *Nieuw Israelietisch Weekblad*, 1st June 1934
30 The sermon would be published, on its own, the following year, with the lithograph at the top of this chapter as its frontispiece.
31 Leaving behind the oldest, 22-year-old Jacob. He would join them for four months in 1859; he, like his father, would become a *Dayan* – a judge – in the *Beth Din* of the Amsterdam community.
32 Mordechai Arbell, *The Jewish Nation of the Caribbean: The Spanish-Portuguese Jewish Settlements in the Caribbean and Guianas*, p.126 (Gefen, 2002)
33 Herbert Bloom, *The Economic Activities of the Jews of Amsterdam in the 17th and 18th Centuries*, p.145 (Bayard, 1937)
34 ib., p.148
35 Jonathan Israel, *Empires and Entrepots: The Dutch, The Spanish Monarchy and the Jews 1585–1713*, p.437 (Hambledon, 1990)
36 Arbell, p.141
37 Emmanuel, p.354
38 *The Occident*, June 1856
39 ib., Dec. 1858
40 Emmanuel, op.cit., p.356
41 ib., p.357
42 *The Occident*, Jan. 1861
43 *The Occident*, August 1863
44 Arbell, p.156
45 Emmanuel, p.375
46 Isaac Emmanuel, *Precious Stones of the Jews of Curaçao*, p.40 (Bloch, 1950)
47 It was written on 27th May, but only appears in the September issue pp.270–4. Aron says his missive will be distributed in Spanish across Curaçao, and translated into English and French for submission across America and Europe.
48 Haham Chumaceiro cites 'Malshinim'- which appears to be a reference to the 12th of 18 blessings in the *Amidah* – the central prayer in a service. In the traditional version of the prayer, this is an appeal for 'slanderers' to lose all hope, for wickedness to perish and that 'the dominion of arrogance do thou uproot and crush'. Current Reform liturgy does indeed tone down the rhetoric in that 12th blessing.
49 Emmanuel, *Precious Stones*... p.487
50 pp.476–8. The report is re-printed in London, in the JC in May 1865.
51 Ron Gomes Casseres, *Van afscheiding tot reünie: Het verhaal van Mikvé Israel, Emanu-El en Mikvé Israel-Emanuel*, De Archiefvriend, Curaçao, 2014)
52 Emmanuel, *History*... p.359

53 ib.
54 ib., p.396 (footnote)
55 As suggested by the Nieuw Israëlietisch Weekblad, 1st June 1934
56 As suggested by Emmanuel.
57 20th Oct. 1882. The American Israelite is the longest-running English language Jewish newspaper in the US; the second longest-running in the world, after the JC.
58 Emmanuel, Precious Stones... p.487
59 I said 'rarely'. Exceptions include Sandy Hook conspiracy theorists.
60 Abigal Namias Lopez Henriquez, b. 1843 (Coro, Venezuela), d. 1930 (Curaçao)
61 Curaçaosche Courant, obituary of AMC 22-08-1902, quoted in Henny Coomans, Ilse Palm-Chumaceiro, et al. A.M. Chumaceiro Az. Praktizijn-Journalist-Publicist: Onpartijdig pionier op Curaçao (1998) p.41
62 The Roman Catholic newspaper Amigoe, obit 23-08-1902, quoted in AMC Az., p.42
63 AMC Az., p.25
64 Curaçaosche Courant, 31-12-1864, quoted in Emmanuel, History... p.381
65 C.CH. Goslinga, Curaçao and Guzman Blanco, A Case Study of Small Power Politics in the Caribbean, p.85 (Nijhoff, 1975)
66 Ib., p.9
67 Emmanuel, History..., p.446
68 Liesbeth Echteld, History of Literature in the Caribbean, Vol.2 pp.505–6 (Benjamins, 2001)
69 Emmanuel, History...., p.399n
70 Ferry de Goey, Consuls and the Institutions of Global Capitalism 1783–1914 (Routledge, 2020)
71 This, and the following brief outline of the slave passage to Curaçao, is drawn from Natasha van der Dijs, The Nature of Ethnic Identity Among the People of Curaçao, pp.105–16 (Drukkerij de Curacaosche Courant, 2011)
72 Willem Klooster, Paths to Freedom: Manumission in the Atlantic World p.169 (USC, 2009)
73 Wim Klooster, Subordinate but Proud: Curaçao's Free Blacks and Mulattoes in the Eighteenth Century, NWIG Vol.68 No. 3/4 pp.288–9 (1994)
74 Cornelis Goslinga, A Short History of the Netherlands Antilles and Surinam pp. 11, 192 (Nijhoff, 2012)
75 J. H. J. Hamelberg, Het Kiesrecht in Curaçao, p.11. Hamelberg is insistent on this point – cannibalism – in his riposte to Abraham's response, published in 'Vragen van den Dag' p.353 (1895)
76 03-12-1867. Retrieved from 'The American Presidency Project' at University of California, Santa Barbara
77 My account (of the Dutch text) is based, gratefully, on another's: J. V. Roitman in 'Mediating Multiculturalism: Jews, Blacks, and Curaçao, 1825–1970', (pp.100–11) – a chapter in 'The Sephardic Atlantic: Colonial Histories and Postcolonial Perspectives' (Palgrave, 2019)

78 See the opening 'Biigftj' question
79 J.V. Roitman, op.cit., p.104
80 Palm-Chumaceiro, p.42
81 *Jewish Roots in Southern Soil: A New History* – eds Marcie Cohen Ferris & Mark Greenberg, p.166 (Brandeis UP, 2006)
82 The entry for the Chumaceiros, father and sons, in JE volume of 1903, says that Joseph took up the post in 1867. *Jewish Roots...* has the date as 1868. But given that the *Jewish Encyclopedia* entry is written by 'J.H.M.C.', I'm more inclined to go with that.
83 *Jewish Roots....*, p.166
84 which 11-page pamphlet fetched $2,600 at auction in 2016.
85 JC, 17-08-1877
86 *The Home Journal* 15-06-1890, as cited by Emmanuel *A History...* p.404
87 ib., p.408n
88 Amy Shevitz, *Jewish Communities on the Ohio River: A History* p.95 (U Kentucky, 2007)
89 Founded in 1890 as a mass-market magazine by Arthur Pearson.
90 It was written in Curaçao in September 1901, published in the Netherlands in 1902.
91 J. H. M. Chumaceiro, *Verdediging is geen Aanval*, p.ii (Rotterdam, 1902)
92 ib., p1
93 *Interaction Between Judaism and Christianity in History, Religion, Art and Literature*, ed. Marcel Poorthuis et al. p.247 (Brill, 2008)
94 He died in 1905.
95 J. H. M. Chumaceiro, op.cit., pp.55–6
96 Delacova 31 Cuban Nationalist Movement meeting New Jersey 1976. [Super 8mm Color Silent Film]. Moving Image Research Collections. University of South Carolina.
97 Palm-Chumaceiro, p29 'Nergens is vermeld welk beroep Chumaceiro in Coro heeft uitgeoefend gedurende zijn vijfjarig verblief in Venezuela.'
98 Isidoro Aizenberg, *The 1855 Expulsion of the Curaçaoan Jews from Coro, Venezuela*, American Jewish History, Vol.72 No.4, pp.495–507 (1983)
99 *Curaçaosche Courant*, 05-02-1876 (quoted in AMC Az.)
100 email exchange, April 2020
101 There's one further, beguiling detail – which adds a little colour to our sepia images: Eneada recalls visiting Abraham, in the 1980s, at his home in Miami. 'He was a very tall man. He had the look of a European Hebrew. Blue or green eyes. Alfredo Sr, my father-in-law, (had) the same look, with green eyes.'
102 *New York Times* 25-07-1976 (Byline: Robert D. McFadden)
103 *NY Daily News*, 9-12-1976
104 *New York Times*, 15-01-1977
105 *The Miami Herald*, 28-11-1987
106 *The Miami Herald*, 03-04-1979

107 ib.
108 The Washington Post, 12-09-1980
109 Newsweek 22-09-1980
110 He is also the first cousin of the political economist, David Ricardo.
111 'To study the laws of history, we must change completely the object of observation, leave kings, ministers and generals alone...' Pevear & Volokhonsky translation, p.823 (Knopf, 2007)
112 Marie Arana, Bolívar: American Liberator, p.123 (W&N, 2013)
113 In contrast, de-mobbed British soldiers would prove to be a key part of Bolívar's revolutionary forces in the years to come.
114 L.W. Statius van Eps & E. Luckmann-Levy Maduro, Bolivar en Curaçao, p.16 (De Walburg, 1988)
115 Arana, op.cit., p130
116 Which beach-side building is now known – for its distinctive design – as The Octagon. As well as operating for a few hours a week as a museum dedicated to Bolívar's Curaçaoan connection, you can also hire it 'for elegant wedding receptions...small concerts and poetry readings'.
117 Arana, p170
118 A facsimile of the original letter is reproduced in Bolívar en Curaçao, p.18
119 De Pool wrote the story while in Panama, and published it in Spanish, along with a translation in Dutch.
120 On the selvage, there are fond words to another of his staunch Jewish supporters on the island: the young Luis Brión, to whom Bolívar writes: 'I don't know what to admire more about you – your generosity, your patriotism, or your goodness.'
121 Obituary in The Economist, 23-04-2020
122 The historian of the Venezuelan Jewish community, Jacob Carciente says 1786 in his 1991 book La Comunidad Judía de Venezuela, p.154; but is then quoted via EJ on encylopedia.com as saying c.1800 – from his 'second edition'; EJ Vol.18, p.750 (Keter, 2007) has c.1795
123 Clarence I. De Sola, The Jewish Encyclopedia, Vol.XI p.434 (F&W, 1905)
124 Arana, op.cit., p.264
125 Jacob Carciente, La comunidad judía de Venezuela: Síntesis cronológica, 1610–1990, y referencias bibliográficas para su estudio: crónicas sefardíes (Asociación Israelita de Venezuela, 1991)

CHAPTER 4

1 OT, p.502 (Penguin, 2017)
2 Vivian Gornick, writing of Hannah Arendt: Taking a Long Look: Essays on Culture, Literature, and Feminism in Our Time, p.131 (Verso, 2021).
3 Isaiah Berlin: Benjamin Disraeli, Karl Marx, and the Search for Identity, presidential address to the JHSE, 15-11-1967, printed in JHSE Transactions & Miscellanies, Vol.22, p.2
4 Swetschinski, p.174

5 Wolf's 1904 lecture to the JHSE, reprinted in *Transactions*, JHSE, Vol.5 (1902–05) p.210. That 'rarity of the surname' will come back, it seems, to contradict a later argument. (see below)
6 Walter Zenner, *Jewish Retainers as Power Brokers*, JQR, Vol.81 No.1/2 (1990) p.128
7 Poul Borschenius, *The Three Rings: The History of the Spanish Jews*, pp.48 & 59 (Allen & Unwin, 1963)
8 Uriel Heyd, *The Jewish Communities of Istanbul in the Seventeenth Century*, Oriens, Vol.6 No.2, p.313 (Dec. 1953)
9 Marc David Baer, 'The Great Fire of 1660 and the Islamization of Christian and Jewish Space in Istanbul', *International Journal of Middle East Studies*, Vol.36 No.2, (May 2004) pp.159–60
10 SAA 334-219-310
11 From 28 family units to 18. (Levie Bernfeld, p.351)
12 Tirtsah Levie Bernfeld, 'Confrontation Between East and West: Balkan Sephardim in Early Modern Amsterdam', *Caminos de Leche y Miel* Vol.1, p.339 (2018)
13 ib., p.335
14 Called *Shomer Cholim*. David Franco Mendes, '*Memorias do Estabelecimento...*', p.103
15 Moses Cohen, 'Et Sofer' (1691), quoted in Levie Bernfeld, FN p.349. She translates פני שוחקות as 'sad faces'. I wonder if the sense is more of abrasion.
16 בסוד צירופי קודש if my Hebrew is correct. From an introduction to a poem written when David Franco Mendes was 20 or 21, and quoted in J. Melkman, *David Franco Mendes*, p.133 (1951).
17 *Memorias do Estabelecimento...* p.108
18 Noah Webster, *A Brief History of Epidemic and Pestilential Diseases*, pp.229–30 (1799). He goes on to record further calamity in 1728 and 1729.
19 Anne E. C. McCants, *Civic Charity in a Golden Age* p.57 (U of Illinois, 1997)
20 *Memorias do Estabelecimento...* p.108
21 SAA 5001-715-49
22 SAA 334-1211-115
23 1156821 Sarah Syprut de Gabay Villa Real, Mrs Benjamin D\'Israeli (1742/3-1825) by Ferrière, François (1752–1839); 78.7x69.9 cm; Hughenden Manor, Buckinghamshire, UK (National Trust); (add.info.: François Ferrière (Geneva 1752 – Morges 1839). © National Trust Photographic Library / Bridgeman Images.
24 *Benjamin Disraeli Letters* Vol.4 pp.152–4 (eds Mary Millar et al. U of Toronto, 1997)
25 *Curiosities of Literature by Isaac Disraeli, a New Edition with Memoir and Notes by his Son, the Earl of Beaconsfield*, Vol.1 p.ix (Warne, 1881)
26 Jane Ridley, *The Young Disraeli 1804–46*, p.10 (Sinclair-Stevenson, 1995); see also Robert Blake, *Disraeli*, p.3 (this Routledge ed. 1969, first pub. 1966)

'Throughout his life Benjamin Disraeli was addicted to romance and careless about facts. His account of his ancestry (is) wrong in almost every detail.' And Stanley Weintraub, *Disraeli*, p.xiii (Hamish Hamilton, 1993) 'Biographers have often charged Disraeli with reckless mendacity in fabricating his past.' And Wolf, *Transactions*, p.202, 'He had very little precise knowledge of his own direct forbears.'

27 Cecil Roth, *Benjamin Disraeli – Earl of Beaconsfield*, pp.7–8 (NY Philosophical Library, 1952)
28 See his signature on the marriage banns 07-11-1698 – SAA 5001.717.87
29 Beth Haim burial register card #8722 – 12-02-1739
30 19-05-1719 – SAA 5001.711.413
31 *The Young Disraeli*, p.26
32 Blake, pp.49–50
33 *Great Lives*, BBC Radio 4 (2004)
34 Anthony Wohl, 'Dizzi-Ben-Dizzi': *Disraeli as Alien*, Journal of British Studies, Vol.34, No.3, 1995 pp.375–411
35 Weintraub, p.22
36 SAA 5075-6450-580
37 SAA 334-1211-115
38 SAA 5075-10734-556
39 SAA 5062-100-156
40 SAA 5062-107-383
41 Ton Tielen – a specialist in Dutch Sephardi documentary research – says that the brothers almost certainly would have bought the houses with an interest-only mortgage. And there's clear evidence that Joseph's income remained or fell low in the 1730s – to the point where he was on welfare and not paying his synagogue subscription (see Chapter Nine)
42 SAA 5062-110-278
43 Unlike Isaac's oldest brother, Jeuda, who had struck out for London with a piffling five guilders to see him on his way. (SAA 334.221.103)
44 Todd Endelman, *The Jews of Georgian England, 1714–1830: Tradition and Change in a Liberal Society* p.119 (U of Michigan, 1989)
45 *Curiosities*, p.x
46 *The Building News and Engineering Journal*, Vol. 109, p.320 (September 1915)
47 Andrew Motion, *Keats*, p.23 (Faber, 1997), quoting E.S. Parker English Society, p.348. The house had become Clarke's Academy – and where the schoolboy Keats lost himself in verse in the garden. AM says the brickwork was dark, not light red. I'm going with the architectural notes in *The Building News* of 1915. The V&A bought the façade – for £50 – when the house was demolished to make way for the railway. It is currently in storage.
48 *Curiosities*, p.x
49 *Curiosities*, p.xi
50 Ester Siprut de Gabay's will of April 1784, held in the National Archives: PROB 11/1203/20

51 The lawyer and historian, Sharon Turner. Weintraub, p.31
52 Berlin, p.16
53 *The Origins of Totalitarianism*, p.43ff
54 *OT*, p.88
55 Berlin, p.6
56 *OT*, p.88
57 Horace Barnett Samuel, *Modernities*, p.57 (Dutton, 1914)
58 Alexander Charles Ewald, *The Earl of Beaconsfield K.G. and His Times*, Vol.1 p.8 (Mackenzie, 1881)
59 *OT*, pp.87 & 101
60 Chapter XX, *Tancred*. Sidonia appeared throughout Disraeli's political trilogy – Coningsby, Sybil, and Tancred (1844–7)
61 *Lord George Bentinck – A Political Biography* pp.496–8 (1852)
62 As he put it in a letter to his sister. *Benjamin Disraeli Letters*, Vol.2 pp.323–4 (eds Gunn et al.). It seems, as a young MP, he wanted to prove his bona fides.
63 *Coningsby*, Book 4, Chapter XV
64 *Daniel Deronda*, p.698 (Penguin, 1967)
65 *Curiosities*, p.xi
66 Letter to John Sibree, 'beginning of 1848', reprinted in *George Eliot's Life, as Related in her Letters and Journals*, Vol.1 pp.123–5. This three-volume set was published after Eliot's death by her widower, John Cross. He blithely prefaces this letter as 'interesting correspondence'. I guess – although he may not be referring to it in this context – it *was* interesting that eight years later, while living in Berlin with her *de facto* husband, George Lewes, she completed the first English translation of that rebellious Jew Baruch Spinoza's *Ethics*.
67 Weintraub, op.cit., p.23
68 Mudge & Sears, *A George Eliot Dictionary*, p.105 (Routledge, 1924)
69 Gordon Haight, *George Eliot, A Biography*, p.488 (OUP, 1968)
70 Gertrude Himmelfarb, *The Jewish Odyssey of George Eliot*, pp.68–72 (Encounter, 2009)
71 Nancy Henry, correspondence with me
72 Isaac's first volume of *Curiosities*, for which the portrait of Sarah was part of the introduction, ran to 12 editions. (From Blake's *Disraeli*, p8.)
73 *Impressions of Theophrastus Such*, p.344 (William Blackwood, 1879)
74 David Kaufmann, *George Eliot and Judaism: An Attempt to Appreciate 'Daniel Deronda'* pp.91–2 (Blackwood, 1877)
75 ib., p.21
76 ib., p.93
77 29th October 1876. *The George Eliot Letters*, Vol.6, 1874–1877 p.300 (Yale, 1954)
78 Haight, op.cit., p.487
79 *The Atlantic Monthly*, Vol.38 pp.684–94

80 A History of the Jews, p.378 (Phoenix, 2004)
81 Modernizing George Eliot, p.139 (Bloomsbury, 2011)
82 Deronda, p.595
83 ib., p.803
84 ib., p.365
85 Modernizing George Eliot, p.144
86 Susan Meyer, 'Safely to Their Own Borders': Proto-Zionism, Feminism, and Nationalism in Daniel Deronda, ELH Vol.60 No.3, p.751 (1993)
87 Impressions..., p.319
88 Bruce Robbins, Death and Vocation: Narrativizing Narrative Theory, PMLA, Vol.107 No.1, p.44 (1992)
89 Monica O'Brien, The Politics of Blood and Soil: Hannah Arendt, George Eliot, and the Jewish Question in Modern Europe, Comparative Literature Studies Vol.44 No. 1/2, pp.106, 99 (2007)
90 Nancy Henry, Ante-Anti-Semitism: George Eliot's 'Impressions of Theophrastus Such', from Victorian Identities, eds Robbins & Wolfreys, p.75 [Palgrave Macmillan, 1995]
91 JR 25-08-1869
92 JC 25-08-1869
93 'F. R. Leavis: The "Great Tradition" of the English Novel and the Jewish Part', Nineteenth-Century Literature Vol.56, No.2 [2001], p.207
94 JC, 20.08.1926
95 Albert Hyamson, The Sephardim of England, p.364 (Methuen, 1951)
96 JR, 11-06-1869
97 Dated 25th June; published in JR, 09-07-1869
98 JR, 16-07-1869
99 JR, 23-07-1869
100 JR, 06-08-1869
101 JR, 13-08-1869
102 JR, 20-08-1869
103 People Love Dead Jews, p.100 (Norton, 2022)
104 America Comes of Age: A French Analysis by André Siegfried pp.25–7, tr. Hemming & Hemming (Harcourt, 1927).
105 We Refugees, 'The Menorah Journal', Vol. 31, p.76 (1943)
106 Hyamson, op.cit., p.366.
107 Maxine Kantor, High Holy Day Melodies in the Spanish and Portuguese Synagogues of London – Journal of Synagogue Music Vol X, No.2 pp.12–44 (Dec. 1980)
108 Gaster, p46
109 Dated 03-12-1813, and reprinted in full in Sketches of Anglo-Jewish History, pp.297–8, James Picciotto (Trübner, 1875)
110 Journal of Synagogue Music, Vol.X No.2, p.28 [Dec.1980]
111 Phone call, 04-07-2016. Benjamin would become the Hazan for the Sephardi congregation in Manchester.

CHAPTER 5

1 I made the lobby/embed comparison in *Not War Reporting – Just Reporting*, a piece I wrote in Iraq for *The British Journalism Review*, Vo.14 No.2 (2003), pp.15–19
2 Isaac d'Israeli, *The Genius of Judaism*, p.251 (Moxon, 1833)
3 *Deronda*, p.875
4 Robert W. Service, *Ploughman of the Moon*, p.302 (Dodd, 1945)
5 His father, Henry Van Ryn, born in 1850 in Amsterdam, moved to London and married three times: Phoebe Myers in 1872, Leah Hamblyn – David's mother – in 1897, and Esther Roco, daughter of Shimshon of Chapter One, in Bevis Marks in 1904.
6 Phoebe died in 1891. Henry's second wife is Leah Hamblyn, born in Castle Cary, Somerset about 1868. She appears, with two siblings but it seems no parents, on the 1871 census in the nearby parish of High Ham. David was born in 1894. Henry and Leah's marriage is recorded as 1897 (sic) in the Westminster marriage register. Leah died in 1902, and is buried at Willesden cemetery.
7 Henry was 54; Esther was 33.
8 And the de facto grandfather he'd had from the age of ten – Shimshon, the father of Esther – 'served his time in the Dutch army' (JC obituary, 20th Aug. 1926)
9 If this is Dave – and a platoon of territorials from the Queen Victoria's Rifles – then the photo would have been taken at his training camp at Crowborough, East Sussex. (Dave himself mentions in his next letter his time at 'Crowboro'.) A century later, I'd be in the same woodlands, 'on scenarios', during my three-yearly BBC-mandated Hostile Environment refresher courses.
10 See letter, below, of 30th May 1915
11 Alan Palmer, *The Salient, Ypres 1914–18*, p.12 (Constable, 2007)
12 Gavin Roynon, *Massacre of the Innocents: the Crofton Diaries, Ypres 1914–15*, pp.203–4 (History Press, 2004). Whatever the motive of the German notes, they made little impression on the British officer who quoted them in his diaries. Sir Morgan Crofton sniffed: 'There are many signs that the Germans are becoming very homesick. As a race they are domestic and inclined to suffer from this sentiment.'
13 Arthur Conan Doyle, *The British Campaign in France and Flanders*, Vol.II p.34 (Hodder & Stoughton, 1917)
14 Brigadier-General Sir James Edmonds and Captain G.C. Wynne, *History of the Great War. Military Operations, France and Belgium 1915*, Vol.III p.168 (Macmillan, 1927)
15 Ib., p.167. Some observers dismissed this multi-volume history, commissioned by the 'Committee of Imperial Defence, Historical Section' as an insiders' snow-job. The criticism here suggests otherwise.

16 Conan Doyle, pp.38–9
17 Edmonds & Wynne, pp.169–70
18 Conan Doyle, p.41
19 The Germans would hold it until June 1917.
20 Declaration (IV, 2), 29th July 1899
21 Edmonds & Wynne, p.176
22 British officer Martin Greener, quoted by Imperial War Museum at www.iwm.org.uk/history/voices-of-the-first-world-war-gas-attack-at-ypres
23 Elizabeth Greenhalgh, *The French Army and the First World War* p.91 (CUP, 2014); the Mordacq quote she cites is from Olivier Lepick, *La Grande Guerre Chimique 1914–1918*, p.79 (PUF, 1998)
24 Conan Doyle, pp.43–4
25 ib., p.174
26 Edmonds & Wynne, p.222
27 Palmer, p.118
28 Reprinted in Appendix 23, Edmonds & Wynne
29 Richard Holmes, *The Little Field Marshal: a Life of Sir John French* p.367 (W&N, 2005)
30 French's diary, March 1915 – cited in ib., p.284
31 A.J. Smithers, *The Man who Disobeyed: Sir Horace Smith-Dorrien and his Enemies*, p.255 (Cooper, 1970)
32 ib.
33 Letter from Smith-Dorrien to 'My dear Field Marshal' Sir John French, 30th April 1915 – quoted in Smithers, p.290. The Commander-in-Chief eventually agreed that a retreat to a shorter line was the best tactic. But not under Smith-Dorrien's command. Within a week, French had forced him out.
34 McMorran letter of 30th May, see below. Nathan is described as 'a friend of the same persuasion'.
35 'He loved books; but even more, he loved men.' From the tribute to Michael Adler, after his death in 1944, by Rev. Arthur Barnett, a fellow chaplain to Jewish soldiers on the Western Front, and collaborator in the JHSE. Rev. Adler was buried in Henry's old manor: Willesden Cemetery.
36 There's probably no contradiction here: St Jean was only ⅔ mile south-west of the smaller hamlet of Wieltje. The letter to Henry on 7th June 1915 from the Territorial Force Record Office says Dave was buried next to the Wieltje–St Julien road.

CHAPTER 6

1 *Ordinary Vices*, pp.22–3 (Harvard UP, 1984)
2 *Eichmann in Jerusalem – A Report on the Banality of Evil*, p.229 (Viking, 1965)
3 He clearly signs his name 'Rocco' in the register of his wedding 28-11-1794 (SAA 5001-761-15)

4 Cecil Roth, *A History of the Jews of Italy*, p.414 ff (Jewish Publication Society of America, 1946)
5 Primo Levi, *The Periodic Table*, pp.158–9 (Penguin, 2000)
6 It was not a neat transition, as shown by near simultaneous entries in the municipal census from the 1850s. Racco (sic) becomes Rococo (sic). (SAA 5000-471-529 & 5000-473-289)
7 Pim Griffioen & Ron Zeller: *The Persecution of the Jews in the Netherlands, France, and Belgium, 1940–1945: Similarities, Differences, Causes* (Boom, 2011)
8 Jacob Presser, *Ashes in the Wind – The Destruction of Dutch Jewry* (first published 1965, paperback ed – Souvenir 2010), *passim*
9 encyclopedia.ushmm.org/content/en/article/westerbork
10 Presser, quoting an unnamed witness, p.461
11 In *Dépôt: Dagboek uit Westerbork* – published as *Waiting for Death: a Diary by Philip Mechanicus*, tr. Irene Gibbons (Calder & Boyars, 1968). Philip Mechanicus (b.1889) was a journalist for *Algemeen Handelsblad*. He had reported from the Soviet Union and Palestine. On 15th March 1944, he was deported to Bergen-Belsen. On 9th October, he was placed on a 'punishment transport' with 120 other men, to Auschwitz-Birkenau. Three days later, he was shot dead.
12 Mechanicus, pp.22–3
13 www.sobibor.org/de-negentien-transporten/
14 Presser, p.492
15 E.g. Marek Bem, *Sobibór Extermination Camp 1942–1943*, tr. Karpiński & Sarzyńska-Wójtowicz, pp.194–6 (Stichting Sobibór, 2015)
16 Rudolf Höss, the commandant of Auschwitz, testified on the witness stand: 'In the summer of 1941 I was summoned to Berlin to Reichsführer SS Himmler to receive person orders. He told me something to the effect... that the Führer had given the order for the final solution of the Jewish question. We, the SS, must carry out that order.' (*Auschwitz* – Debórah Dwork and Robert Jan Van Pelt, p.279 [Norton, 1996])
17 Christopher Browning, *The Origins of the Final Solution*, p.312 (U Nebraska, 2004)
18 Bem, p.117. The previous year – 15th July 1942 – Himmler had inspected the new instrument of mass murder at Auschwitz, watching through a peephole a gassing of Dutch women. On that same day, he'd written a letter of cloying vapidity to his wife, with the sign-off – 'have a nice trip and enjoy your days with our little daughter. Many warm greetings and kisses! Your Daddy'. (*Die Welt*, 25-01-2024)
19 Bem, pp.210–11
20 Presser, p.492
21 See Anne Frank's diary entry of 9th October 1942: 'The English radio says they (the deported Jews) are being gassed. *Perhaps that's the quickest way to die*.' (my italics)
22 Presser, p.493
23 Dwork & Van Pelt, p.327
24 Photo attached to the back of Isaac's market permit, held in municipal archives (SAA 30187-51)

25   The market prohibition was Article 2 of *Generalkomissar*, H. Rauter's detailed and extensive 'Proclamation on the Movement of Jews', cited in Presser, p.83
26   It purported – perhaps genuinely – to be a way of preventing utter chaos and destruction, of attempting to mitigate the worst depredations of the Nazi overlords. It was widely, at the time and particularly subsequently, disparaged for being self-serving and barely useful: indeed, far more useful as a tool for the Nazis.
27   Presser, p.85
28   As with so much in this chapter, I owe this account to Presser's forensic and first-person history.
29   *Eichmann…*, p.11
30   Ronen Bergman, *Rise and Kill First: The Secret History of Israel's Targeted Assassinations*, pp.11–12 (Random House, 2018)
31   Thomas Harding, *Hanns and Rudolf*, p.147 (Simon & Schuster, 2013)
32   *Eichmann…*, p.47
33   ib., pp.93, 95 & 126
34   ib., p.175
35   ib., pp.287–8
36   *Hannah Arendt and Karl Jaspers Correspondence 1926–1969*, eds Köhler & Saner, p.54 (Harvest, 1993). I'm indebted to Lyndsey Stonebridge and her superb book on Arendt – *We Are Free to Change the World* (Jonathan Cape, 2024) – for highlighting this exchange.
37   ib., p.62
38   The letter was datelined New York City, 24-07-1963, and reprinted in *The Jewish Writings – Hannah Arendt*, eds Kohn & Feldman, pp.465–71 (Schocken, 2007)
39   Testimony on www.joodsmonument.nl
40   Dwork & Van Pelt, op.cit., p.322
41   Yad Vashem archive 15000/14109261
42   Interview #21695 with Annette Roco, Visual History Archive, University of Southern California
43   The World Jewish Congress records: D50.7.a.5
44   Presser, pp.224–5
45   *The Rescue of Jews with the Aid of Passports and Citizenship Papers of Latin American States*, Nathan Eck, YV Studies, Vol.1 pp.125–152 (1957)
46   Richard Dimbleby's despatch for the BBC, 17th April 1945. His level tones are remarkable, and a lesson. You can sometimes hear the edits: he broke down repeatedly while recording the piece. In London, his bosses initially – and famously – refused to broadcast the despatch: they found it unbelievable. Dimbleby threatened to resign. Two days later, it was broadcast, albeit – according to his son Jonathan (interview in *The Times* 07-06-2015) – with the references to Jews edited out.
47   Anne Frank, *The Diary of a Young Girl*, ed. Otto Frank & Mirjam Pressler, tr. Massotty, pp.340–1 (Doubleday, 1995)

48 USHMM ID:25721
49 www.jewishgen.org/databases/holocaust/0170_lost_train.html
50 www.bergenbelsen.co.uk/pages/PDF/Lost_Transport.pdf
51 ib.
52 See Endnote 42, above
53 This, and other information, from Elisabeth's post-war de-briefing ('verklaring') with two Dutch officials, in Rotterdam on 12th September 1945. Testimony held in NIOD: Archive 250d, inventory no. 793
54 Adriana 'Jeanne' Valkenburg. It is estimated that she betrayed 50 Jews, of whom 33 died.
55 Eichmann..., p.168
56 Presser, p306
57 ib, p.297
58 Martin Woodroffe, 'Racial Theories of History and Politics: the Example of Houston Steward Chamberlain', *Nationalist & Racialist Movements in Britain & Germany Before 1914*, pp.143–53 (Palgrave Macmillan, 1981)
59 *Foundations of the Nineteenth Century*, pp.272–3 (Fertig, 1968)
60 Which are both included at the end of the loose-leaf English translation of a history of *The Portuguese Jewish Congregation in Amsterdam, on the occasion of the 275th anniversary of this synagogue* by Dr J. Meijer (1950), held in LMA.
61 YV M.31.2/12996
62 Archive of Hanns Albin Rauter, the *Höherer SS und Polizeiführer* (HSSPF) in the Netherlands, No. 077, file 186a, NIOD.
63 '*Hartefälle zur Portugiesische Israeliten Liste*' – undated, from Rauter archive, NIOD.
64 Zöpf 'took his direct orders from Eichmann' according to Presser, p5
65 Presser, pp.310–11
66 Zöpf's submission to *Brigadeführer* Naumann and (apparently now promoted) *Obergruppenführer* Rauter, 21-02-1944. (Original letter, from Rauter archive, NIOD). Chillingly, at the top left of the first page is 'IV B 4' – the department for 'Jewish Affairs' that Eichmann supervised.
67 Mechanicus, op.cit., p.262
68 As would be Ribca Chumaceiro, Lea Chumaceiro, Abraham Roco and Sara Roco (see below) – prisoner records from Rauter archive, NIOD
69 USHMM RG-14.053M, reel 1
70 Anna Hájková, '*Poor Devils' of the Camps: Dutch Jews of Theresienstadt, 1943–1945*, p.11 (YV, 2015)
71 encyclopedia.ushmm.org/content/en/article/theresienstadt-final-weeks-liberation-and-postwar-trials?series=18010
72 H.G. Adler, *Theresienstadt 1941–1945:The Face of a Coerced Community*, tr. Belinda Cooper, p.162 (CUP 2017, from original German pub. 1955)
73 ib.
74 An undated account by S. Israel, quoted in Adler, p.683
75 ib.
76 USHMM: RG-58.001M

77 Presser, p.162
78 22-06-1942 letter from Eichmann to follow up telephone call of 20-06. From Nuremberg Documents, International Military Tribunal, NG-183
79 Published in 1959, and winner of the Prix Goncourt. I saw this extract painted on the wall of an exhibition at YV in 2008.
80 Via joodsamsterdam.nl & joodsmonument.nl
81 Lucy Dawidowicz, *A Holocaust Reader*, p.87 (Behrman, 1976)
82 ib, pp.133–4
83 'Rebecca (Mendes) Chumaceiro' is transportee number 75 on the list. Lea, below, is no. 74 – from the NIOD archives #077 (HSSPF), file 186a.
84 Eg 01-03-1943 and 09-07-1943 – from the Rauter archive, NIOD
85 Laurence Rees, *Auschwitz: The Nazis & The 'Final Solution'*, p.224 (BBC Books, 2005)
86 Harding, p.164
87 Martin Gilbert, *Auschwitz and the Allies*, p.270 (Mandarin, 1981). An academic debate continues to this day over the desire for and feasibility of air strikes on Auschwitz.

CHAPTER 7

1 Alfonsas Eidintas et al. *The History of Lithuania – Revised Second Edition* p.223, 'Published on Behalf of the Ministry of Foreign Affairs of the Republic of Lithuania' (Eugrimas, 2013)
2 Rūta Vanagaitė and Efraim Zuroff, *Our People: Discovering Lithuania's Hidden Holocaust*, p.41 (Rowman & Littlefield, 2020)
3 Herman collapsed and died while driving on Vauxhall Bridge Road, on 16th August 1939, aged 59.
4 Stanley Vardys & Judith Sedaitis, *Lithuania: The Rebel Nation*, p.52 (Westview, 1997)
5 Dina Porat, 'The Holocaust in Lithuania', from *The Final Solution: Origins and Implementation*, p.160, ed. David Cesarani (Routledge, 1994). The write-up of a 2004 symposium at the USHMM on the Holocaust in Lithuania presents two other figures: upwards of 90 per cent, and 'almost 95 per cent'.
6 From the 1931 survey of 'Jewish Merchants of Vilkaviškis', published 26-08-2017 on Ralph Salinger's wonderful blog, *Jewish Vilkaviškis* (salingerblog.wordpress.com/2017/08/)
7 Proclamation 18855, *Correspondance de Napoléon I*, Tome XXIII, pp. 618–19 (Imprimerie Impériale, 1867)
8 Mendel Sudarski, *Lite* ('Lithuania'), Vol.1 pp.1633–1644, (NY Jewish Cultural Society, 1951) translation via www.jewishgen.org/yizkor/lita/Lit1614.html#Page1633
9 Nancy Schoenberg, *Lithuania Memorial Book: Lithuanian Jewish Communities*, p.363 (Garland, 1991). She says the proportion was 30 per cent in 1921; by 1939, that had halved, as Jewish families left the town.
10 Sudarski, op.cit.

11 Yohanan Petrovsky-Shtern, *The Golden Age Shtetl: A New History of Jewish Life in Eastern Europe*, pp.39–40 (Princeton UP, 2015)
12 Sudarski, op.cit.
13 Glenn Dynner, *Yankel's Tavern: Jews, Liquor, and Life in the Kingdom of Poland*, p.39 (OUP, 2014)
14 Timothy Snyder, *Black Earth: The Holocaust as History and Warning*, p.163 (Little, Brown, 2015)
15 Porat, pp.162–3. Also Vanagaite and Zuroff, op.cit., pp.4–5: 'in many locations, especially throughout provincial Lithuania, the majority of the killers were Lithuanian volunteers, and in quite a few places, it was Lithuanians alone who carried out the murders without any Germans or Austrians present…in Onuškis, Vilkaviškis, and Virbalis, the only Nazis present at the murder sites were photographing the crimes.'
16 Matilda Kulikauskienė, quoted by David Bankier in *Expulsion and Extermination: Holocaust Testimonials from Provincial Lithuania*, pp.199–200 (YV, 2011).

PAUSE

1 *Réflexions Sur La Question Juive*, (Éditions Gallimard, 1954) p.184
2 Ludwig Börne, 74th letter, *Paris 1832* (www.projekt-gutenberg.org/boerne/briparis/chap074.html)
3 *Réflexions*, pp.45–6
4 ib, p.64
5 ib, p.164
6 ib, p.182
7 *The Jew as Pariah: A Hidden Tradition*, Jewish Social Studies, April 1944, Vol.6 No.2, pp.107 & 109 (Indiana UP)
8 *Close Readings: 'The Second Sex' by Simone de Beauvoir*. (LRB podcast, 2024)

CHAPTER 8

1 From "My Parents' Lodging Place", from *Open Closed Open* by Yehuda Amichai, translated by Chana Bloch and Chana Kronfeld (Harcourt, 2000) Compilation copyright © 2000 by Yehuda Amichai. English Translation Copyright © 2000 by Chana Bloch and Chana Kronfeld. Used by permission of HarperCollins Publishers. Reprinted by permission of Georges Borchardt, Inc., on behalf of Chana Bloch, Chana Kronfeld, and the Estate of Yehuda Amichai. Audio rights reproduced with permission of The Deborah Harris Agency.
2 also commonly romanised to 'Orel'
3 'Orrel' on John's naturalisation certificate
4 EJ, 1st ed., Vol.15, p.464 (MacMillan, 1971)
5 Leon's mother, Minnie (Mindla) Ettleson could trace her great-grandfather Jeziel back to what was then, probably, just a clutch of houses
6 ANU Museum of the Jewish People, Tel Aviv dbs.anumuseum.org.il/skn/en/c6/e178840/Place/Sakiai

7 EJ, Vol.17, p.679
8 Handwritten notes on the family by Rivelyn, passed on to me during the 1990s. She entitled the sheets: *Tales from the Haim*. (This was a different *Haim* to Leon's Hebrew name. This was the Yiddish for 'Home' or 'Homeland' – חיים – which tends to be transliterated as 'Heym'.)
9 Isaiah Berlin, in his introduction to *My Past and Thoughts: the Memoirs of Alexander Herzen*, tr. Constance Garnett p.xv (Vintage, 1974)
10 Simon Schama says this would have been unusually young; conscription was meant to start no younger than 12. For introducing me to Herzen's memoirs, as well as much else, in his sparkling history of the Jews, *Belonging: 1492–1900*, he has my thanks and admiration.
11 Herzen, op.cit., pp.170–1. What's more, by the time Leon was becoming old enough to be conscripted, in late imperial Russia, Jews were both over-represented (compared to their number in the general population) in the army, and subject to increasing Judeophobia ordained by the new War Ministry. Yohanan Petrovsky-Shtern, *Jews in the Russian Army, 1827–1917: Drafted into Modernity* p.184 & p.202 (CUP, 2008)
12 William J. Fishman – *East End Jewish Radicals 1875–1914* pp.34–8 (Duckworth, 1975)
13 *Menorah Journal* 31, no.1 (1943), pp.69–77
14 The title of a BBC documentary, broadcast 2016
15 www.iwm.org.uk/history/voices-of-the-first-world-war-winter-1916
16 It seems difficult to account for – but that length of time is what his medical records clearly state. 403 days to be precise.
17 The census incorrectly has her age as 18
18 Josef Rosin, *Preserving our Litvak Heritage*, p.667, ed. Joel Alpert, (JewishGen, 2005)
19 Present-day Kaunas.

CHAPTER 9

1 Lyndsey Stonebridge, *We Are Free to Change the World: Hannah Arendt's Lessons in Love & Disobedience*, p.183 (Penguin, 2024)
2 Abigail Dias da Pina Fonseca, cited in *Genio e Ingenio del Poeta Judeo-Andaluz, Miguel/Daniel Leví de Barrios (Montilla, Córdoba 1635 – Amsterdam 1701)* by Francisco Javier Sedeño Rodriguez and Kenneth Brown, p.89 (Universidad de Malagá, 2024). Again NB: my schoolboy translation.
3 Anthony Julius, *Idolizing Pictures: Idolatry, Iconoclasm and Jewish Art*, p.34 (Thames & Hudson, 2000)
4 1748, Amsterdam. For the wedding of Jakob Teixeira de Mattos and Sara Levi Ximenes. 'Written and illustrated by Jozef Šiprut de Gabay', according to L. Fuks and R. G. Fuks-Mansfeld in *De Handschriftenverzameling Van de Bibliotheca Rosenthaliana*', SR Vol.14, No.2, p.173 (July 1980). Image reproduced with permission of Bibliotheca Rosenthaliana, Allard Pierson, University of Amsterdam

5   SAA 334-1102-317, dated 5471, i.e. 1710–11
6   SAA 334-1102-274; '...classi più avanzate della yeshivà Ets Haim', according to Bernfeld in 'Verso la "Gerusalemme dell'Ovest"': Incontri tra Diaspora Sefardita Occidentale e Orientale ad Amsterdam', La Rassegna Mensile di Israel, Vol.76 No.3 (2010) p.91
7   eminent enough and prolific enough to warrant 435 mentions in the collection of the National Portrait Gallery in London.
8   Gaster, p.21
9   ib., p.27
10 JE Vol.2, pp.359–60 (1902)
11 SAA: 5001-710-292 (19-06-1716)
12 She signs the wedding register SAA 5001-699-102 (15-07-1695)
13 According to a notarised statement from her neighbours SAA 277-7470-334-5. For this, and some other key research, I have to thank the generosity, experience and expertise of Ton Tielen, in Amsterdam. Ribca's burial record says that Manuel died in Paris, but provides no source.
14 Engraving by Christian van Hagen (after the Jewish painter Aron de Chaves), from Imperio de Dios en la Harmonia del Mundo by 'Don Miguel de Barrios', 1670. (Koninklijke Bibliotheek, Nationale Bibliotheek van Nederland) Ets Haim – Livraria Montezinos, Amsterdam
15 Timothy Oelman, Marrano Poets of the Seventeenth Century, p.219 (Littman, 1982)
16 Romeyn de Hooghe 1665–8, Besnijdenis-scène ('Circumcision Scene'). Public domain. Downloaded from the website of the Rijksmuseum, Amsterdam.
17 'The Circumcision' – a Drawing by Romeyn de Hooghe, 'Master Drawings', Vol.13 No.3 pp.250–8 (1975)
18 Frustratingly, Zwarts just says he reached the conclusion 'after an extensive examination, that does not matter here'. The Significance of Rembrandt's 'The Jewish Bride', p.21 (Amersfoort, 1929)
19 Memorbook: History of Dutch Jewry from the Renaissance to 1940, p.62 (English translation – Bosch & Keuning, 1977)
20 Francisco Javier Sedeño Rodriguez and Kenneth Brown, pp.70–6
21 ib., pp.7–8
22 Judith Belinfante: The Esnoga: a monument to Portuguese–Jewish culture, p.30 (D'Arts, 1991)
23 Steven Nadler, Spinoza: A Life, pp.145–6 (CUP 1999)
24 Wilhelmina Pieterse, Daniel Levi de Barrios als Geschiedschrijver van de Portuguees-Israëlietische Gemeente te Amsterdam in zijn 'Triumpho del Govierno Popular', p.30 (Scheltema en Holkema, 1968)
25 Into what, I don't know (SAA 334-223-175). Thirty years later, Joseph receives two guilders for inscribing two names (SAA 334-970-648), suggesting that – even allowing for inflation – he has become a rather more sought-after calligrapher.
26 Hava Tirosh-Samuelson, JQR Vol.89 No.1/2 (1998) pp.251–2
27 Levie Bernfeld, FN 83, p.353

28 SAA 5004-112-137 (21-08-1736)
29 Melkman, pp.115, 154
30 ib., p.116
31 ib., p.95
32 J. S. da Silva Rosa, *Geschiedenis der Portugeesche Joden te Amsterdam, 1593–1925*, p.126 (Menno Hertzberger, 1925)
33 EH 47-B-03 p.2
34 Melkman, p.115
35 Melkman, p.33
36 ib., p.40.
37 ib., p.47
38 Melkman, FN p.144
39 Kenneth Brown found, transcribed and annotated this treasure from the Ets Haim archives. It appears in his (as I write) yet-to-be-published paper: *Superior Genius, Wondrous Inventiveness, Divine Guidance: An Illustrated Medley of 17th–18th century 'New' Sephardic Texts by and about Amsterdam-Based Literati*
40 SR Vol.40, 'Epigonism and the Dynamic of Jewish Culture' (2007–2008) pp.147–158
41 Berger and Zwiep, pp.149, 151, 156
42 ib., p.154
43 c.1750, Amsterdam. Omer counter, held in Ets Haim library, EH V0297. It has not been formally attributed. But the library's curator, Heide Warncke, was the first to suggest to me that it may well have been the work of Joseph: the illustration and calligraphy seemed similar. It's a view backed by the London-based *sofer* (religious scribe and calligrapher) Bernard Benarroch, who says that the lettering is tellingly similar (eg: the ayin, lamed and aleph), and that the scrolled bordering as well as the flowers seem to be very close to Joseph's other output. Images on pp.232 & 239 reproduced with permission of Ets Haim – Livraria Montezinos, Amsterdam.
44 Chapter 20:4
45 *Aesthetics and History*, p.157 (Pantheon, 1948).
46 *Almas en Litigio*, 'Clavileño' I (1950), pp.14–26
47 'de voornaamste leden', J. da Silva Rosa, p.126
48 Exodus 16:12 and Leviticus 23
49 Melkman, p.12
50 J. H. Chajes, 'Diagramming Sabbateanism', *Images* Vol.13, No.1 (Dec.2020), p.108
51 ib.
52 Gross Family Collection 028.012.024, Object ID #45451. Courtesy of William Gross, Photography by Ardon Barhama.
53 Chajes, p.134

54 *The Classical Style*, p.142 (Norton, 1997)
55 *Music, Sense and Nonsense: Collected Essays and Lectures*, p.217 (Biteback, 2015)
56 Bom Judesmo: The Western Sephardic Diaspora, in 'Culture of the Jews: A New History', Vol.2 pp.227–67 ed. David Biale (Schocken, 2006)
57 Levie Bernfeld, p.353 FN82
58 Herbert Bloom, *The Economic Activities of the Jews of Amsterdam in the 17th and 18th Centuries* p.212 FN30 (Bayard, 1937)
59 SAA-334-07-559 (04-04-1745)
60 Levie Bernfeld's definition from 'Portuguese Women in Amsterdam's Golden Age' p.85, in *The Religious Cultures of Dutch Jewry*, eds Kaplan & Michman (Brill, 2017)
61 Lydia Hagoort, *Het Beth Haim in Ouderkerk aan de Amstel*, p.132 (Hilversum Verloren, 2005)
62 Levie Bernfeld says that in the mid-eighteenth century, a family on 180 to 200 guilders a year was 'on the edge of the poverty' op.cit., p.340 FN41
63 Hagoort, op.cit., p.136
64 *De Zeven Provinciën in Beroering: Uit de Jiddische Kroniek 1740–1750*. The text in Yiddish was written by Abraham Chaim Braatbard. The translation by Lajb Fuks was published in 1960.
65 See Chapter Four
66 'geweldige ruzie' pp.126–7
67 *Memorias...*, pp.118–19
68 Israel Adler, 'A Competition for the Office of Hazzan in the "Great" Portuguese Synagogue of Amsterdam in the 18th Century', *The Journal of Synagogue Music* (Fall 2013), pp.31–2
69 EH 48 E 44. See also L. & R. Fuks, notes to Mendes' *Memorias*, FN249 p.167
70 EH 49 A 14
71 *Memorias...*, p.119
72 Israel Adler, 'Hebrew Writings concerning Music, in manuscripts and printed books from Genoic Times up to 1800', p.101 (Henle Verlag, 1975), cited by Joshua Jacobson, *Journal of Synagogue Music* Vol.XXV No.2 (1998) pp 42–3
73 Don Harrán, 'Dum Recordaremur Sion: Music in the Life and Thought of the Venetian Rabbi Leon Modena', *AJS Review* Vol.23, No.1 (1998) pp.17–61. Also Kobler, p.418 (see footnote p.238)
74 EHV0297, image courtesy of Ets Haim – Livraria Montezinos, Amsterdam.
75 He died on 30th December 1766, at the age of 71. Three months before his death he was earning a bit of cash as an 'inspector of cheeses': checking whether the produce of local farms was kosher (SAA 334-27-12)
76 27th & 29th June and 2nd July 1765; the concert was on 3rd July
77 See Otto Jahn's *W.A. Mozart*, Vol.1 pp.2–3 (Leipzig, 1867) – from where the 'excellent violoncellist (sic) comes'; also *Mozart und Haydn in London*, p.109 [Pohl, 1867], *Quellen-Lexikon der Musiker und Musikgelehrten*, Vol.9 p.183 [Eitner, 1903], EJ Vol.18, p.642

78 SAA 5501-734-471.
79 Sources have him variously born in Venice, Verona and Livorno. Northern Italy, then. And between 1680 and 1682. He probably came to London in the 1720s. He died, astonishingly, in 1783. His son, James, was another talented cellist, who premiered Haydn's second cello concerto.
80 Her grandfather Salomone was, it seems, Giacobbe's brother.
81 The Public Advertiser, 27-02-1758
82 ib., passim, 1760–1764
83 She was charged in 1771 with keeping a 'common disorderly house'. A Biographical Dictionary of Actors, Actresses, Musicians, etc., 1660–1800, Vol.3 p.598 – Highfill et al. (Southern Illinois UP, 1973)
84 Hannah Templeton, The Mozarts in London: Exploring the Family's Professional, Social and Intellectual Networks in 1764–1765 p.52 (PhD thesis, King's College London, 2016)
85 Perhaps Isaac's son, Jeuda?
86 Letter from Leopold Mozart to Lorenz Hagenauer, written in Chelsea, 13th Sept. 1764. Mozart Briefe und Aufzeichnungen, Vol.1 p.164, eds Bauer & Deutsch (Bärenreiter Kassel, 1962). My translation. Now: rhubarb, you say? Well given that you ask, an early sixteenth-century Portuguese New Christian called Garcia d'Orta – 'apparently a far from convinced convert' (M.N. Pearson, Hindu Medical Practice in Sixteenth-Century Western India: Evidence from Portuguese Sources – 'Portuguese Studies', Vol.17, 2001, pp.100–13) wrote 'the first European medical book published in India' (D.V.S. Reddy, Medicine in India in the Middle of the XVI Century – 'Bulletin of the History of Medicine', Vol.8 No.1 pp.49–67) in 1563. D'Orta relates one incident – where, clearly contrary to the treatment offered by the indigenous court physicians – he cures a prince's son of his severe gastro-intestinal complaint by advising him to 'take some rhubarb and whey'. The Jewish Museum in London holds two enticing prints of turbanned Moroccan Jewish pedlars selling rhubarb in the eighteenth century. So medicinal rhubarb appears to have had a Jewish provenance.
87 i.e. the Sephardim who attend Bevis Marks
88 Mozart Briefe... p.181 (19-03-1765)
89 ib., p.165
90 Advertised in the Amsterdamse Courant.
91 The Duchess Countess by Catherine Ostler (Simon & Schuster, 2021)
92 Its full, venomous title: Original Anecdotes of the late Duke of Kingston and Miss Chudleigh alias Mrs Harvey, alias Countess of Bristol, alias Duchess of Kingston (Bladon, 1792)
93 Original Anecdotes.... pp.16–17
94 ib., pp.17–19
95 ib., pp. 20–1

96 Émile Ouverleaux, *Notes et documents sur les Juifs de Belgique sous l'Ancien Régime*, 'Revue des Études Juives', Vol.9, no.18, (octobre-décembre 1884), p.272
97 That would soon change, with the French and then Napoleonic revolutions
98 Archives of the City of Brussels, Collection of the Historical Archives, Liasse 698
99 (SAA 2075-15259-177)
100 State Archives of Belgium, Archives du Royaume, Conseil privé, carton 1293.
101 *The Musical Times*, p.540 – 01-08-1903
102 *Early Music* Vol.7 No.3, p.10 (July 1979)
103 *Cello Sonatas Op.III & Op.V* (Urania, 2022)

EPILOGUE

1 *As I Ebb'd With the Ocean of Life* (1860)
2 'To A Young Reader', from *Other People's Trades* p.209. tr. Raymond Rosenthal (Michael Joseph, 1989)
3 JC, 08-06-1962
4 Quoted by Galen Strawson in *Just Live*, Dublin Review of Books, Feb 2024.
5 'The Jew as Pariah: a Hidden Tradition', *Jewish Social Studies* Vol. 6 No. 2, p.120 (April 1944) (In the collection *The Jewish Writings: Hannah Arendt* [eds Kohn & Feldman, Schocken 2007], the essay is re-printed with 'nominal' replaced by 'normal'. I've stuck with the version of the original journal, whose managing editor, coincidentally, was Theodor Gaster, son of Haham Moses Gaster – Shimshon Roco's colleague, and the rabbi who married Henry Van Ryn and Esther Roco. And – more importantly – in the inside front cover of the journal, published by the 'Conference on Jewish Relations, Inc.' is its manifesto, which states: '...we cannot afford to rely either on *a priori* convictions or on muddling through.' Amen.)
6 viz. Yuval Noah Harari: *Homo Deus* (Harvill Secker, 2016) and John Gray: *Straw Dogs*, p.16 (Farrar, Straus and Giroux, 2007)
7 *Not So Black and White: A History of Race from White Supremacy to Identity Politics*, pp.290–1 (Hurst, 2023)
8 *Black Skin, White Masks*, p.61 (Penguin translation, 2008)
9 ib., p.59